# America's Best
# Fresh Water Fishing

RAY OVINGTON

## Other Fishing Books By the Same Author

*How to Take Trout On Wetflies and Nymphs*
*Tactics On Trout*
*More Tactics On Trout*
*Tactics On Bass*
*Freshwater Fishing*
*The Trout and the Fly*
*Basic Fly Fishing and Fly Tying*
*Introduction to Bait Fishing*
*The Young Sportsman's Guide to Fresh Water Fishing*
*The Young Sportsman's Guide to Salt Water Fishing*
*The Young Sportsman's Guide to Fly Tying*
*Spinning America*

# America's Best Fresh Water Fishing

By
Ray Ovington

Illustrated by the author
Maps by Moraima Ovington

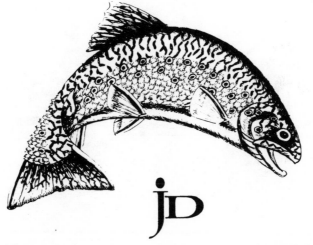

JONATHAN DAVID PUBLISHERS, INC.
MIDDLE VILLAGE, NY 11379

America's Best Fresh Water Fishing

Copyright © 1978
by
Ray Ovington

No part of this book may be reproduced in any manner without
written from the publisher. Address all inquiries to:

Jonathan David Publishers, Inc.
68-22 Eliot Avenue
Middle Village, New York 11379

Library of Congress Cataloging in Publication Data

Ovington, Ray
America's best fresh water fishing.

1. Fishing—United States. 2. Fishes, Fresh-water—
United States. I. Title.
SH463.09          799.1'2'0973          77-24740
ISBN 0-8246-0219-6

Printed in the United States of America

## A Note On the Drawings

My good wife, Moraima, labored far into many nights drawing these maps. They are composites of maps supplied by guides, outfitters, conservation departments and private concerns. They are simplified as much as possible, but do contain enough direction for you to follow—right to the fishing area.

The decorative line drawings are by the author.

# Table of Contents

Acknowledgments......................... vii

Introduction.............................. xi

## 1. THE NORTHEASTERN STATES

Maine....................................... 1
New Hampshire ........................... 8
Vermont................................... 13
Massachusetts ............................ 21
Connecticut ............................... 27
New York ................................. 38
New Jersey ................................ 51
Pennsylvania............................. 57

## 2. THE SOUTHEASTERN STATES

Virginia—West Virginia................. 69
North Carolina........................... 71
South Carolina ........................... 73
Georgia................................... 77
Florida ................................... 83

## 3. THE EAST CENTRAL STATES

Indiana—Ohio ............................ 89
Kentucky ................................. 95
Tennessee................................101
Alabama .................................105
Mississippi ..............................107

## 4. THE CENTRAL STATES

Michigan..................................112
Wisconsin ...............................125
Minnesota ...............................135
Illinois—Iowa ...........................141
Missouri .................................143
Arkansas.................................147
Louisiana................................153

## 5. THE WEST CENTRAL STATES

North Dakota .............................157
South Dakota .............................157
Nebraska..................................157
Kansas—Oklahoma......................158
Texas .....................................158

## 6. THE INTERMOUNTAIN STATES

Montana ..................................163
Colorado ..................................173
Wyoming .................................177
New Mexico .............................183

## 7. THE ROCKY MOUNTAIN STATES

Idaho......................................187
Utah.......................................193
Nevada ...................................197
Arizona....................................197

## 8. THE WEST COAST STATES

Washington ..............................199
Oregon ...................................205
California..................................217

APPENDIX ..............................228
INDEX ...................................239

# Acknowledgments

This is to offer my sincerest thanks to the many authorities on fishing and streams who have helped me over the years in compiling the data and information contained in this book. There are also many unknown anglers and local residents who have added to the treasury of information gathered here while the author was fishing the streams and states. Special thanks go to Duncan Campbell, who, after much urging, wrote the first book of its kind: *88 Top Trout Streams of the West*, plus of course my publishers: Alfred Knopf, Thomas Nelson, J.L. Pratt, Digest Books, Hawthorn Books, Little-Brown, Freshet Press, and to the editors of *Field & Stream*, *Sports Afield*, *True*, *Argosy*, *Saga*, *Outdoors* and *Pennsylvania Angler*, and the now defunct *New York World Telegram & Sun*.

Much appreciation goes to: Frank Amato, editor, *Salmon, Trout and Steelheader* magazine; Cyrus Brown, fishing guide, Caribou, Maine; E. Kliess Brown, Chief, Information and Education, Idaho Fish & Game Department; Virginia Buzek, fly tyer, Visalia, California; Angus Cameron, editor/sportsman, Wilton, Connecticut; Duncan Campbell, member, Orange County Fly Fishers, California; Paul Collier, member, Inglewood Fly Fishers, California; Bernard W. Corson, Director, New Hampshire Fish & Game Department; Harry Darbee, fly tyer, Roscoe, New York; Jim Deren, Anglers' Roost, New York City; Eli L. Dietsch, Supervising Aquatic Biologist, N.Y. State Department of Environmental Conservation; Richard G. Diggins, District 1 Fisheries Biologist, Vermont Fish & Game Department; William E. Easte, Assistant Aquatic Biologist, Massachusetts Division of Fish & Game; James Eriser, President, Federation of Fly Fishermen; Art Flick, fly tyer, Westkill, N.Y.; George Forrest, former editor, *Pennsylvania Angler*; Alvin Grove, Editor, *Trout*, Trout Unlimited; R.C. Holloway, Chief, Information and Education Division, Oregon Wildlife Commission; Willard T. Johns, Director, Pennsylvania Fish Commission; George A. Kaminski, Chief, Information & Education, Wyoming Game & Fish Department; Mark Kerridge, Vice-President, Federation of Fly Fishermen; Harry Kime, member, Orange County Fly Fishers, California; Tom Knight, Information Officer, Washington Department of Game; the late Larry Koller, angler, Neversink, New York; Don Leyden, angler, Holyoke, Massachusetts; Stanley Lloyd, a founder of Cal Trout, California; T.M. Lynch, Fish Manager, Colorado Division of Wildlife; G. W. McCammon, Chief, Inland Fisheries Branch,

California Department of Fish & Game; John McKean, Wildlife Director, Oregon Wildlife Commission; Jim Petersen, sportsman, Hartford, Connecticut; Martin H. Pfeiffer, Associate Aquatic Biologist, New York State Department of Environmental Conservation, U.S. Geological Survey Water Resources Invest. 8-73, Department of the Interior; Steve Raymond, editor *Flyfisher*, Federation of Fly Fishermen; Michael Riedell, officer of Cal Trout, California; Jack Samson, editor, *Field & Stream*; Ed Sens, fly tyer, Bronx, New York; Phillip Vallarine, member, Inglewood Fly Fishers, California; Cole W. Wilde, Chief, Connecticut Department of Environmental Protection; Dick Wolfe, Vice-President, Garcia Corp., N.J.; J.F. Yoder, Editor, *Pennsylvania Angler*.

# Introduction

I've personally fished most of the waters written about in this book; some more often than others; some for a one-time-only try. I've come away from them amazed that the 48 contiguous states of America can offer such a variety, and in some cases, an unbelievably large amount of natural environment that still produces top-flight angling. In some instances the newer impoundments created by dams have added immeasurably to the store of angling prospects, even at the sacrifice of valuable streams.

In writing and compiling the facts in this book, I have, in addition to my personal notes, consulted many experts and particularly the conservation departments of the states in order to offer a more rounded appraisal of the waters described or referred to in the text. Some states are loaded with first class fishing and others are not.

The one main point I wish to make here is that this book is a collection of what I consider the best, most famous and *most consistently* productive waters that contain and produce the best catches of the biggest fish. In selecting specific waters I've asked myself: "Would I travel 500 miles to fish such-and-such lake when a really top lake is right in my home state or at least within an easier, shorter drive?" For example, there is some fairly good trout fishing in West Virginia, but would I go there in preference to a top Pennsylvania or New York State stream if I lived say, in Boston? The answer is, No.

Now, I fully realize that many readers might feel abused if I do not mention a specific lake or stream that they consider to be tops. I found it very difficult to eliminate some very good waters from the editorial stockpile, but, again, I have had to hold fast to my present specific guidelines. Some states are not included here, and some mentioned only briefly because they are not important in the context of this book.

In several instances, such as the Rangeley Lakes in Maine, the St. Lawrence River section of New York State, or a myriad of lakes and streams, say in Wyoming, I have referred to the AREA as being famous and tops rather than to mention twenty or more fishing "spots" in that area. A book that mentions all the waters leaves me in a confusion into which I don't want to lead you.

The state, stream, area and in-text maps will help you to recognize and locate the waters so you can readily reach them by car, and without confusion. Trout stream maps have labels of large block lettering with arrows pointing to the stream. Maps with lightly shaded areas indicate lakes and streams where other game fish besides trout are found. Where necessary and possible, I've given dependable information sources for more detailed up-to-the minute statements of prevailing fishing conditions. I've also not fallen too many times into the trap of relating a personal anecdote when writing about pet waters. Neither have I wanted to involve the how-to of fishing techniques. I assume the reader knows how to fish, or will avail himself of the needed research on fishing, boating, camping, hiking and RV travel. I've added an appendix to the book which covers most of these subjects in general. It also offers insights into the various fish species you'll be catching on "my" waters.

I've also written this book with the hope that all of us will grow to appreciate these waters, protect them and guard them from exploitation, destruction or pollution.

# MAINE

The entire state of Maine is famous for its fishing. It is the symbol of wilderness and unshaven guides wearing plaid wool shirts, red caps and leather boots. For many years the traditional first salmon to be caught from Bangor Pool on the Penobscot River was sent to the President of the United States. Sportsmen from New York and other eastern cities made these waters famous for over a period of nearly a hundred years. Famous angling authors extolled the virtues of the Pine Tree State to add further fame to the area—a fame richly deserved.

From one end of the state to the other, it is true north country with timbered ridges, some very high (for the East) mountains and a landscape that seems to be more water than land—chains of lakes with winding, connecting streams.

I've fished most of the best midstate waters in the Sebago Lake Chain with its many streams just outside of Portland to the Rangeleys and toward the center of the state dominated by the state's largest lake, Moosehead Lake. While most good trouting is in the main ponds and lakes of this region, the connecting streams and lake feeder brooks produce well enough to supply many a camp dinner. The upper part of the state from Greenville on the southern shore of Moosehead clear up to Canada, Quebec on the west and New Brunswick on the north and east, is my favorite country. It may be true that some bigger trout can be had further south in the state, but I favor the north because of its absence of civilization and overdevelopment.

Maine is the home of the native brook trout, lake trout and landlocked salmon, and in a few remaining streams in the extreme northeast, the Atlantic salmon.

1

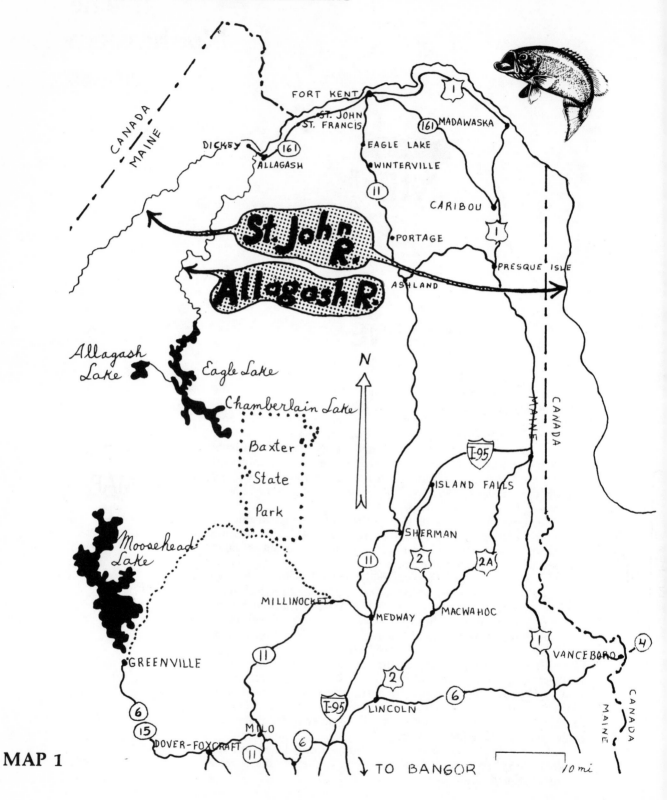

MAP 1

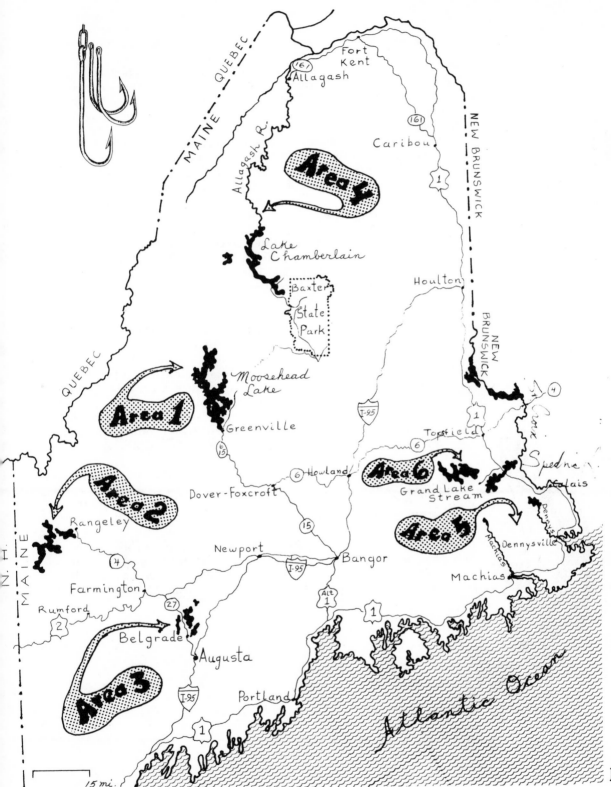

Area 4

Fort Kent

Allagash

161

161

Caribou

QUEBEC

MAINE

Allagash R.

NEW BRUNSWICK

1

Lake Chamberlain

Houlton

Baxter State Park

NEW BRUNSWICK

St. Croix R.

4

QUEBEC

Area 1

Moosehead Lake

Greenville

15

I-95

1

Topsfield

6

Spednic R.

Area 6

6

Howland

Grand Lake Stream

Calais

Dover-Foxcroft

Denny's R.

Area 2

Area 5

Machias

Dennysville

Rangeley

15

Newport

Bangor

I-95

Machias

4

Farmington

Alt 1

Rumford

27

1

2

Belgrade

Augusta

Area 3

I-95

1

Portland

Atlantic Ocean

1

N.H.

MAINE

15 mi.

**MAP 2**

Part of the fishing flavor of this country is the background and atmosphere. Actually the trout are simply not as many or as big as they used to be. But it is famous country and it can produce for you some big ones if you are persistent.

My first encounter with Maine was when I was a boy. I'd like you to experience the trip my father and I took with two guides in canoes from Greenville, Maine. We paddled and portaged the entire run, some 450 miles up the lakes and through the Allagash (East Branch), which finally joins the St. Johns River along the New Brunswick border. From there we canoed all the way to the Bay of Fundy at the city of St. John. We had to rely on the trout, bass, perch and lake trout as staple diet. Even then the trout were small, with the exception of two 4-pounders I caught below a falls one evening.

The Allagash, then, is the epitome of what Maine has to offer, in my opinion.

Beginning in the headwater lakes of Allagash, Eagle and Chamberlain, the waterway is fed by hundreds of streams and broken by countless lakes and ponds all the way to the junction with the West Branch. There are public campgrounds all along its course, but most of it is miles from the nearest road.

Trouters educated on waters of Pennsylvania and the Catskills and even anglers from the West will have to discard some of their techniques when hunting for big brook trout in Maine. These fish have their own way of doing things, and I've been skunked trying to apply sophisticated casting and fly patterns that work well elsewhere. The conventional Down Easterner usually fishes with two or three wet flies on a leader, always the classic patterns, such as the Royal Coachman, Parmachene Belle, Black Gnat and Silver Doctor. You can catch the fish on others, but the traditionals usually produce. Short casts, long drifts are the techniques.

The best way to fish the Allagash is from a canoe, especially if you have to do any portaging.

This is blackfly country in May, June and into July, and the mosquitoes come along in June through the summer, so go equipped.

I should also recommend as famous and profitable the extreme eastern portion of the state, and also nearby portions that border New Hampshire as being tops especially for smallmouth bass as well as trout and salmon. Most of this, again, is wilderness

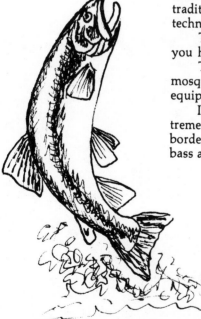

and the best waters are available by portage or flying in. There are many access roads into the privately owned timberlands, but these roads do not appear on commercial maps, since they are not maintained by the county or state. Get maps from the Maine Tourist Development Commission, Augusta, or from the lumber companies such as Brown, and International Paper Co. These are available at local chambers of commerce.

Basically, the fishing season opens when the ice goes out from the lakes, which happens about the middle of April in the lower portions of the state. This is the best time for landlocked salmon fishing if you intend to take them on the surface. When the water warms up, they go deep to hold company with the lake trout and big brook trout. The bass season is a summer proposition.

Late summer finds Atlantic salmon fishing in Maine's two very good reclaimed salmon rivers, the Dennys and the Machias, in the extreme northeastern section of the state. Extensive progress has been accomplished by joint efforts between New Brunswick and Maine to also develop the St. Croix watershed to again provide magnificent runs of Atlantic salmon as well as superb smallmouth bass and landlocked salmon-trout fishing. Fly fishing only is allowed on these waters.

Despite the fact that modern highways have made Maine quickly available to millions of tourists and sportsmen from the major cities of the East and guests from farther away by plane, the area has resisted overdevelopment, thanks, in large part, to the lumber and wood industries who owned major portions of the northern section. This has limited the hot-dog-stand era from entering and despoiling.

Unlike many other areas of the country, there are well-established information sources, and I list a few here.

For complete information on canoe outfitting and trips into the Pleasant Lake and Washington County wilderness waterways and the Grand Lake Chains, write Maine Wilderness Canoe Basin, Box F, Carroll, Maine, 04420.

In the Grand Lake Stream Area, write Weatherby's, Box F-74, Grand Lake Stream, Maine, 04637. Trout, bass, lake trout and salmon.

For Allagash canoe trips and fishing, write Greg Jalbert, P.O. Box 126, Ft. Kent, Maine, 04743.

For all species of game fish near Princeton, Maine, write Long Lake Camps, Princeton, Maine, 04668.

For famed China Lake, contact Nelson Bailey, China, Maine, 04926.

For information on Moosehead Lake area, write Moosehead Hotel, P.O. Box 235, Rockwood, Maine, 04478.

Since the State of Maine contains so many famed fishing areas, the reader will find it helpful to check the 6 areas below, for easy access.

Area 1. The best way to the Moosehead Lake region is by State Routes 6 and 15, north from Bangor to Greenville and Rockwood. There is also a scenic private road down from Baxter State Park.

Area 2. The Rangeley Lake area is best reached from State Route 4, northwest from Farmington.

Area 3. The Belgrades are easily reached by State Route 27 off Interstate 95, just north of Augusta.

Area 4. The Allagash River System is in a roadless area, with only two access points; one by a private road across Lake Chamberlain at the south end (coming out of Baxter State Park) and the other by State Routes 11 and 161 at the north, near the New Brunswick border.

Area 5. The Atlantic salmon rivers, the Machias and the Dennys, are located in the extreme eastern portion of the state. The stream is reached from Machias on U.S. 1 on the Atlantic Coast, and the Dennys about 25 miles further north along U.S. 1, at Dennysville.

Area 6. The Grand Lake Stream area is north and west of Calais. Rich in tradition for its trout, bass and landlocked salmon fishing, this area blends into the Spednic Lake area and the fabulous St. Croix River system, which also includes some Atlantic salmon fishing. Numerous resorts, guides and outfitters serve the region.

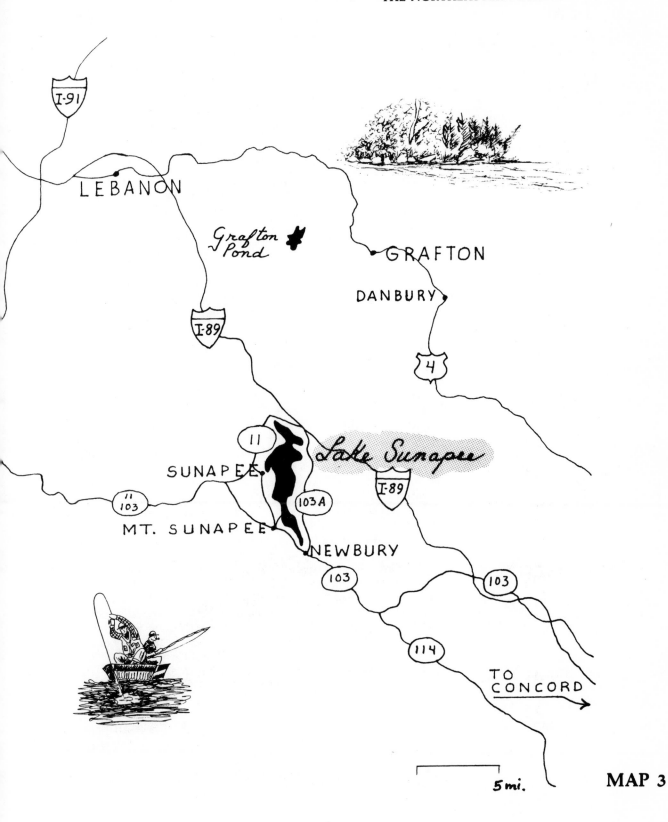

I-91

LEBANON

Grafton Pond

GRAFTON

DANBURY

I-89

4

11

SUNAPEE

Lake Sunapee

I-89

11
103

103A

MT. SUNAPEE

NEWBURY

103

103

114

TO
CONCORD

5 mi.

MAP 3

# The Northeastern States

# NEW HAMPSHIRE

Like the state of Maine, New Hampshire has varied fishing and fishing conditions. In the northern and central parts of the state, you'll find brown, rainbow, brook and lake trout, landlocked salmon, and smallmouth bass. Largemouths are in the south, however. The famed and most beautiful golden trout (not to be confused with the golden trout of California) is a prize worth going after, even just once! The golden is native to Lake Sunapee. Big Dan Hole Pond near Ossipee (which is near the Maine border) and Tewsbury Pond near Grafton, east of Lebanon, are also good spots for brown and brook trout.

The largest lake in the state is Lake Winnipesaukee in the center of the state in the famed "lakes region." It's crowded in vacation season. Brook trout, lake trout, bass and panfish are the fare.

Northern New Hampshire has good fishing all around. North of U.S. 2 are the Connecticut River lakes, including Back Lake and Lake Francis (formed by Murphy Dam from the headwaters of the Connecticut). Also in that area is the Connecticut River along U.S. 3 near Pittsburg, just below the dam at the junction of State Route 3 and U.S. 3. The river is good for many miles—all the way down to Stratford. Brown and rainbow trout abound.

The White Mountain zone south of U.S. 2 is excellent territory for bass and trout, and you can get the up-to-date facts from the publication, *Outdoors in the White Mountains.* This is available from White Mountains Region Associates, Lancaster, N.H. 03584. It lists 100 rivers and ponds. The best take-off point is at Woodsville, on U.S. 302, or Franconia Village on Interstate 93. This is gorgeous vacation country.

For further details write the Economic Division of Tourism, Concord, New Hampshire 03300.

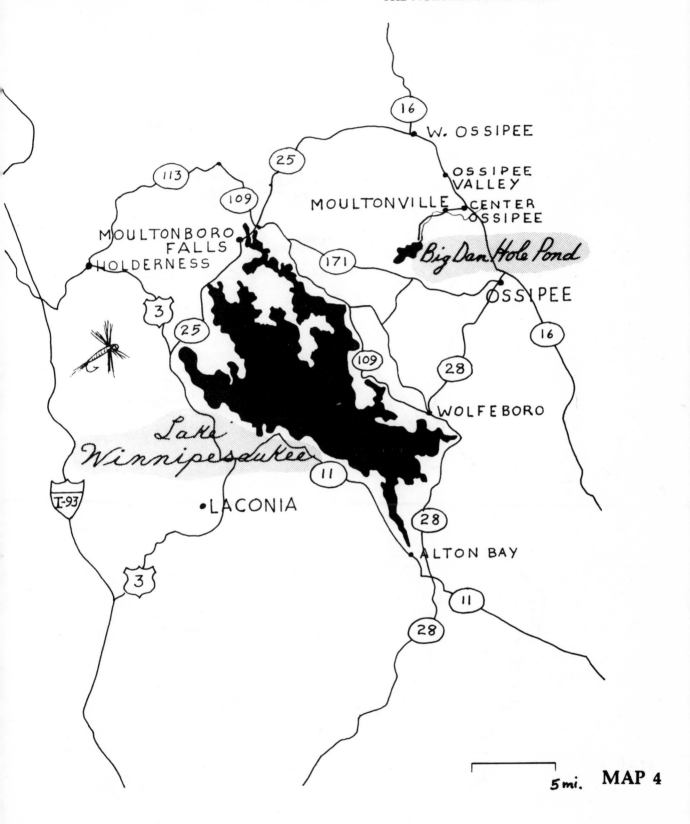

MAP 4

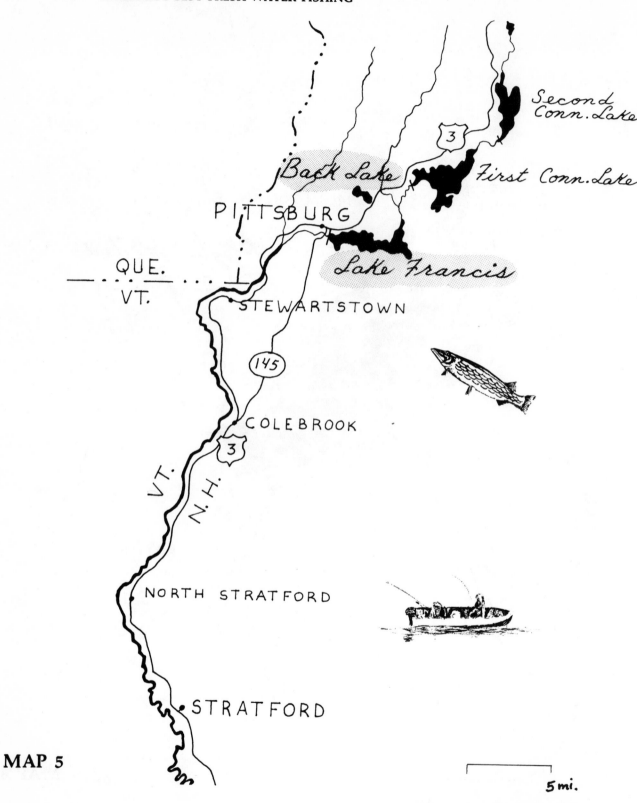

Second Conn. Lake

First Conn. Lake

3

Back Lake

PITTSBURG

QUE.
VT.

Lake Francis

STEWARTSTOWN

145

COLEBROOK

3

VT.

N.H.

NORTH STRATFORD

STRATFORD

MAP 5

5 mi.

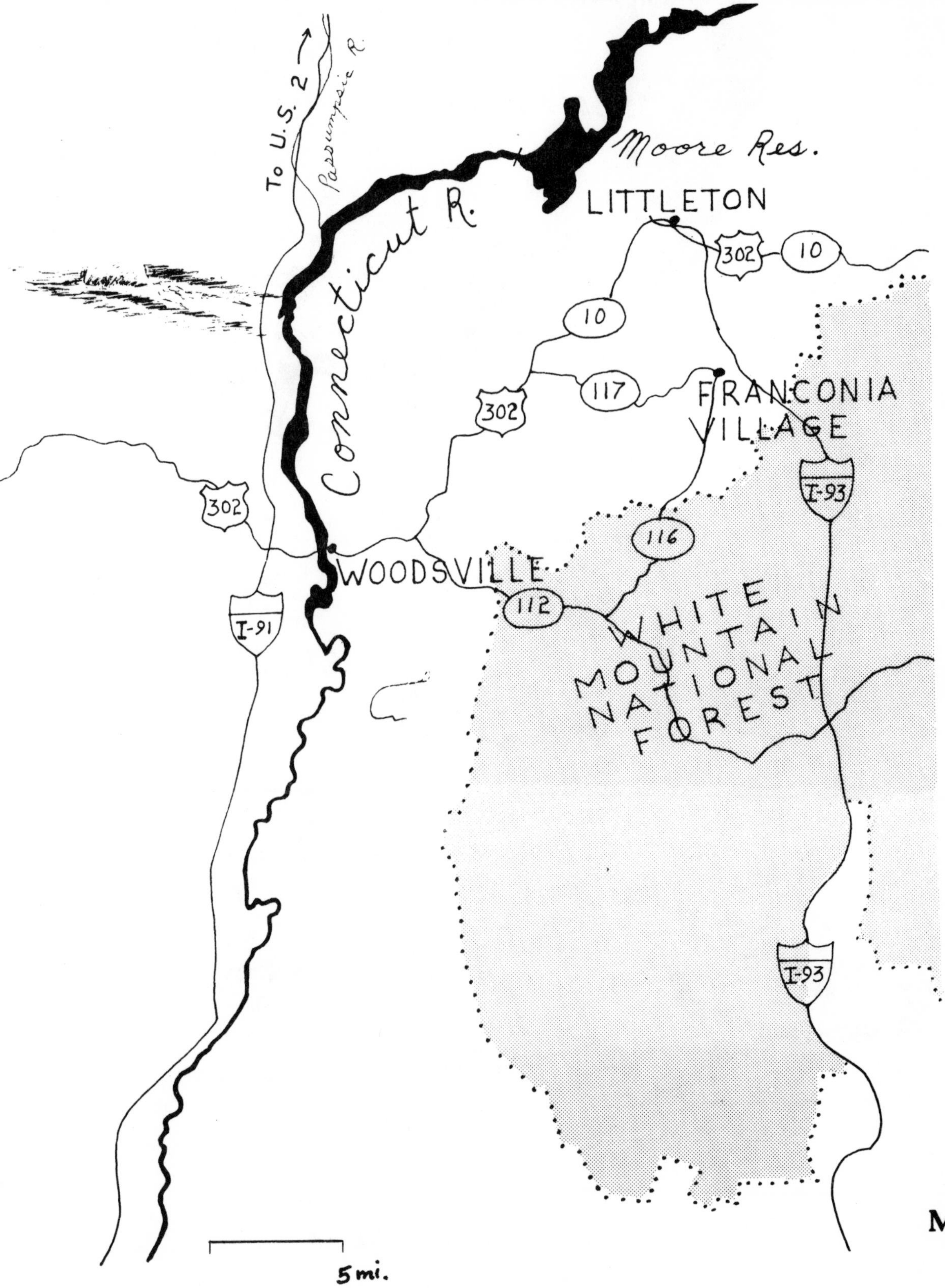

To U.S. 2

Passumpsic R.

Moore Res.

Connecticut R.

LITTLETON

302

10

10

117

FRANCONIA
VILLAGE

302

I-93

302

116

WOODSVILLE

112

I-91

WHITE
MOUNTAIN
NATIONAL
FOREST

I-93

5 mi.

**MAP 6**

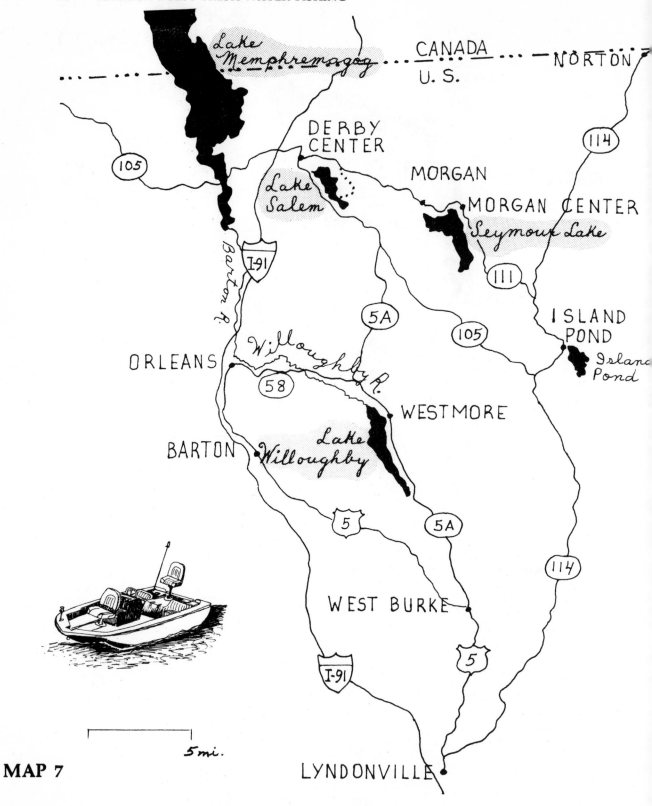

**MAP 7**

5 mi.

# The Northeastern States

# VERMONT

The Granite State's eastern border is the Connecticut River. Lake Champlain covers 100 miles of the state's northwestern border and then flows south into Poultney River for another 50 or so. In between are the ever-gorgeous Green Mountains with their 4,000-foot elevations, clear, sparkling streams; small lakes and ponds. There are also the medium-sized streams where trout fishing is excellent-to-good in the upper reaches and some good bass fishing is found further downstream.

Vermont's Battenkill, the White, the Mad, the Lamoille and the Dog are among the best known for brook, brown and some rainbow trout.

Lake Champlain and Lake Memphremagog on the Quebec border are lake fishing bests for trout, landlocked salmon, lake trout, plus limited muskellunge, pike and walleye pike.

Fortunately for the hurried angler, Vermont is well networked with excellent roads despite its often rugged terrain. The best north-south route is Interstate 91 along the Connecticut River for most of the state. Interstate 89 crosses the northern section of the state from Burlington on Lake Champlain to Barre. U.S. 2 goes from Barre straight across the state to the New Hampshire border. In the south, U.S. 4 offers the same ready access from New York State to Rutland and so on to Lebanon, New Hampshire. U.S. 5 goes along the entire eastern section of the state.

Lakes Champlain and Memphremagog, and Willoughby, which is joined to Lake Memphremagog by the Willoughby and Barton Rivers, is one of the finest territories for both trout and smallmouth bass. Heavy lake trout are also taken up to 25 pounds or more. There is public fishing reachable at Westmore, on State Route 5 A, which is reached by coming north from the junction of State Route 5A with U.S. 5 at West Burke, or by coming east on State Route 58 from the junction with U.S. 5 at Orleans.

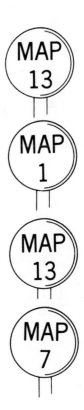

I've had good days on this one, and I caught the first lake trout of my career here.

Another top lake in the region is Seymour Lake, with some very good lake trout, landlocked salmon, rainbow, brook and brown trout plus a generous portion of smallmouth bass. Public fishing areas, boat launching sites and boat liveries are available at the town of Morgan Center on State Route 111, which can be reached easily from I-91 at Interchange #28, or north from Island Pond, also on State Route 111.

While you are there, try Lake Salem, near the town of Derby Center. There is a public fishing area at the end of a dirt road off State Route 111. The Salem Lake Camps are excellent for you and the family. They offer boats and guides. Landlocked salmon fishing is excellent in May, and you can also catch lake trout, bass and walleyes in the summer.

Quimby's Camp, a world-famous caterer to anglers, is on Averill Lake, also called Great Averill Pond, almost upon the Canadian border and reached by State Route 114.

One I've fished many times is Crystal Lake, a beauty spot that contains rainbows, lake trout, salmon and smallmouth bass. It is just west of Lake Willoughby on U.S. 5 at Barton. Take Interchange #25 off I-91 to Barton and Crystal Lake Park.

For your river fishing, the Connecticut River is the main waterway, and its tributaries offer very good angling for bass, trout and walleye the full length of the state. From my own experience, the Nulhegan River tributary is a beautiful run in wild timbered hills with rainbows and brook trout. State Route 105 from Bloomfield on the New Hampshire border to as far up as Island Pond on State Route 114 is good for bass and trout. An also-ran, for brook and brown trout, is the Moose River, one of the better tributaries of the Passumpsic River, entering the Connecticut River south of St. Johnsbury.

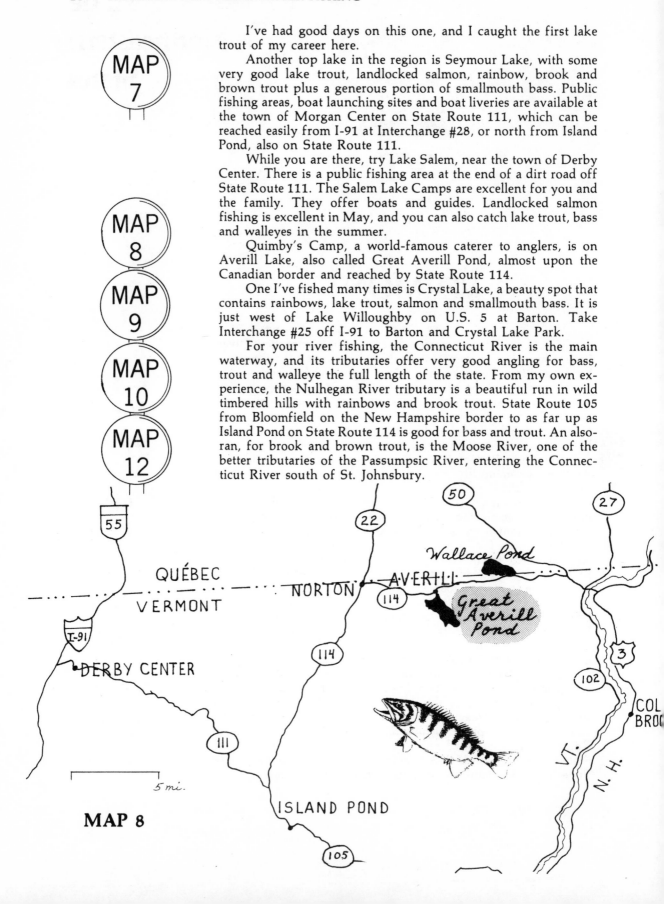

MAP 8

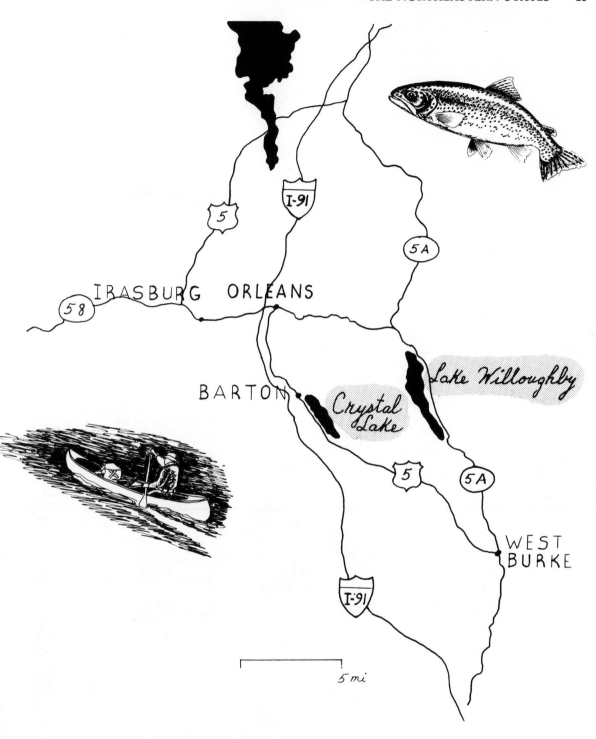

IRASBURG   ORLEANS

58

5

I-91

5A

BARTON

Crystal Lake

Lake Willoughby

5

5A

WEST BURKE

I-91

5 mi

**MAP 9**

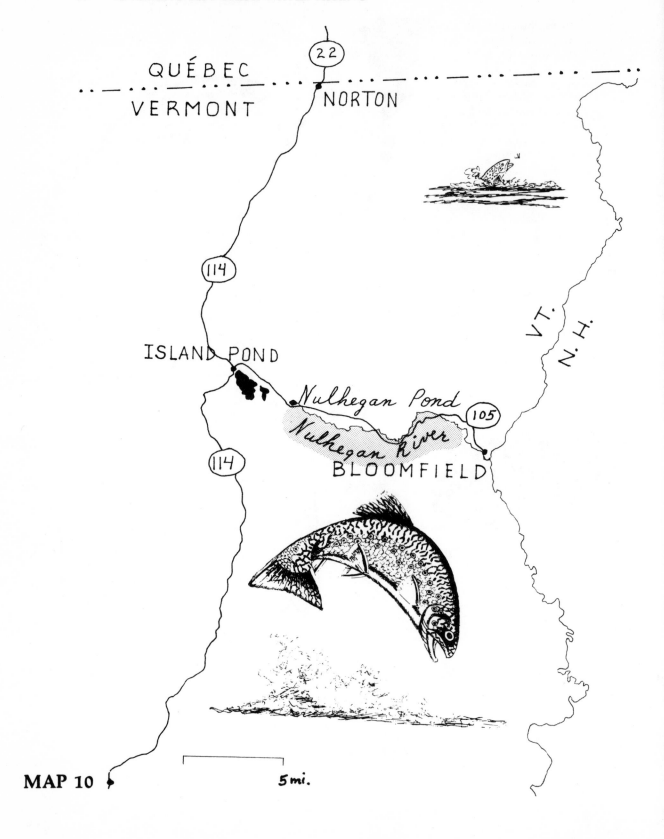

QUÉBEC

VERMONT

22

NORTON

114

ISLAND POND

Nulhegan Pond

Nulhegan River

BLOOMFIELD

105

VT.

N.H.

114

MAP 10

5 mi.

A famous river for trout is the White, between Royalton and Rochester in the center of Vermont. State Routes 107 and 100 parallel this stretch of the river. Its entry into the Connecticut River is at White River Junction, now the junction of I-91 and I-89 as well. Back in more innocent times, decades before the Interstates, White River Junction consisted of a post office, a one-pump gas station and a small general store where my dad and I would always go for bottled birch beer. Take Interchange #3 from I-89 for Royalton and State Route 107. For other good but not famed waters contact the Fish and Game Department, Montpelier, 05602.

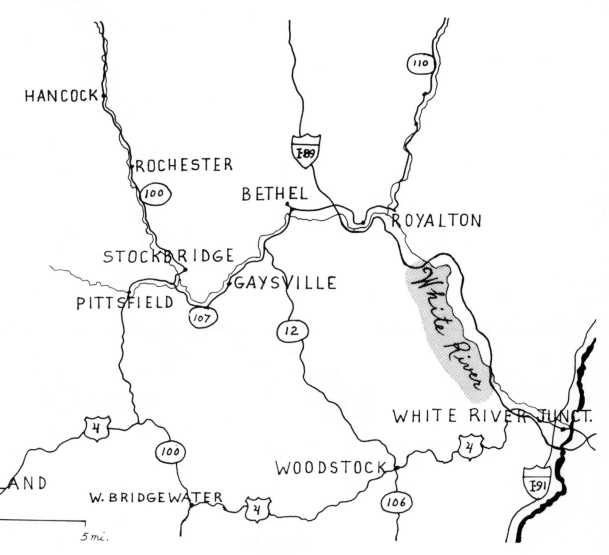

**MAP 11**

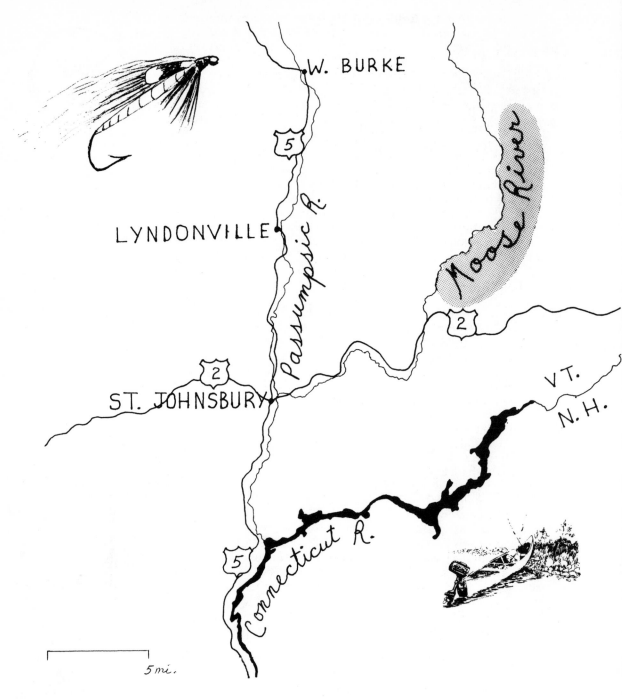

W. BURKE

5

Moose River

LYNDONVILLE

Passumpsic R.

2

2

ST. JOHNSBURY

VT.

N.H.

5

Connecticut R.

5 mi.

**MAP 12**

## Battenkill River

The Battenkill is definitely Vermont's most famous trouting river, and when one thinks of that stream, the name of one particular man comes to mind. Sharing his fishing know-how and talent for fly tying and illustrating, John Atherton wrote extensively on the Battenkill and worked hard for conservation efforts there. His name and love are linked with that famed water.

Like many Eastern streams, though, the Battenkill is not what it once was, if you consider a stream that is wild as being worthy of higher esteem than a more civilized one. Before mounting fishing pressure reduced the quality of the fishing, there were plentiful brook and brown trout that were born in its tributaries. Today, under the pressures of put-and-take trouting, the Battenkill has to be constantly resupplied from the hatcheries and the Vermont Fish and Game Commission takes special interest in this stream, keeping it in top shape, improving it and supplying the needed fish to keep the hordes of anglers happy. These anglers come from the local towns, yes, but experts from as far away as California also visit the Battenkill's banks and wade its famous pools and riffles for some of the most sophisticated trouting to be had anywhere, especially those big browns that have made it famous. In this respect, the Battenkill should be revered in the same class as the Beaverkill in New York State.

It is prime water for fly fishing as well as bait and spinning. The hatches of caddis, stonefly, may fly and other aquatics in great, constant, dependable numbers are found especially in the upper sections. The stream has a varied character, being born in areas of solid granite hills with dramatic gorges, steep falls, long runs in the valleys and deep, slow-moving pools down below where it enters the State of New York. Upstream it can be as narrow as 20 feet, though with a constant fast, turbulent flow bent on tearing its bottom apart. It can also be wide and handsome, all the way decorated by rocky outjuts, crags and overhangs that support both hardwoods and evergreens. It is a stream to be photographed and painted, as well as fished. Lying as it does in the lower half of this sport-orientated state, it is in the heart of prime ski country in the East. Resorts are busy all season long, catering to fishing, boating, skiing, hunting and sight-seeing. With wide and fast roads, it is not remote even for weekend visitors from New York City.

The Battenkill becomes fishable at East Dorset, on Route 7 about halfway from Bennington to Rutland. It flows southerly into a group of lakes, mainly Dufresne Pond, where it breaks loose again to flow into its beautiful course south to Arlington, after which it heads west to West Arlington, where it is joined by Terry Brook. It then flows north and west to Greenwich, N.Y., and then down to finally empty into the Hudson River.

The stretch on Highway 313 above Cambridge and into West Arlington and north Manchester is the most popular, but the upper reaches should be investigated. The lower reaches in New York State begin to deepen and slow down, with bass and other fish dominating the river.

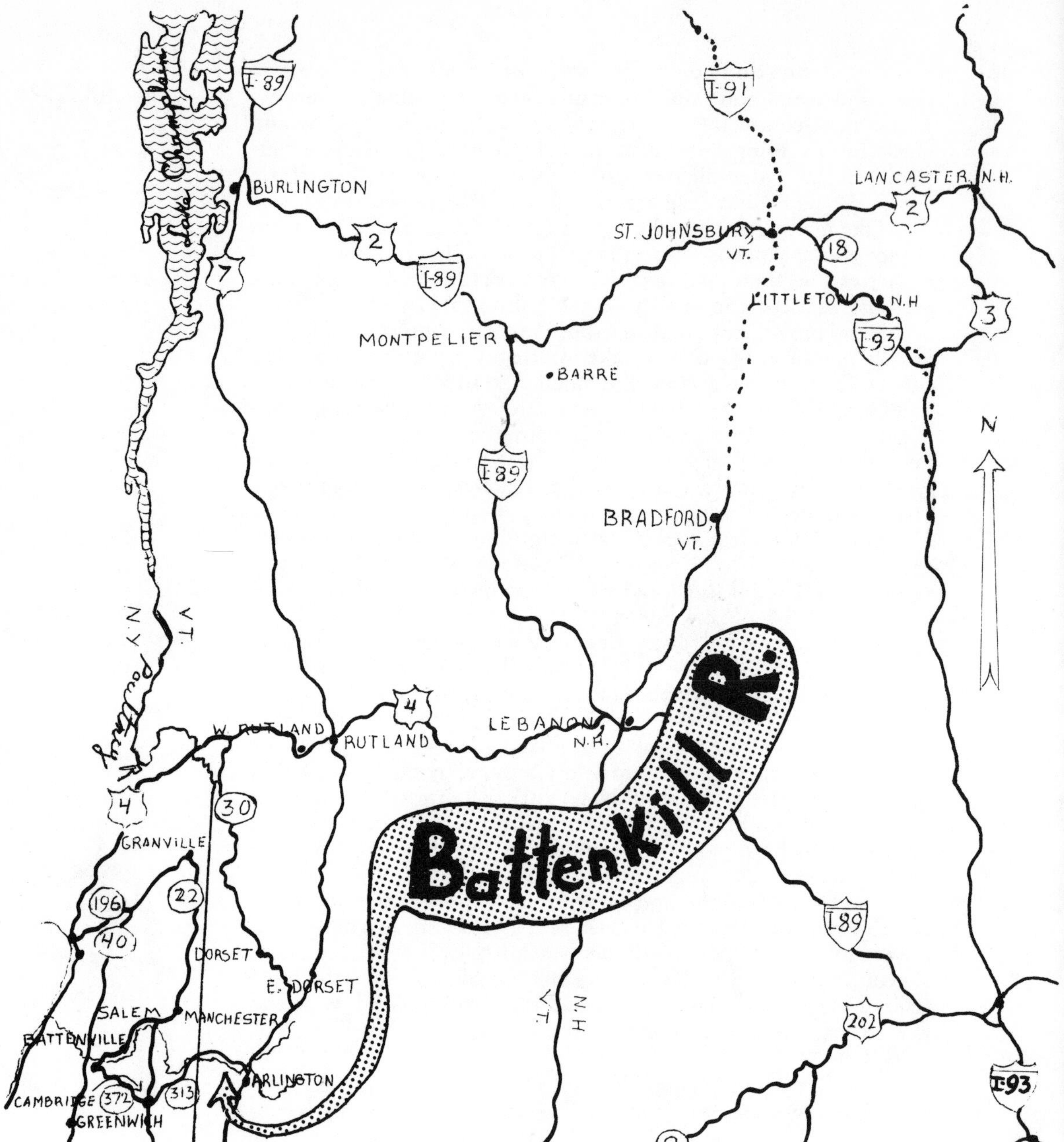
BURLINGTON
ST. JOHNSBURY, VT.
LANCASTER, N.H.
LITTLETON, N.H
MONTPELIER
BARRE
BRADFORD, VT.
N
W. RUTLAND
RUTLAND
LEBANON, N.H.
Battenkill R.
GRANVILLE
DORSET
E. DORSET
SALEM
MANCHESTER
BATTENVILLE
ARLINGTON
CAMBRIDGE
GREENWICH
SCHAGHTICOKE
BENNINGTON
TROY
VT.
N.H.
MASS.
N.Y.
5mi 15mi.

MAP 13

# MASSACHUSETTS

It is surprising that Massachusetts fishing has held up and even more surprising that it has actually improved in some areas. It is a heavily populated state with much industry and pollution, but thanks to its topography and drainage systems, it is blessed with much good fishing water that has gained fame and retained it through the years. All popular game fish abound. Brook trout, brown trout, rainbows, lake trout, largemouth and smallmouth bass, walleye, pickerel and some pike head the list, with shad as an extra in some rivers during their spring run from the ocean.

The major river running through the center of the state is the Connecticut, and the tributaries leading into this mainstream offer excellent fishing all year, from the top of the state to the Connecticut border. Major highways whisk you quickly from one end of Massachusetts to the other. Interstate 90 crosses the state from east to west, and Interstate 91 from north to south.

Lake fisherman in quest of bass, lake trout, pickerel and pike should remember Quabbin Reservoir, the largest impoundment in the state. It was created in 1939 and stocked in 1953 with fingerlings of lake trout. The Swift River is its source, and I can remember fishing this wondrous trout stream as a boy, long before the dam was put in. Even though much good stream fishing was sacrificed, Quabbin has gained a reputation of being a top Eastern fishing water, with brown trout up to 15 pounds, rainbows up to 8 pounds, lake trout to 10 pounds, plus bass up to 5 pounds.

The lake is reached by State Route 122 north and west of Worcester, or by U.S. 202 north and east of Holyoke. Boats and motors are available and you'll find three or four good launching sites plus many good accommodations locally. A very helpful chart of the lake with complete details of available services can be gotten from the Bureau of Wildlife Research and Management, Division of Fisheries and Game, Westboro, Mass., 01581.

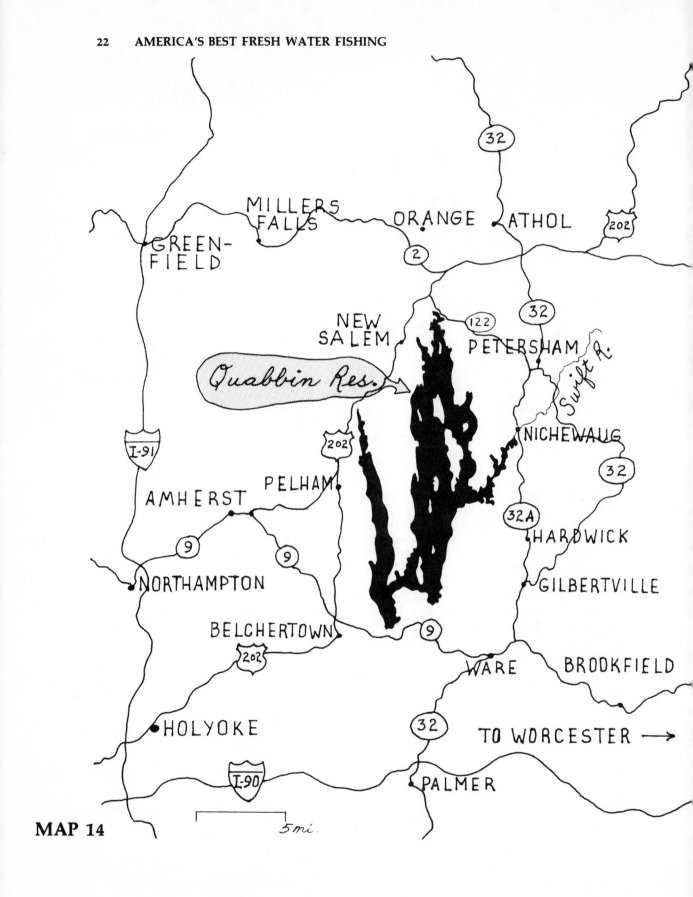

MAP 14

A much smaller lake is found near the Connecticut border, with the large name of Chaubunagungamaug (or Lake Webster, as some prefer), which is reached by taking State Route 12 south from Worcester, or superhighway 193 when finished. Black bass, pickerel and panfish abound but they are not sensational.

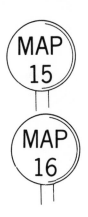

My father introduced me to the Deerfield River some forty years ago. In those days, the winding roads, quaint little villages and pastoral countryside, blended nicely with the special appeal of the Berkshire Hills and mountains. Today, the mountains are still there, but there are wider roads, more signs and many resorts catering to the vacation crowd. Back in the early days there were big trout in the river, hard to catch, but there. Then, over the years, the fishing declined from overpressure, pollution, and the incoming of trash fish. The stream was then purposely poisoned by the state conservation department and stocked anew with the know-how of modern conservationists and ecologists. Since then, it has blossomed into a fine trout fishery with generous help from the remote and well-protected tributary streams as well as from the repeated stocking of browns and rainbows. While the natural spawn could never support the take-out of meat-hungry anglers, it is a big help to the hatchery men who have to keep the stream loaded with hatchery fish. In this respect, the Deerfield is not an exception as far as Eastern streams are concerned. This is the story all over, including the best streams in New York and Pennsylvania. Until fly-fishing-only and no-keep limits are imposed, our fishing will be largely put-and-take.

But the Deerfield is a pretty stream, even if the fish will not be too plentiful or monstrous—one of the prettiest in New England. Like all such streams, the challenge to the angler is a great one and the angler who can fare well here can be considered an expert.

I rate the Deerfield as the best stream in the state partly because of its fame. Famous anglers have fished it and written about it and have used it as a laboratory for the development of their flies and rods and techniques. It is also, as mentioned, a tribute to scientific fisheries management.

This trout stream begins its flow in southwestern Vermont and winds through timbered ridges and broad valleys and farms in a southwesterly direction into Massachusetts for miles and then turns abruptly southeast for 35 miles until it joins the Connecticut River at Greenfield, Massachusetts. Rainbow trout fishing is strictly put-and-take, with little carryover from one year to the next. Because of this, and because most of the hatchery fish are released prior to opening day, the best time to fish for rainbows is in the spring. The patient angler can reserve his time for morning and evening in June and July, when the best hatches of aquatics are in progress. Here is the real test of skill. The hatchery fish are used to their new environment and become especially selective and wary. If you wish to experiment on the numerous feeder streams for more off-beat fishing, the tributaries offer large populations of native brook trout and browns that are often ignored in favor of the mainstream hatchery trout. These smaller streams offer delights in scenic beauty and solitude, as well as difficult tests of casting skill.

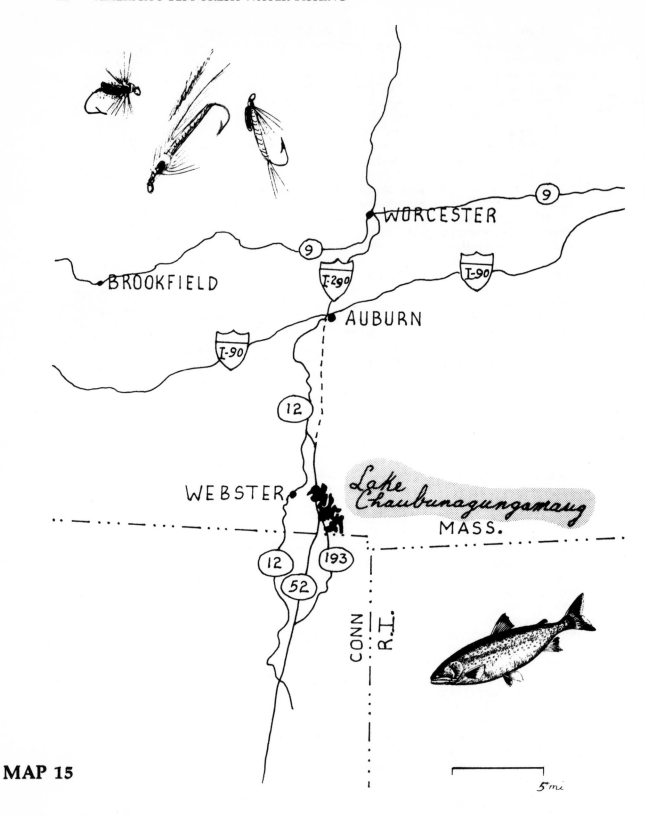

**MAP 15**

5 mi

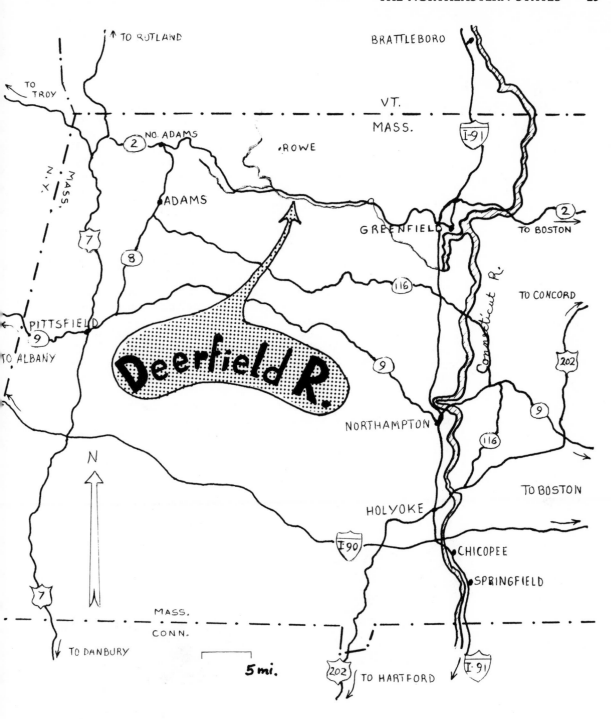

TO RUTLAND

BRATTLEBORO

TO TROY

VT.

MASS.

I-91

② NO. ADAMS

ROWE

⑦

⑧

ADAMS

GREENFIELD

TO BOSTON ②

MASS.
N.Y.

116

Connecticut R.

TO CONCORD

PITTSFIELD

⑨

TO ALBANY

Deerfield R.

⑨

202

NORTHAMPTON

116

⑨

N

TO BOSTON

HOLYOKE

⑦

I-90

CHICOPEE

SPRINGFIELD

MASS.

CONN.

TO DANBURY

5 mi.

202

TO HARTFORD

I-91

**MAP 16**

Except during periods of heavy runoff, the Deerfield River flows are regulated by hydroelectric station releases from storage reservoirs in Vermont, a newly constructed pumped-storage plant in Rowe, Massachusetts, and a network of reservoirs, dams and diversion canals. Water is released from these various impoundments in accordance with daily power requirements, and you should be on the lookout for rapidly rising waters. The general pattern of operation is one in which the plants operate continuously during the late fall, winter and spring, but only during periods of peak power use at other times of the year. There is considerable variation in these periods of peak power use, but they generally occur during week-day business hours and evenings and, to a lesser extent, on Saturdays. Consequently, river flows are lowest on weekends, particularly Sundays.

There are thirty listed streams in the Deerfield drainage system, telling us that this area is rich in trout waters that flow amid Berkshire hills whose scenic beauties defy description . . . and they all have what the serious trouter can enjoy. While the Deerfield is not a sensational trout stream, as is the case with larger, wilder streams in less civilized areas, it is nonetheless a prime trout stream for the serious angler.

There are numerous public and private camping grounds, resort facilities and tackle shops all along its course. State Route 2, running from North Adams at the extreme northwest corner of the state, follows the stream throughout its course to the Connecticut River at Greenfield.

Other fine Massachusetts streams include the Blackstone, Chicopee, Farmington, Millers and Westfield.

For more information, write the Division of Fisheries and Wildlife Field Headquarters, Westboro, Mass. 01581.

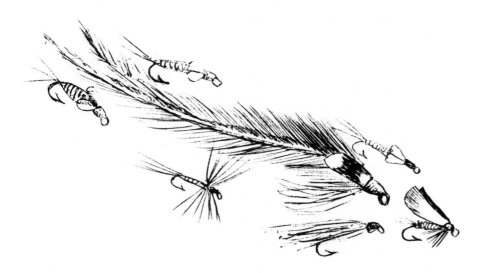

# The Northeastern States

# CONNECTICUT

Connecticut is filled with people and industry, many roads and much pollution, but it boasts a countryside loaded with timbered hills and valleys, swamps and rivers, streams and creeks. It is surprising that good trout water could survive this close to New York and in such developed conditions, but it does. Connecticut certainly cannot be considered to have wilderness or wild trout water, per se, but the fishing is there and the streams are attractive from a scenic point of view. In fact I've taken some browns and brook trout in rivers such as the Housatonic and Farmington that would rival those of the Beaverkill and the Pennsylvania streams . . . not many, not often, but I have taken them, which means that there are many, many more to be had.

While all methods of angling are practiced, there is a very high percentage of fly fishermen who live in the state and partake of the bounties. They are joined by anglers from the New York and other big city areas. Many of these are technicians enjoying the challenge of working over fish that are constantly having all manner of food and lures thrown at them. These anglers are after sport . . . fun with trout. If they can manage to make a 10-incher in Connecticut rise to a dry fly, this is parallel to a similar victory over a 5-pounder from the Yellowstone. Much effort on the part of private clubs and associations, plus the efforts of an alert state Department of Environmental Protection, have been responsible for the fact that the quality of Connecticut streams has remained high.

The west branch of the Farmington River in central Connecticut is fine trout water, with about eighteen miles open and well stocked with browns and rainbows in addition to brook trout. The bottom is mixed: big boulders, rocks and gravel stretches, then sandy and muddy bottoms. There are many runs, eddies, indented banks, long glassy pools and some white water. The river is typically bordered by thick brush and trees. There are no special fishing restrictions and there are few posted areas.

MAP 17

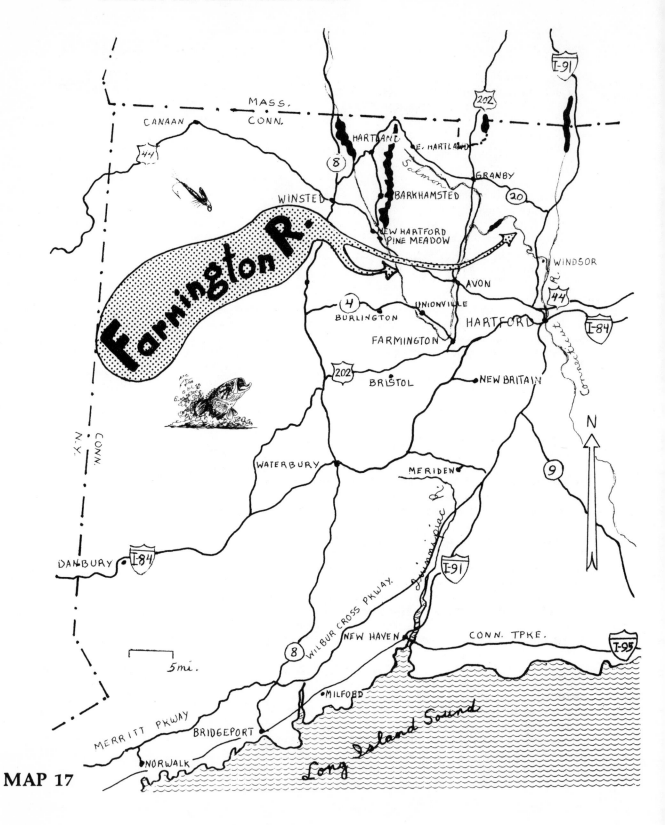

**MAP 17**

The upper reaches vary from a width of 20 to 40 feet, while the lower river is fishable in widths of over 100 to 200 feet. It is wadable water unless in high state, sometimes fast, with innumerable holes and mucky spots, but the careful wader can make it much easier than in most of the heavy waters of Catskill streams. I like the stretches in and around the towns of Hartland, Barkhamsted, New Hartford, Burlington and Unionville where you can enjoy a mixture of church steeples with your trouting.

The insect hatches on this water, as is the case with waters that are disturbed by controlled flow from dams and power stations, are quite unpredictable. But they are there, all the aquatics, and fortunate is the angler who is present when one of the hatches occurs. As is the case under these conditions, a few flies are hatching all the time, and during the highwater times, the nymphs are being washed downstream, making that time excellent for wet fly fishing. The stream also has its quota of minnows, so the streamer and bucktail are good takers on this water. The many tributary streams too small to fish in their upper reaches, afford some natural spawning, and there is a fair holdover of stocked trout from year to year, accounting for the presence of some big fish in this water. In such civilized country it is not difficult to find lodging and tackle stores for your needs. The American Legion State Forest and Barkhamsted Park, right on the stream, are good places to squat.

The Farmington can easily be reached via Route 44 north of Pine Meadow and Route 20 goes through the American Legion State Forest. To orient, the stream lies north of the cities of Bristol and New Britain and northwest of Hartford.

The Housatonic River is long, having its source in Massachusetts and flowing down to Long Island Sound at Stratford, but there are only a very few miles of what can be called excellent trout water. Like many stretches in Eastern streams, however, it can be a gem.

Flowing as it does through some of the prettiest of Connecticut's gentlest rolling hills, it wends its way down through forested lands, bubbling and gushing over big rocks and many boulders and gravel along its curvy course and offers big pools; slick, long glides; and other varied water and fishing. The 8 miles that are prime lie in the townships of Sharon and Cornwall in northwestern Connecticut. There you'll find a gracious allotment of 3½ miles of fly-fishing-only water, with 4½ with no restrictions.

In similar fashion to the way it splits Massachusetts, the broad and deep Connecticut River splits its own state. While much of it is highly developed and industrialized, the fishing still remains good, but not exceptional. The sea-run shad is, of course, the main attraction, migrating upstream as it does in the spring months of March and April. Upwards of 50,000 shad are taken from its waters by lure fishermen every year. A man with a boat has unlimited fishing, but there are few entrance places in the upstate portion that are practical.

The town of Enfield at Enfield Dam is one good spot for shad. One mile northwest of the junction of I-91 and U.S. 5 there is

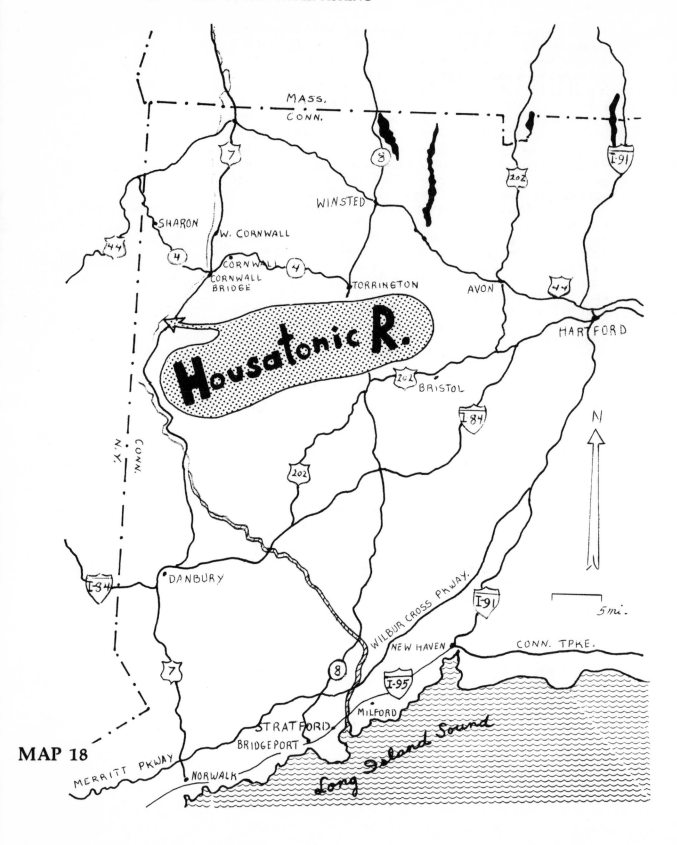

MAP 18

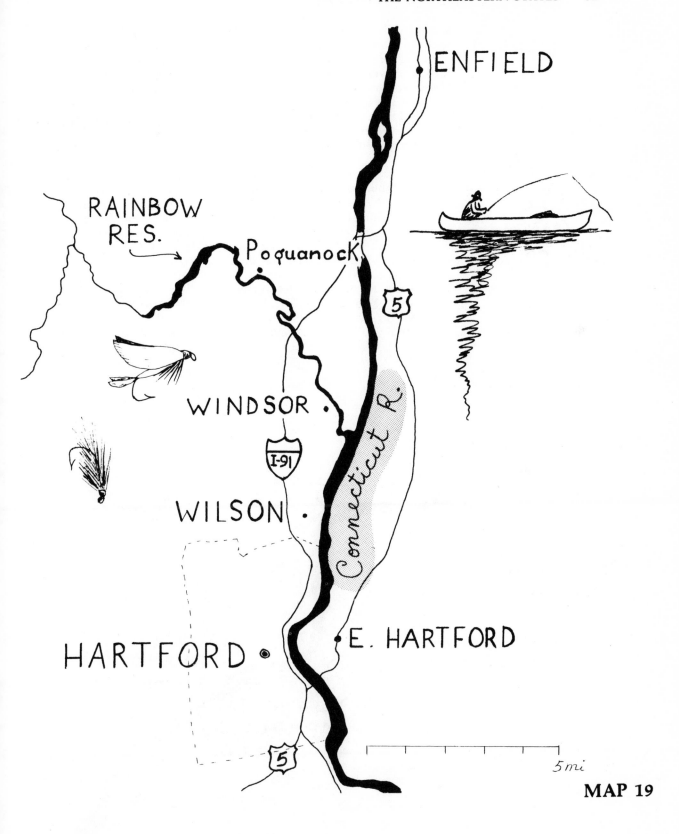

RAINBOW RES.

Poquanock

ENFIELD

5

WINDSOR

I-91

Connecticut R.

WILSON

HARTFORD

E. HARTFORD

5

5mi

**MAP 19**

access for fishing below the dam. More chances are at Wilson, just north of Hartford. Fishing here is best north or upstream of the bridge. There's also entry at Middletown off State Route 9 and further downriver at Haddam Island State Park and Haddam Meadows Park, east of Route 9. The Farmington has already been mentioned as a top trout stream, but shad do enter this tributary and good fishing can be had from Windsor up. Shad also spawn in the Salmon River, another good trout stream up in the north-central part of Connecticut. There's also good catfishing in this water.

The largest river in the eastern segment of the state is the Thames. Public access is at Stoddard Hill State Park on State Route 12, south of Norwich. There are also good brook and brown trout.

Lake fishing for bass, walleye and pickerel can be enjoyed in a number of good lakes, though only Candlewood Lake and Rainbow Reservoir can be highly rated or of sufficient interest to the out-of-stater. Candlewood Lake, on the western border, can be reached by following State Routes 37 and 39 north from Danbury. There are many marinas, boat launching facilities, bait and tackle shops and, of course, excellent lodgings. Rainbow Reservoir has produced for me. It's due north of Hartford on the Farmington River; here you'll find largemouth bass, pickerel and panfish.

MAP 20

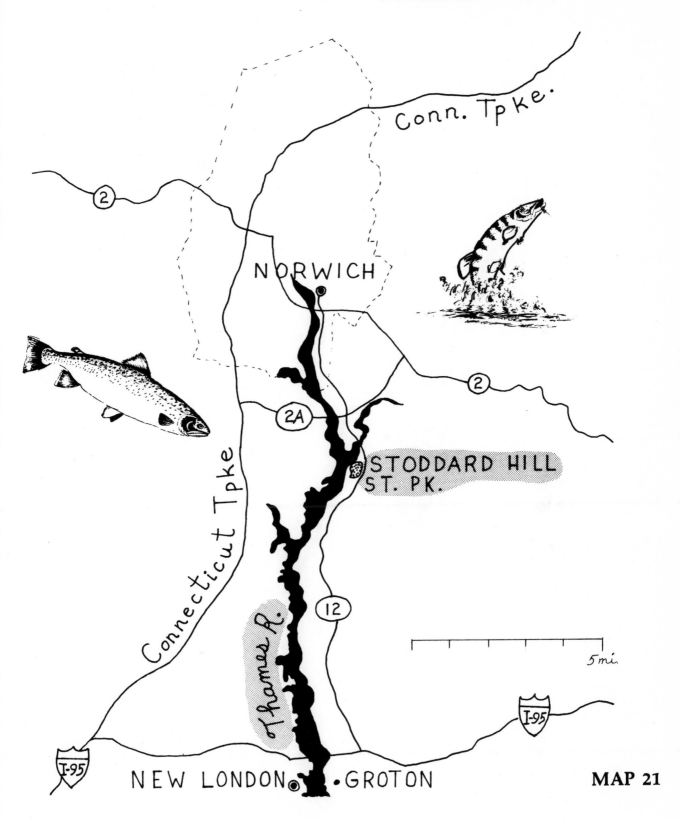

Conn. Tpke.

2

NORWICH

2

Connecticut Tpke

2A

STODDARD HILL ST. PK.

12

Thames R.

5 mi.

I-95

I-95

NEW LONDON    GROTON

**MAP 21**

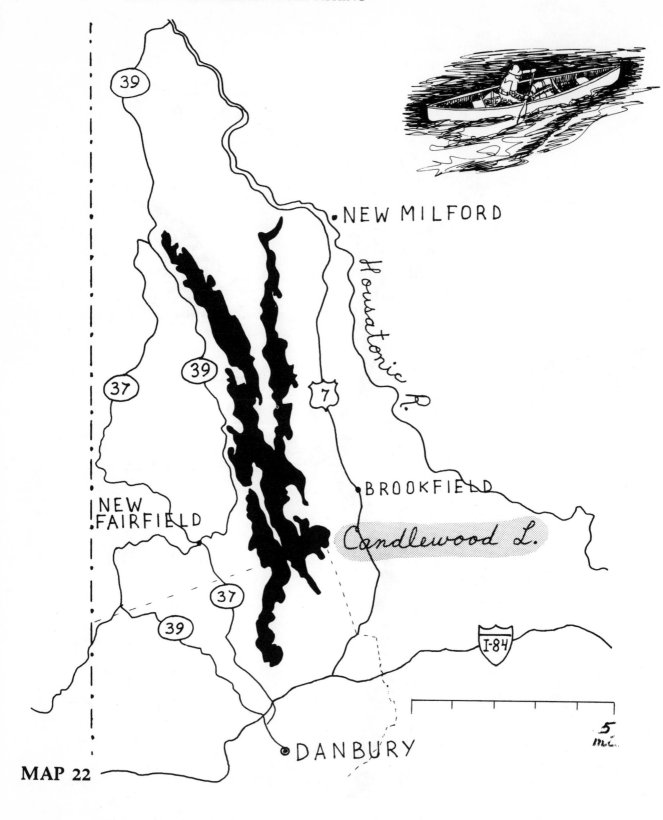

39

NEW MILFORD

39

37

7

BROOKFIELD

Candlewood L.

NEW
FAIRFIELD

37

39

I-84

5
mi.

DANBURY

**MAP 22**

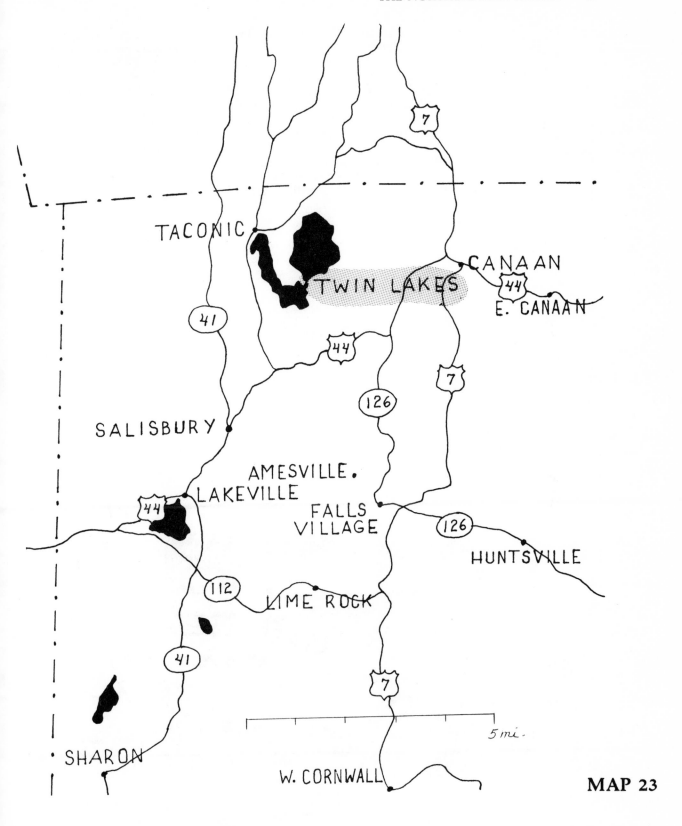

TACONIC

CANAAN

TWIN LAKES

E. CANAAN

SALISBURY

AMESVILLE.

LAKEVILLE

FALLS
VILLAGE

HUNTSVILLE

LIME ROCK

SHARON

W. CORNWALL

5 mi.

**MAP 23**

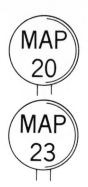

South from Middletown on the Connecticut River, look for Dooley Pond on State Route 17. The lake is normally not heavily fished, and contains largemouth bass and pickerel of good size.

An unusual experiment is being conducted by the Connecticut Board of Fisheries and Game. They've stocked kokanee and landlocked salmon in Twin Lakes, north of Salisbury on U.S. 44, up in the best part of the state, the northwest portion. It is worth a try. In this same area there are still lakes tucked away in the hills. It is not sensational or famous fishing, but you can have a good time with bass, panfish and some trout.

For more information, write Department of Environmental Protection, State Office Bldg., Hartford, Conn. 06115.

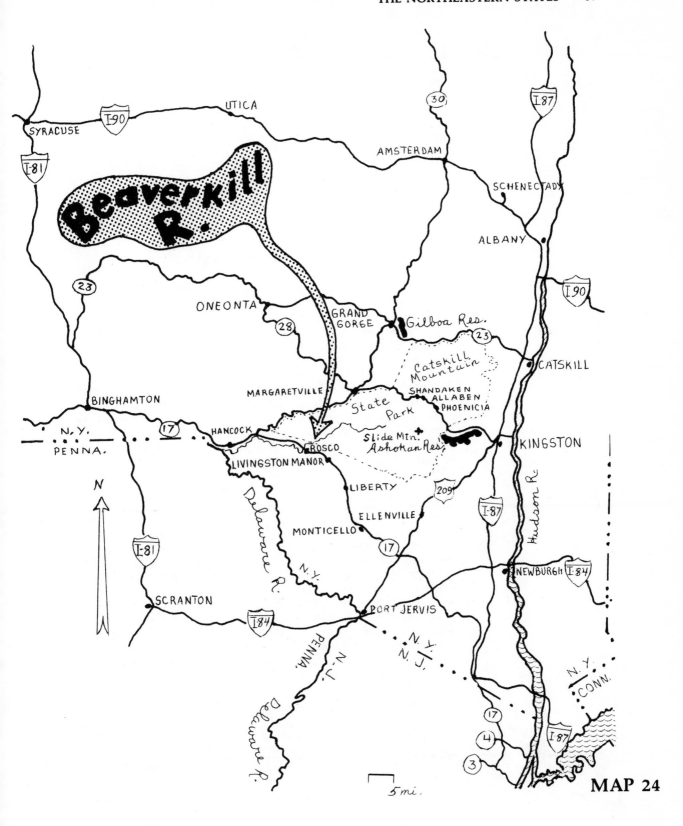

MAP 24

# The
# Northeastern
# States

# NEW YORK

### Beaverkill River

MAP
24

It would be difficult to write about the famed Beaverkill River in Sullivan County, New York, without writing about the Catskill streams in general, since so many find their births almost within shooting distance of each other. The Beaverkill and the other Catskill streams, like all traditional trouting in this country, sprang from nearby or distant sources, in this case, in the nearby streams of New Jersey and Pennsylvania.

I have fished the Beaverkill and its cousins for nearly forty years. Many famed anglers of the East and a number of the experts from foreign countries, mostly England and France, have done likewise. Some of my first books were based primarily on the experiences gained on these cherished watercourses where I was able to learn from prominent anglers and angler-authors such as Edward Hewitt, George LaBranche, Jim Deren, Bill Schaldach, Al McClane, Larry Koller and Harry Darbee, to mention only a few. The legendary Theodore Gordon, probably the first man to develop specific fly patterns for the Beaverkill, such as his Quill Gordon, lived out his life on this stream, as did Louis Rhead.

So, the Beaverkill is rich in the tradition of trout lore in America, and this includes it as the birthplace of bamboo fly rod development and a ready-made laboratory for many fishermen, since it is only a few hours from New York City.

Unlike most other streams, the main pools on the Beaverkill have been named. This cataloging is well recorded in Bill Schaldach's immortal book, *Currents And Eddies* and remains the best writing about the Beaverkill I have ever read. Borrowing from his chapter, "The Bountiful Beaverkill," here is a condensed version of the stream description:

The Forks or Junction Pool at Roscoe is where the Willowemoc joins the Beaverkill. This is the start of the big water all the way to the Delaware. Then comes Ferdons Pool with good pocket water at its head and a long, slick tail. Hendricksons is next with its huge boulders, deep holes and treacherous wading. Horse Run Pool is named from a small tributary that joins with its flow here. A good

spot for dry fly fishing in late June. Cairns is one of the most popular because it is easily fished. This is wide, open, flat water with one very deep side. Wagon Wheel Pool has been considered as part of Cairns . . . again, big water. The well-fished Schoolhouse Pool, yet, below, is beyond a patch of woods. Long, with glassy runs, perfect dry fly water during the Green Drake hatch in mid-June. Next is Lockwoods, a long, deep run with center glassy stretches. Big browns here and they come up well to a Hendrickson, or even an early blue dun or Quill Gordon hatch. It has a good, wadable bottom. A real beauty spot is next, one that has been appreciated over and over by photographers and artists. This is the Mountain Pool . . . cliffs, laurel and a backdrop of sheer mountains. Tricky currents for the dry fly man, but see it when the rhododendron is in bloom! Painter Bend is next downstream (named for a panther, pronounced 'painter' in the old days) another test of skill for the fisherman. Cook's Falls is next with a good, long run of variable water. Cemetery and Barrel Pools are next . . . lots of flat glides broken by boulders and tricky currents. Chiloways is another beauty spot. (I've spent many a lunch hour on the bank here, watching the casters go by. Nice fish, but I've been skunked too many times here!) Almost the last important pool is Baxter's, with every type of water close to the road.

Rocks, gravel, boulders, shelving riffles, deep runs, rapids, still pools, long, slick glides—100 to 200 feet wide in the big river, from 20 to 50 feet wide in the headwaters, wadable most of the way, but arm yourself with a wading staff—and watch out for deep holes and swift currents. That's the Beaverkill!

To really get the lay of the land where the Beaverkill carves its way one has to visualize an almost distinct and separate mountain grouping, separated from the Jersey mountains and those of Pennsylvania to the south and west and well below the beginnings of the more northern Adirondack mountains.

## Other Streams

Seven principal fishing streams arise in the Catskill Mountains. The famous Beaverkill is only one. To the north, the Schoharie runs south from the town of Amsterdam and has good trout fishing all the way to Gilboa Dam and reservoir. There is a portal through the mountains to where it joins the Esopus at Shandaken. Another fringe river just outside the state park is the Delaware. Its East Branch is the most famous, although the West Branch is good also. They flow southwesterly and then angle southeasterly to Hancock, where the Beaverkill enters. The Willowemoc joins the Beaverkill at Roscoe, on Route 17, the main thoroughfare of the southern tier of the Catskills. To the east are two more famous streams: the east and west branches of the Neversink, that flow into Neversink Reservoir. Below the reservoir is the famed big water flowing down to the town of Ellenville and below.

MAP 25

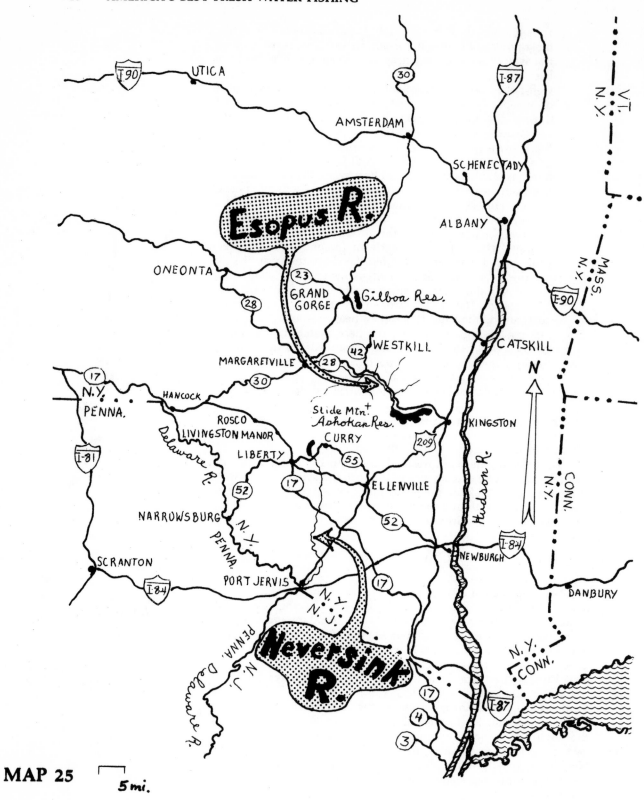

MAP 25      5 mi.

A look at a detailed map of the area shows that the Willowemoc, Esopus, Beaverkill and Neversink Rivers start basically at the very top of Slide Mountain, some 4,200 feet above sea level. The little Oliveria flows north to circle down and form the Esopus. The others flow in a southerly course between the dramatic gorges leading down from the peaks.

To approach the Beaverkill from either Albany or New York, take the New York Thruway to the Kingston area, then proceed southwest on Route 209 to 52, a secondary road heading west; or you can go down to Route 17, a superhighway heading west. Route 17 takes you through the famed resort area, across the Neversink and on to Roscoe. The Upper Beaverkill starts at Roscoe and is mainly club owned, but there is much good open water. The famed lower section from Roscoe to Hancock (along Route 17) is all big water containing large fish.

Several famed fly tyers live in the area: Walt Dette, at Livingston Manor, and Harry and Elsie Darbee of Roscoe. On the Schoharie, contact Art Flick, a famous author and fly tyer, owner of Westkill Tavern in Westkill, on Route 42 within the Catskill State Park, just off Route 23. The Folkert Brothers' store in Phoenicia is headquarters for excellent flies and tackle in Phoenicia, on the Esopus on Route 28. For detailed maps of the streams, write to the New York State Department of Environmental Conservation, 50 Wolf Road, Albany, N.Y. 12233.

If you have the time, take the high mountain road up the east branch of the Neversink from Curry on Route 55, over the "top" and down the north side of Double Top Mountain to Oliveria, the beginning of the south branch of the Esopus. When you reach Route 28 you can go west to the East Branch of the Delaware or east and follow the magnificent Esopus all the way downstream to Ashokan Reservoir. The Upper Beaverkill can be viewed from the car from Livingston Manor up a winding road to Beaverkill, Lewbeach and Turnwood.

During the Catskill's early history, all of the mountains were forested with a generous and tenacious covering of hemlock, spruce and pine, with a sprinkling of hardwoods. But in the late 19th century the mountainsides were lumbered first for the wood and then for the tannic acid found in tree bark. Add to this the cultivation of broad areas of the sloping mountainsides, and the quality and temperature of the waters gradually changed.

Before the importation of the brown trout in 1886 and later the rainbow, these streams were teeming with bright, plump and big brook trout. Anglers from New York City would make the two- or, sometimes, three-day trek from the city in order to angle for them in this untamed wilderness. But then came better roads and the march of civilization, and soon the streams were bordered by railroad beds and road beds, altering the characteristics and conditions of the streams. The last big change for these famed streams has come with the need for water for New York City. Reservoirs were plugged into the streams and the roads—once twisting, winding, two-way hardtops—became the present four- and six-lane highways that will take only a few hours from city desk to stream bank. But still, these streams survive and in some cases are even better fish producers than they were with only

brook trout as the fare.

Hurricanes and floods have also taken their toll. During the past twenty years many of the classical Eastern trout streams have almost met their death, partly because of intense weather. Strong and flash washouts wreak havoc in the mountains, causing gushing of water down well-carved drainages, widening and in some cases straightening them into veritable ditches. When these undercut a large section of clay, a landslide can alter the entire course of the stream. This can result in loss of insect hatches, for it takes many years for a streambed to restore the former ecological balance which had been built up over the years. Damaging effects have just barely been overcome on waters such as Pennsylvania's Brodhead and New York's Catskill streams.

Another horror is the U.S. Army Corps of Engineers, with its many and ingenious plans and formulas for "proper flood control." That these schemes differ from those of Mother Nature doesn't seem to occur to the computers. As a result, the Corps has made worse the job that nature started in one of her raw moments.

But nature repeatedly tries to heal herself despite crises, and, believe it or not, with the help of local rod and gun clubs, some of the best and most interesting trout fishing is still to be had in these famed Eastern streams, rivalling anything to be found in many of the touted streams west of the Great Divide.

In fact, I've had more interesting times and more times where my skills were stretched to the limits on the Beaverkill, and especially the Esopus, than I've had on Oregon's Klamath or on Idaho's Silver Creek. There's something cagey about Catskill streams. I've gone fishless more times than I care to mention on these waters and I've seen experts, used to fishing the teeming waters of the West, totally depressed as they wade ashore from the -kill without having felt a rise.

Catskill feeder streams are quite remote from road traffic. Much of the mountain area is either too difficult to reach or is owned by private landowners and is heavily posted. Native brook trout are still to be found there. Several clubs, mainly on the Beaverkill, post much of the headwaters of Catskill Mountain streams. While these restrictions do tend to concentrate the fishing activity to the broader and more open lower river sections, they do help to preserve the fish population and allow unhampered spawning activity. The reservoirs grow big trout that ascend the upper rivers and spawn in the highest mountain tributaries, allowing many natural "wild trout" to form the basis of the fish population, which is augmented several times each year by the hatchery trucks. Cold water below reservoir dams assures much good trout water for many miles.

In the case of the Esopus, a stream which flows into the Ashokan Reservoir, the water was stocked with rainbow trout some fifty years ago and the fish took hold almost immediately, growing to 22 inches in length in the reservoir and making tremendous spawning runs upstream for a constant natural restocking. The brown trout also found the reservoir to its liking, some fish growing to ten pounds or more in weight and taking advantage of the secluded spawning tributaries high atop the neighboring mountains.

The word "rugged" sums up, I believe, the character of all these streams. They are born of ice-cold springs far up in the heavily wooded and rocky peaks, then carve their twisting ways through clay banks and shale and harder rock formations, tumbling all the way until they reach the comparatively rolling, gravel-and-boulder valleys in their lower reaches. In these fast-moving stretches before the streams reach the bottomlands, are pools of quiet water, often and abruptly broken by step-down pools and many fastwater rapids.

Though this is a generalization, each of the streams has its special appeal because of the unique path it takes from its source to its confluence with a stream or river below. Along their way, each has many excellent tributaries that are fishable and contain good-sized trout. The extreme lower reaches, particularly just above the reservoirs, also produce excellent smallmouth bass and walleye pike fishing.

It is also a wonder how well the fishing holds up under a constant barrage of anglers who visit these streams from the biggest population center in the United States. All methods of fishing are allowed on most of the water, with only a few stretches reserved for fly fishing only. In the early season the baiters and spin fishermen have constant, big fish success on waters such as the Esopus, for they are working over the early spawning rainbows and a few browns that have ascended in early February. In this stream the browns often ascend the tributaries in spring, and some rainbows ascend with the bulk of the browns in the fall, which makes for quite a mixture and sometimes a two-spawn season for many of them. In the case of the Esopus, the water below the portal coming in at the town of Allaben from Gilboa Dam on the Schoharie, keeps the river abnormally high in the spring, and smart anglers work the edges with bait and spinning lures, and with bucktails and streamers. Later on, when the hatches occur and the water clears a bit from the snow run-off, the whole stream is fair game, especially the holds behind the enormous rocks found all along the broken water, and sometimes in the center of the long, slick runs. Later in the season when the upper river is down, the portal water is a blessing, since it maintains a normal level throughout the season. When dry weather of July and August lowers other streams, many anglers desert the Beaverkill and come over to the Esopus.

There are miles of good water on the lower Neversink, below the reservoir. Here too, the cold flowage from the bottom of the dam keeps the water cool and high enough for big stream angling. The same is true below the dam on the East Branch of the Delaware. Both of these streams profit from the reservoir, even though the reservoir lakes have replaced miles of good trout stream. The big fish that have grown big in the reservoir are taken in the upper reaches.

Everything from worms to live bait to spinning tackle to the finest leaders and midge flies can be used. The choice is yours. The fly hatches follow a very steady pattern from April right through to the closing days of September. Upper New York State is graced with the large Adirondack State Park, which encompasses some of the finest fishing to be found in the East. It is dotted with lakes and

is criss-crossed by streams that are born of mountains and high hills. The native brook trout still holds its ground here, and good catches can be had in the numerous lakes and brooks accessible only by long hikes from the road, even though this park is the most-used recreation area in the East.

The Ausable River (West Branch) is probably the best trout stream in the Adirondacks. Certainly it is the most famous, having gained its reputation because well-known angling writers have made it so. Almost all of its length is fishable, and brook, brown and rainbow trout are plentiful. Some very big trout can be had. While the local clansmen take a constant amount of big trout, the experts who visit it even for a day can connect with trout of magnificent size. The fly hatches on this river are constant from the earliest days in April right on through the season until September. Of course, bait fishermen and spin fishermen as well as fly fishermen pound this stream constantly. As is usual with most well-traveled waters, the time for the best fly fishing is from two to three weeks after the opening days of the season.

The Ausable is a wondrous stream, filled with contrasts. It is a fast stream, rock- and gravel-strewn, with big boulders breaking its course. It is born in the mountains south of Lake Placid and flows northeastward into Lake Champlain. The Ausable has two branches: East and West. The West Branch is more favored and contains better fishing and scenery. It is a classic trout stream, and voluminous studies have been done to keep it that way. It has one state campground at Wilmington Notch, possibly the most beautiful stretch scenically as well as from the fishing point of view. It runs from 60 to 100 feet in width and from 2 to 8 feet deep, from Lake Placid to Wilmington Notch. From there downstream to Wilmington Pond, the river becomes a series of rapids and falls. The wadable bottom is mainly gravel and sand in the upper reaches, with larger boulders and slick bedrock in the lower section. Here, wading is a hazard because the bedrock is extremely slick and smooth. The stream is graced with a mixture of conifers and hardwoods. The water flow is fast and deep. Many anglers fish from canoes, but this is restricted to the upper reaches because of rapids and waterfalls. Most popular canoe-fishing is in the vicinity of Monument Falls.

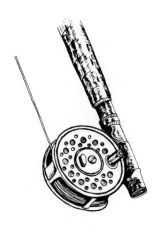

This (West) branch is 29 miles in length, from Marcy Dam Pond to Ausable Forks, with only about 5 miles of posted river. The best area for fishing is from Wilmington Pond to the Route 73 bridge. Reports claim that there is about 10% natural reproduction in the upper portion, with some 80,000 trout stocked annually in a mixture of the three main species, brook, brown and rainbow. From Monument Falls a length of 2.2 miles is designated "trophy trout water" for artificial lures only; minimum length 14 inches, one per person, per day. Six-pound browns have been taken in this section.

To reach the Ausable from the Albany region, take the New York Thruway north. It is a gorgeous ride to sample the glories of the area. Thruway Route 87 parallels Lake Champlain, but before you reach the northern border of Adirondack State Park, take Route 73 west to Lake Placid and there transfer to Route 86, which borders the West Branch all the way to the Forks. The East Branch

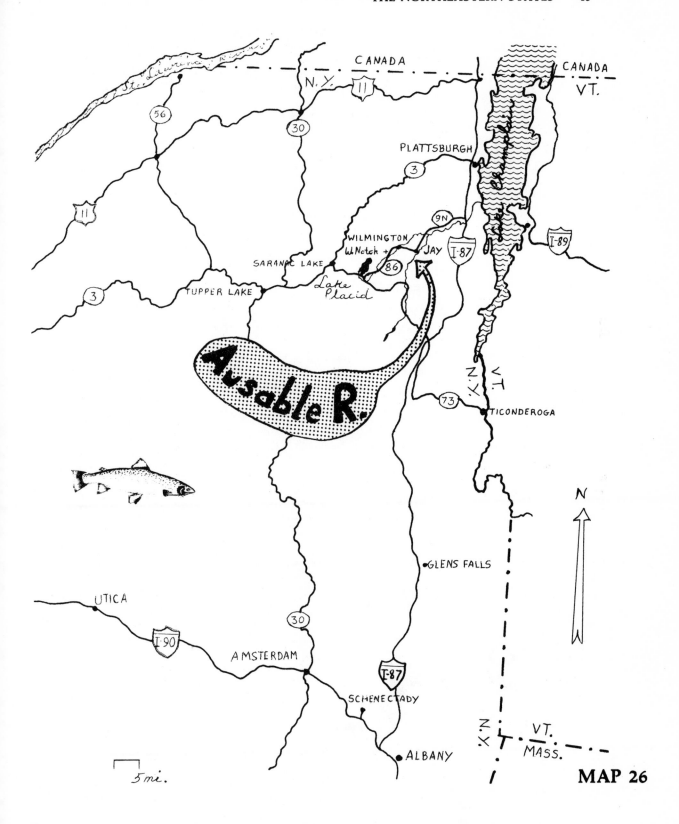

MAP 26

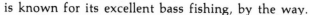

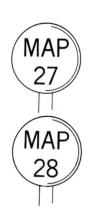

is known for its excellent bass fishing, by the way.

As you can see by looking at the map, there are hundreds of other streams within a few miles' drive from Lake Placid. They should be investigated if you have the time. Since this is resort country, there are all kinds of accommodations and tackle stores to choose from.

My fondest memories of the Ausable have occurred the second or third week in June. While insect hatches of may flies and caddis occur before then, this period brings out the biggest of the may flies, the famed Green Drake. If you can hit the river during this hatch, you see and possibly connect with some of the really big trout that reside in that stream. They are big because they are smart.

There are a lot of chubs in the river and they also like dry flies, so the trick is to snatch your fly away from the chub if you think that is what is tickling it. Or it may be a monster brown nudging it. You'll know when the leader tightens and the rod bends.

Best bets for bass, pike, salmon and trout fishermen are in the large lakes such as Lake Champlain, the largest (shared with Vermont), the headwaters of the Mohawk, waters such as Lake Oneida and the famed Finger Lakes: Seneca, Cayuga, Onandaga, Canandaigua, Skaneateles, Owasco in North Central New York. Far to the west near Lake Erie at the border of Pennsylvania is famed Lake Chautauqua. Anglers wanting to fish from canoe or boat should definitely write to the State Department of Environmental Conservation, Albany, N.Y. 12233, and ask for "Your Outdoor Recreation Map," for it offers all details needed.

In Lake Ontario, bass fishing is excellent all along the shore and particularly near the St. Lawrence River, especially from Sackets Harbor, off Pillar Point and Dexter on State Route 3 and off Chaumont. State Route 12E goes through Cape Vincent, another touch-off point for good pike, walleye and bass fishing.

The St. Lawrence area is world famous for smallmouth bass, muskie, northern pike, walleye and panfish as well as trout, and is, in my opinion, the most productive and interesting section of the state to fish.

Actually a whole book could be written on this area, yet no really specific spot should be singled out as the "best" in the territory. You have to go there year after year, and even then, you'll have hardly scratched the surface.

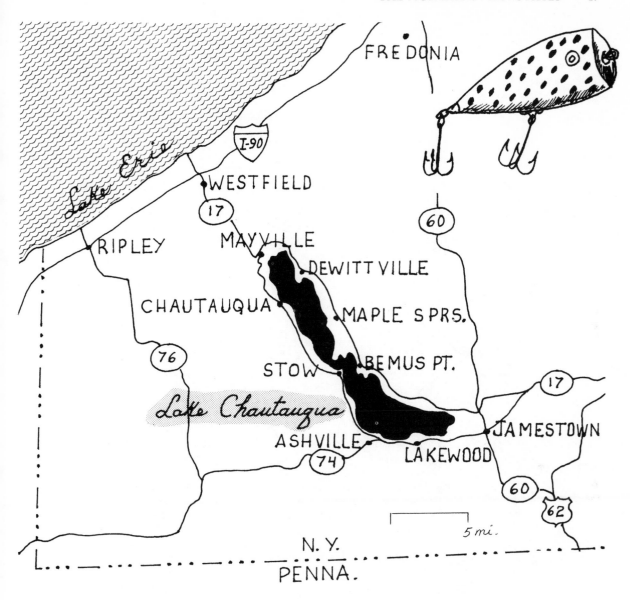

FREDONIA

Lake Erie

I-90

WESTFIELD

17

RIPLEY

MAYVILLE

DEWITTVILLE

CHAUTAUQUA

MAPLE SPRS.

76

BEMUS PT.

STOW

17

*Lake Chautauqua*

JAMESTOWN

ASHVILLE

LAKEWOOD

74

60

62

60

5 mi.

N.Y.

PENNA.

**MAP 27**

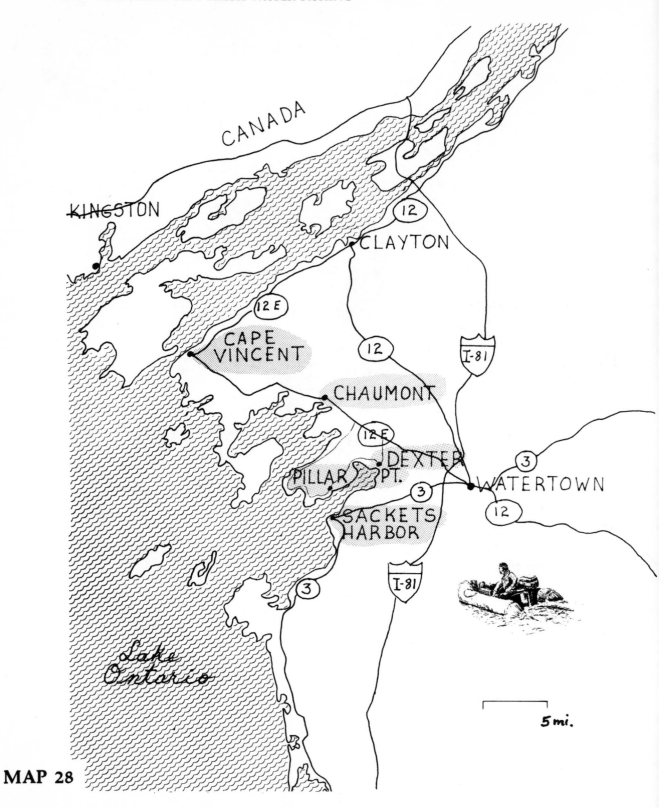

CANADA

KINGSTON

12

CLAYTON

12 E

CAPE
VINCENT

12

I-81

CHAUMONT

12 E

DEXTER
PT.

3

WATERTOWN

PILLAR

3

12

SACKETS
HARBOR

I-81

3

*Lake
Ontario*

5 mi.

**MAP 28**

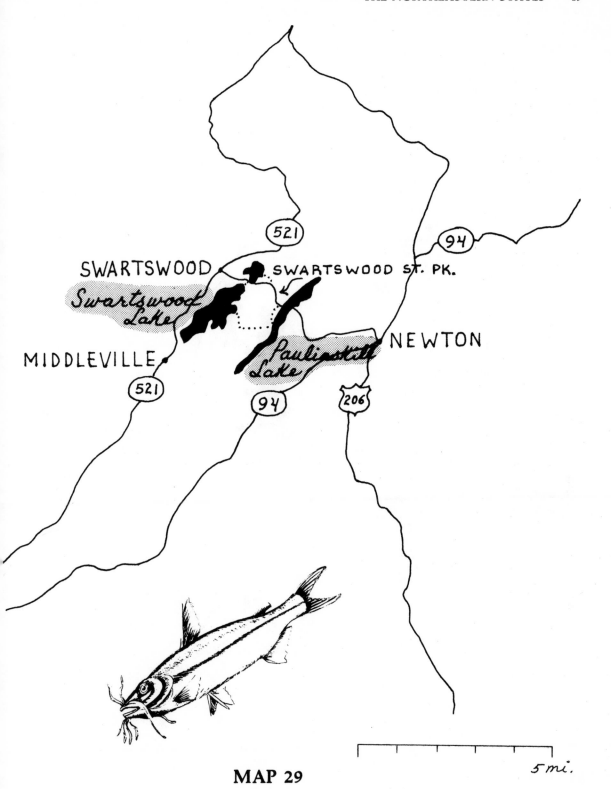

521

94

SWARTSWOOD    SWARTSWOOD ST. PK.

*Swartswood Lake*

MIDDLEVILLE

*Paulinskill Lake*    NEWTON

521

94    206

5 mi.

**MAP 29**

**MAP 30**

# The
# Northeastern
# States

# NEW JERSEY

While I have deep roots in the streams and lakes of New Jersey, since I've fished them from school days, I can say with all honesty that "it ain't what it used to be." True, the upper Delaware of my memory, shared by New Jersey with New York State, still produces excellent bass fishing and some good trout fishing, further up. But for the most part the state of New Jersey is a matter of put-and-take fishing. While I would not intentionally visit New Jersey for its fishing over some of the better states, it does provide unbelievable recreational fishing and outings for its residents from the highly crowded cities as well as for anglers from neighboring New York.

A look at the map shows networks of highways big and small literally covering every inch of the state, so access is more than adequate to any waters. With such easy access you will find crowds of anglers and, in summer, hikers and campers too.

New Jersey, New York, and Pennsylvania are the birth-states of angling history in America. Many notable angler-writers lived there and formed their part of the angling culture. A hundred years ago the waters of New Jersey and, likewise, the Catskills in New York State were "country" and "remote" and much sport was to be had. It was here that Ray Bergman, one of the most famous angling authors, resided and did his fishing and learned the techniques that made his reputation.

A brief rundown of the lakes and rivers of northern New Jersey should mention the waters north of Interstate 80 and west of U.S. 202. A species of trout is found, as well as largemouth and smallmouth bass, plus panfish, in Lake Hopatcong, which lies north of Interstate 80 and east of U.S. 206. This is the most famous of all lakes. Trout can be had also in Lake Musconetcong, adjacent to it, and in Swartswood and Paulins Kill Lakes, near Newton on U.S. 206 and State Route 94. To the northwest, Big Flat Brook,

MAP 33

MAP 30

MAP 29

MAP 31

51

DINGMANS
FERRY (PA.)

Delaware R.

521

521

LAYTON

206

Big Flat Brook

Kittatinny Lake

WALLPACK CTR.

Culver Lake

BRANCHVILLE

521

206

FLATBROOKVILLE

5 mi.

SWARTSWOOD

NEWTON

**MAP 31**

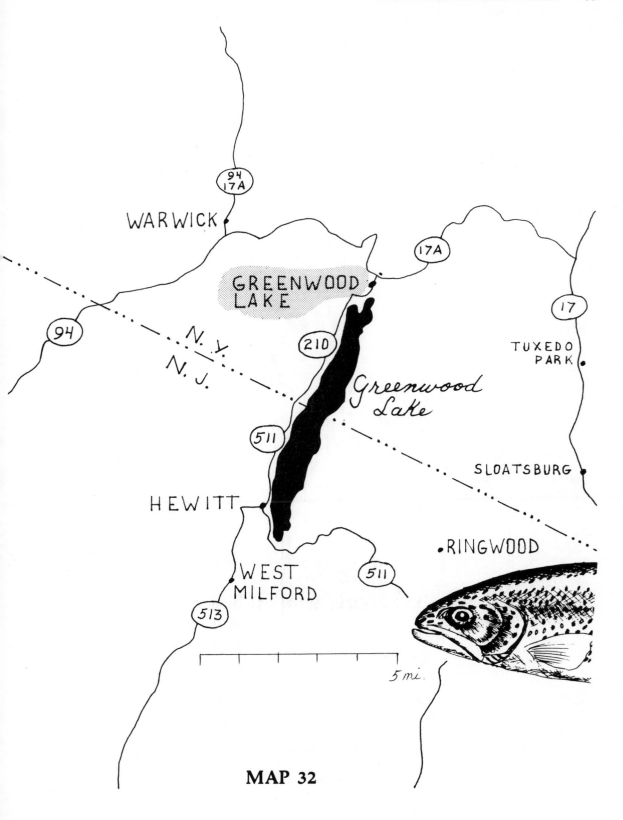

MAP 32

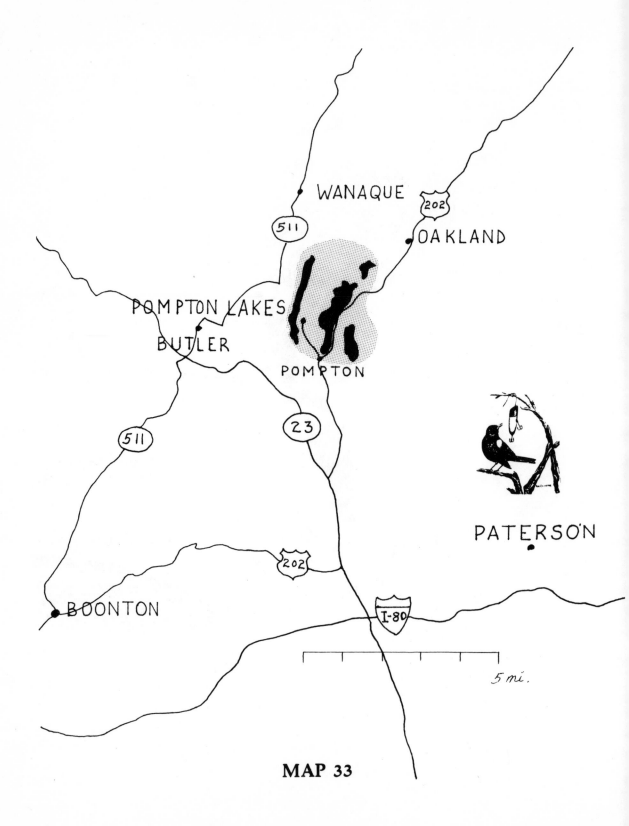

**MAP 33**

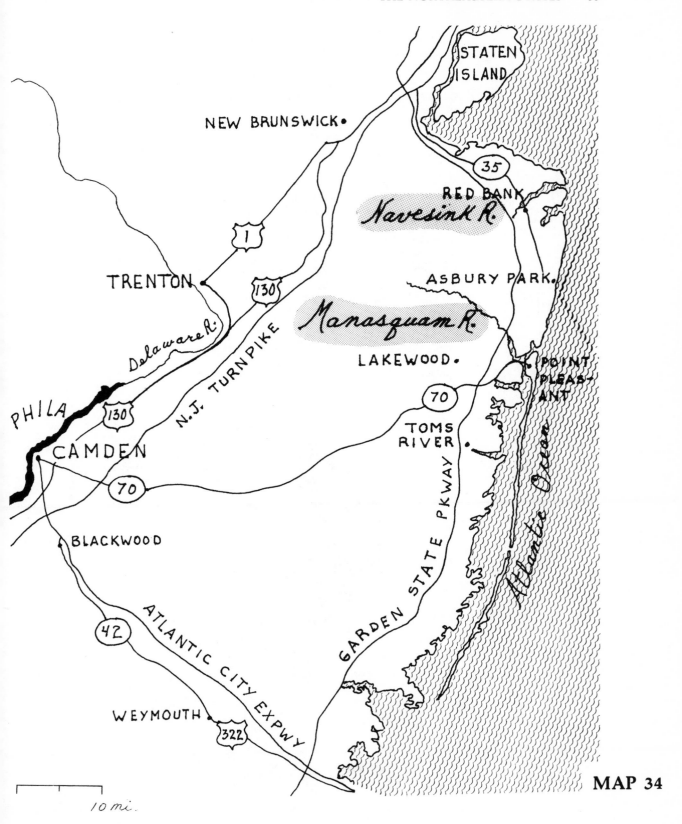

STATEN ISLAND

NEW BRUNSWICK.

35

RED BANK.

*Navesink R.*

ASBURY PARK.

*Manasquam R.*

1

TRENTON.

130

LAKEWOOD.

*Delaware R.*

N.J. TURNPIKE

70

PHILA

130

CAMDEN

70

TOMS RIVER.

POINT PLEASANT

*Atlantic Ocean*

BLACKWOOD

GARDEN STATE PKWY

42

ATLANTIC CITY EXPWY

WEYMOUTH.

322

10 mi.

**MAP 34**

Kittatinny Lake and Culver Lake—all close to Pennsylvania, have produced through the years despite shore development and hordes of anglers.

I can remember as a boy fishing Greenwood Lake, which is along the New York State border. Those were big trout then, and stocking today keeps this water producing.

Smaller, very pretty lakes are in the Pomptons, northwest of Paterson, accessible from State Route 23 and U.S. 202. All the trout, and both bass and panfish abound.

If you wish to fish New Jersey for its tradition of trout and bass angling, write for the list of streams available from the Division of Fish, Game, and Shellfish, Box 1809, Trenton, New Jersey 08625. Also get the regulations, because they are quite complicated, even on a day-to-day fishing basis, due to the stocking programs.

Southern New Jersey is bass country with hundreds of lakes. The best, in my opinion, is still Blackwood Lake southeast of Camden. Good bass also exists at Navesink near Red Bank and the famed Manasquam, entering the ocean at Point Pleasant.

# PENNSYLVANIA

On a long magnificent curve, the main ridge of the Appalachian Mountains traverses the central part of the state. Cutting through between the Alleghenies from north to south is the famed Susquehanna River, draining northeastern Pennsylvania through its West Branch. The other major river system is the Allegheny, noted for its muskie fishing, draining the entire western portion of the state. The tributaries of these two rivers offer angling that has become famed all over the world. There are not too many big lakes, but a number of rivers have been dammed to make excellent impoundment fishing for bass, muskellunge and walleye pike, as well as rainbow and brown trout. Lake trout are present but are not of spectacular size.

In the northeastern part of the state, the Delaware River offers some of the most famed smallmouth black bass fishing in the United States. In fact it was on the Delaware that the pioneers of bass bugging, that is, casting lightweight, fluffy, "bug"-type deerhair flies with a fly rod, was introduced many years ago. The river can be floated by canoe or john boat for miles as far down as Phillipsburg. Port Jervis, New York, or Milford, Pennsylvania, on U.S. 209, or Dingman's Ferry or Bushkill, farther south along 209, are good starting points—all of which happen to be in the area of the controversial Tocks Island Dam project. The Delaware Water Gap is the famed hot spot, and I urge you to fish this water if you ever come to this state.

The Susquehanna and its tributaries are also famed for bass and walleye. All the way to Conowingo Lake on the Maryland border, some few miles above the Conowingo Dam, you'll also find muskies and rock bass. It is a big river, a mile wide in stretches, and the upper waters are famed as the birthplace of fly rod fishing for bass.

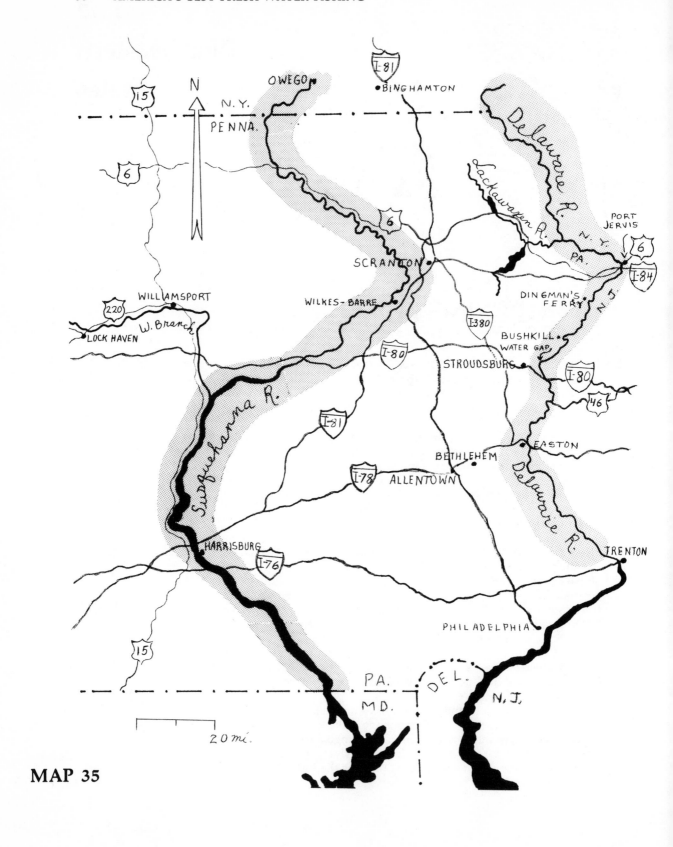

**MAP 35**

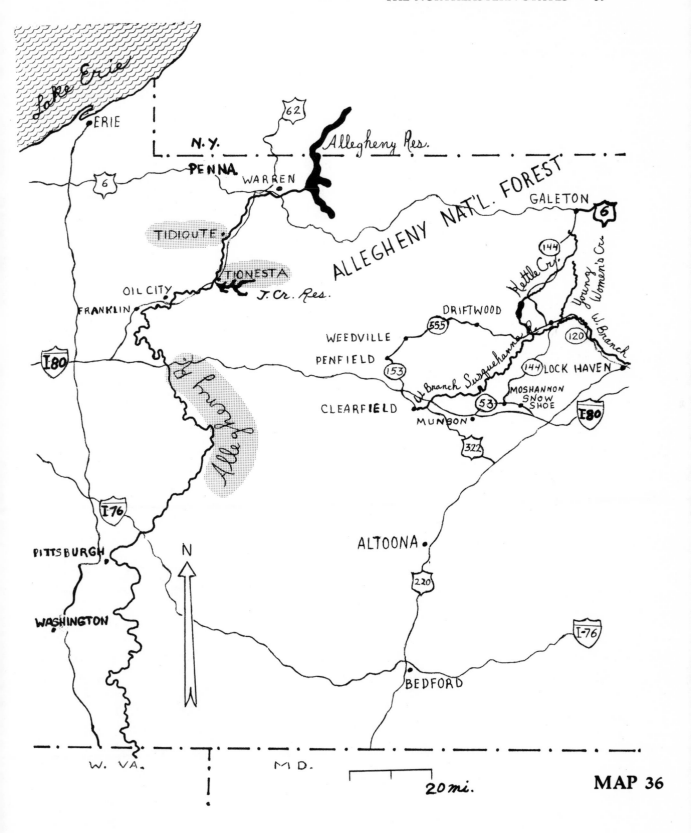

Lake Erie

ERIE

62

N. Y.

PENNA.

WARREN

Allegheny Res.

6

GALETON

ALLEGHENY NAT'L. FOREST

6

144

Kettle Cr.

Young Women's Cr.

TIDIOUTE

TIONESTA

J. Cr. Res.

OIL CITY

DRIFTWOOD

W. Branch

FRANKLIN

555

120

WEEDVILLE

Allegh.

PENFIELD

153

W. Branch Susquehanna

144 LOCK HAVEN

I80

MOSHANNON SNOW SHOE

I80

CLEARFIELD

53

MUNSON

322

I76

ALTOONA

PITTSBURGH

N

220

WASHINGTON

I-76

BEDFORD

W. VA.          M. D.

20 mi.

**MAP 36**

The best muskie fishing in the state is on the Allegheny between the towns of Tidioute and south to the Tionesta Creek Reservoir, on the borders of the Allegheny National Forest in northwest Pennsylvania. U.S. 62 follows the river, and there are boat landings along the way, together with varied public access spots in case you want to bring your own craft. The fish also are found in the water below the dam on the Tionesta Creek. Walleyes, generally large, are found here and some bass. Boats are to be had for rent above the dam.

Bass, walleye and muskie are also to be had in French Creek, which rises about 20 miles away from the shore of Lake Erie and flows in a long curve to the Allegheny River at Franklin. U.S. 322 travels beside the river almost for its entire length. Interstates 79 (north-south from Erie to Pittsburgh) and 80 (east-west) intersect southwest of Franklin.

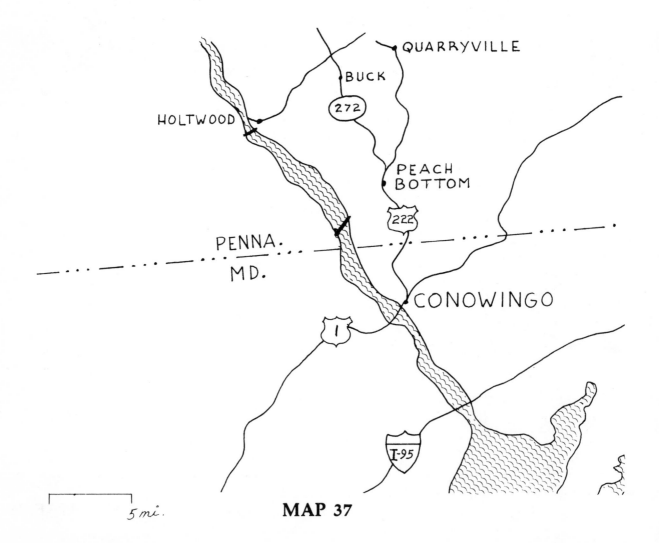

5 mi.

**MAP 37**

Lake fishermen will enjoy its 50 miles on Lake Erie, but better fishing is to be found above three large dams on the Susquehanna River system just above the Maryland border. Lake Conowingo, Holtwood Lake and Safe Harbor Lake are all reached by country roads off State Route 272 on the east and State Route 74 on the west. U.S. 30 between Lancaster and York also crosses part of Safe Harbor Lake, making it quite accessible. Boats are available at Drumore, which is on a secondary road west of the Peach Bottom junction of U.S. 222 with State Route 272, at the riverbank town of Holtwood, which is on State Route 372 west of Buck on S.R. 372, at Safe Harbor on State Route 441 and at Columbia at the junction of U.S. 30 and State Route 441. Many local accommodations are available.

Nine miles from where I used to live is Pennsylvania's largest man-made lake: Lake Wallenpaupack, created in the 1920's. The scenic route on its east shore is accessible from I-84 at Greentown and at the northern end from U.S. 6 at Hawley, directly east from Scranton. This lake is hard fished but does contain some good bass and some particularly good walleye.

Harvey's Lake on State Route 415 offers trout, lake trout and walleye. It is reached out of Wilkes-Barre westward via State Route 118 to Dallas and thence to Idetown and State Route 415. Coming from the west on State Route 118, you turn north on 415 near Lehman.

The largest natural lake in Pennsylvania is Pymatuning on the Ohio border about 25 miles south of Lake Erie. Some 18,000 acres in size, it contains 72 miles of shoreline, harboring muskellunge, bass, some pike and walleye.

The Pennsylvania Department of Commerce and the Pennsylvania Fish Commission in Harrisburg have combined efforts for a broad-based publication listing nearly every fishable lake, pond and stream in the state, including the species found in these waters, plus directions on how to get there.

In addition to its fishing, this state is one of the most beautiful in the U.S. Not sensational scenery as is found in Wyoming, but a sense of quiet, pastoral farmland and well-wooded, long lines of mountain ridges. Despite the fact that Pennsylvania is heavily populated and industrial, the woodlands and open country are readily available and relatively uncrowded.

One big advantage to fishing in this state is the fact that there is always some kind of fishing available year-round.

When discussing Pennsylvania trout streams, we are in delightful trouble. If we pinpoint any stream and leave out any, we are up for criticism from the greatest angling authorities in and out of print. As a matter of fact, the state of Pennsylvania has probably produced more angling writers of immortal fame than it has trout streams. The list of streams is long and any angler seriously considering fishing this state, no matter upon what stream, had better bone up via the exhaustive pages of art and fact that have been published by such as Ernie Schwiebert, *Matching The Hatch*; Charlie K. Fox, *Wonderful World of Trout*; Vincent Marinaro, *Dry Fly Code*; Emlin Gill, *Practical Dry Fly Fishing*; Charles Wetzel, *Fishing The Wet Fly*; Preston Jennings, *Book of Trout Flies*; Alvin Grove, *Lure and Lore of Trout Fishing*; John

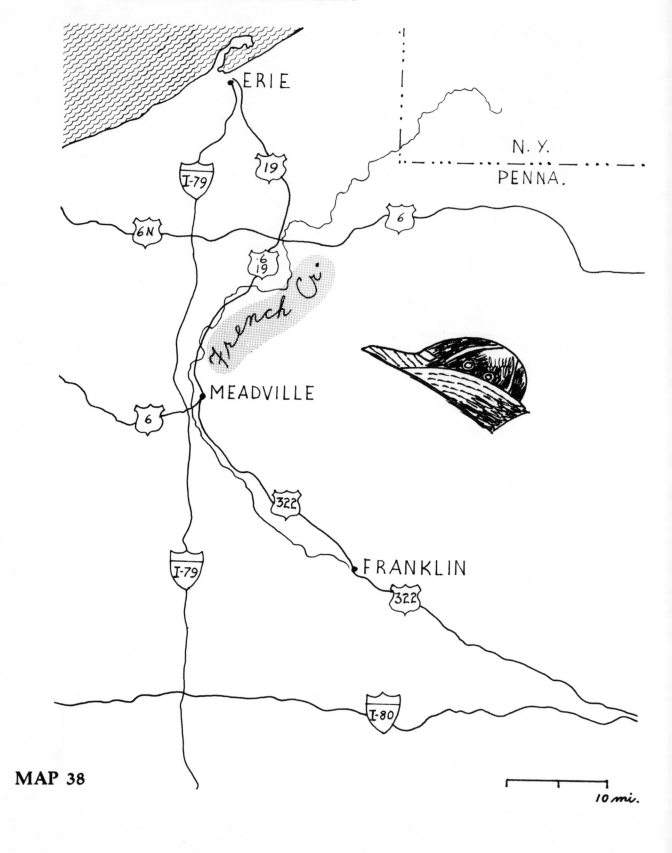

ERIE

N. Y.
PENNA.

I-79
19
6N
6
6
19
French
MEADVILLE
6
322
I-79
FRANKLIN
322
I-80

**MAP 38**

10 mi.

MAP 39

Alden Knight, *Modern Fly Casting;* Eugene V. Connett, *Any Luck?;* J. Edson Leonard, *Flies;* and Fred Everett, *Fun With Trout.* And I've probably missed some good ones.

All these anglers have spent their lives on Pennsylvania trout streams and with obvious good reason. They have minute acquaintance with these streams, as have their cohorts who are so far unwritten and who include such stalwarts as Roy Steenrod, George Harvey, Ross Trimmer and Dr. Henry Stebbins, just to name a few.

In a sense, Pennsylvania streams should be known as the American birthplace of serious angling authors. As a result of the energy and dedication of these angling mentors, there is a big program of "Fish for Fun," which should be mentioned here as an example of the kind of fishing we could have in many states if such policies were accepted. The areas set aside are also an indication of the best streams in the state for all-around trout fishing.

Charlie Fox, a famed angler and authority, knows the state's angling scene perhaps better than most, and was quite descriptive about it in a letter he sent to me as this book was being written. I quote from that recent letter:

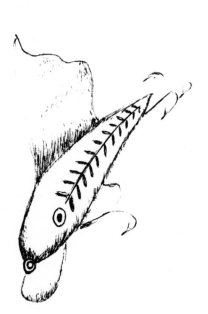

> In the west is the Allegheny River, down the center is the large Susquehanna and in the east, the Delaware. All have wonderful cold water feeder streams—thus three great water systems. That's the good part. Now comes the bad. With the daily creel limit of eight trout and a size limit of six inches, the streams are fished down to almost nothing and held there. The Fish Commission publicizes just when and where the next dumping truck of trout will be and the fishermen are right behind the fish truck.
>
> About two decades ago I gave up on open catch-and-restock waters. It became too discouraging to intercept a hatch under favorable conditions at a beautiful place and see little or nothing, where sometimes in the past under similar conditions you saw the surface broken by rings made by feeding fish. The only places I bother with are the stringently regulated killing areas which the Fish Commission designates as "Fish For Fun." In these waters there is very little killing and no closed season, so no crowds on opening day. For the most part, these sections are short and at times crowded but they all carry a head of good sophisticated fish of fine average size and do present a real challenge.
>
> In the 'Fish For Fun' areas you can fish the rise and match the hatch and in the summer you can show the incessant feeders your idea of the imitations of the various terrestrials. It is pretty fishing. I love this regulated fishing over good-sized, sophisticated trout. That's why I leave the open water to the 'mess of fish' crowd.
>
> The Commission has another deal called 'Fly Fishing Only.' Here the creel limit is six fish per day and minimum size of nine inches. These waters offer fair chances at decent size browns once in a while.

Information on Pennsylvania fishing is available from the Game Commission, P.O. Box 1567, Harrisburg, Pa. 17120.

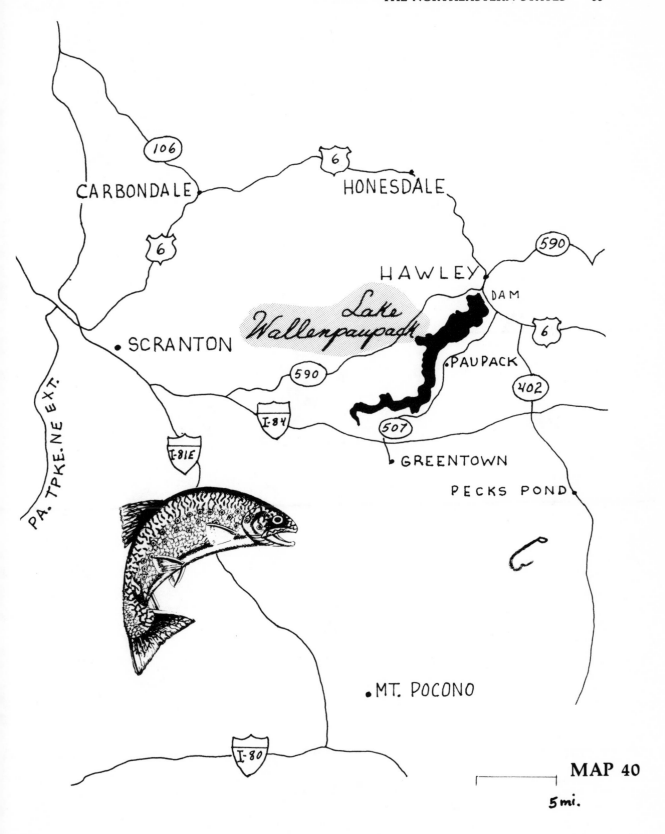

CARBONDALE

106

6

6

HONESDALE

6

590

HAWLEY

DAM

Lake
Wallenpaupack

SCRANTON

590

PAUPACK

6

402

PA. TPKE. NE EXT.

I-84

507

I-81E

GREENTOWN

PECKS POND

MT. POCONO

I-80

MAP 40

5 mi.

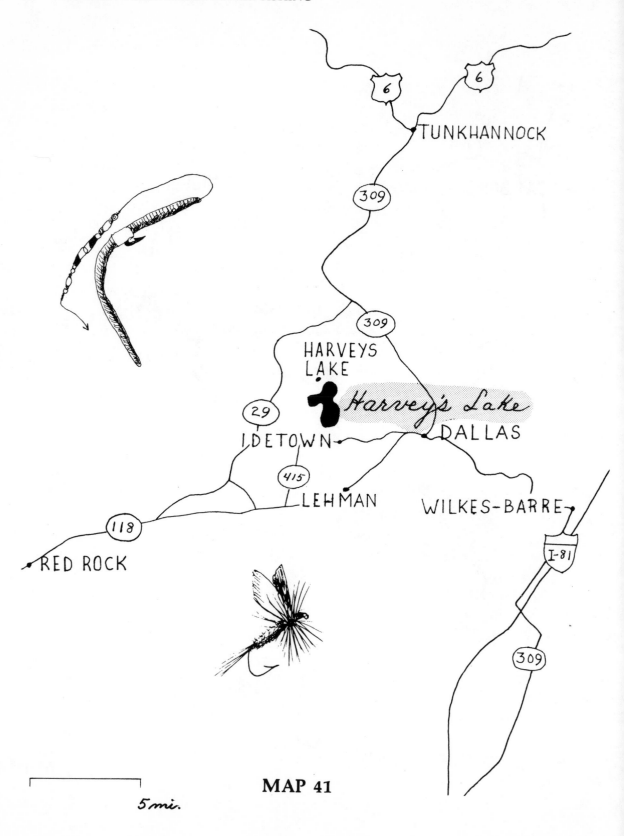

TUNKHANNOCK

6    6

309

309

HARVEYS
LAKE

*Harvey's Lake*

29

IDETOWN    DALLAS

415

LEHMAN    WILKES-BARRE

118    I-81

RED ROCK

309

**MAP 41**

*5 mi.*

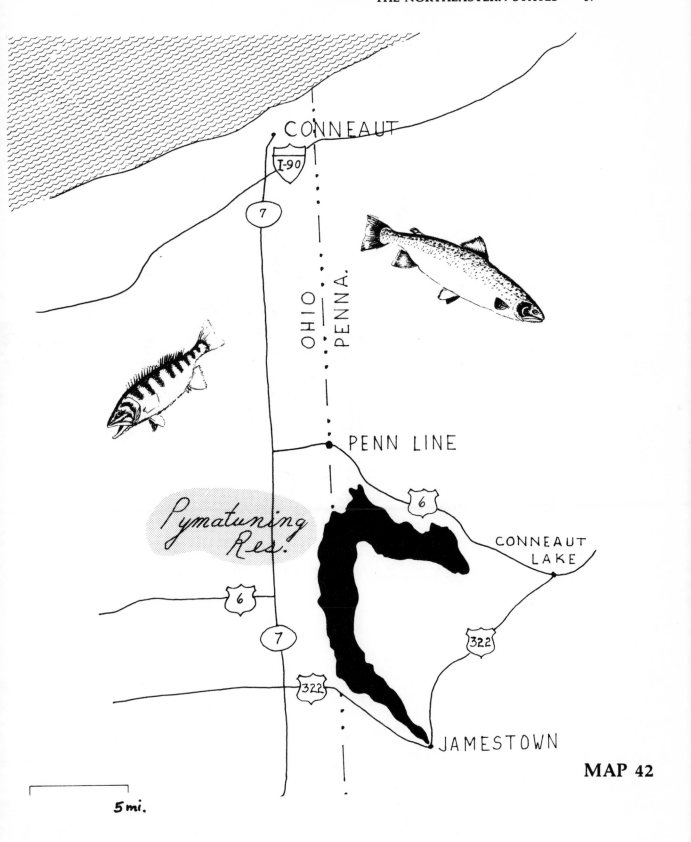

CONNEAUT

I-90

7

OHIO

PENNA.

PENN LINE

Pymatuning Res.

6

CONNEAUT
LAKE

6

7

322

322

JAMESTOWN

**MAP 42**

5 mi.

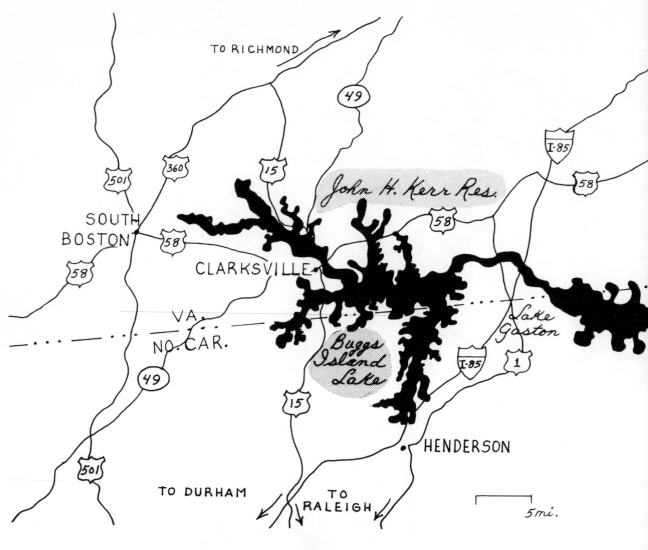

**MAP 43**

# 2. The Southeastern States

# VIRGINIA
# WEST VIRGINIA

These two states form a bridge between the Northeastern States and the South, in terms of sport fishing. They are both mountainous and scenically beautiful, containing hundreds of mountain streams and small brooks that contain some fine back-country type trout fishing with the largemouth bass found in the lakes along with sunfish, crappie and catfish. While the residents might differ with me, none of these waters are famous, nor are they as heavily fished as comparable areas in the Northeast or South. In other words, an angler who lives in New York City, for instance, would not single out either of these two states for a jaunt to famed or big-fish waters. A scenic vacation trip with the family yes, definitely, with fishing as a side issue but not as the prime interest.

Due to the mountainous terrain, much of the best fishing is not readily accessible from the major highways and most of it is gained only from second-and third-class roads with little of the deluxe type of motel and facilities demanded by most vacationers.

Buggs Island Reservoir, also known as the John H. Kerr Reservoir, straddling the North Carolina-Virginia border, provides some 50,000 acres of bass fishing in the 7- to 9-pound class.

March and April, when the 800 miles of willow-bordered shoreline is budding, are good as are September and October.

Lake maps can be had from the Corps of Engineers, J.H. Kerr Reservoir Manager, Route 1, Box 76, Boydton, Virginia, 23919.

A detailed Map-Atlas by the Alexandria Drafting Company is also available. Write to the "Tacklebox," P.O. Box 697, Clarkesville, Virginia, 23927.

MAP 43

69

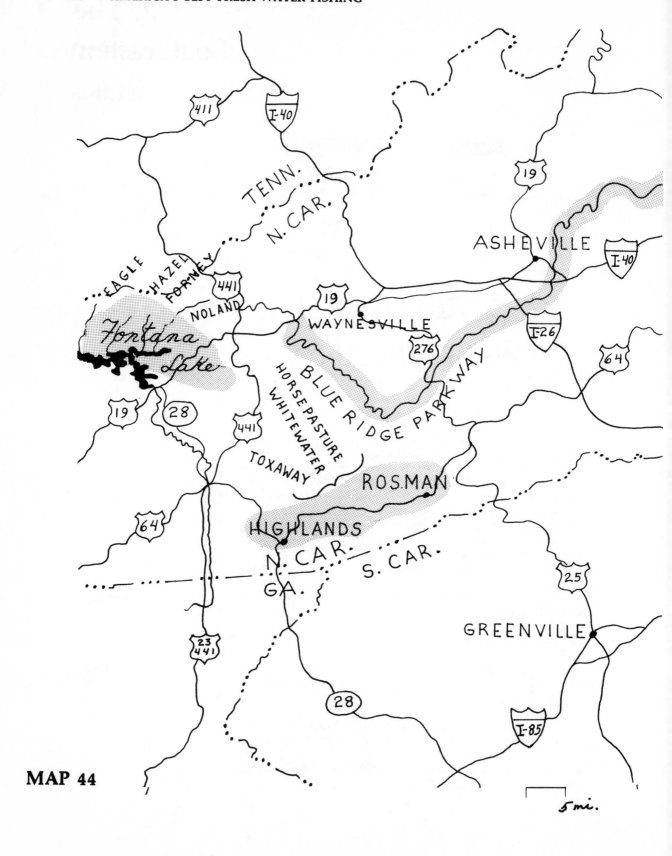

**MAP 44**

5 mi.

# The
# Southeastern
# States

# NORTH CAROLINA

I remember excellent bass fishing in this state in the Blue Ridge Mountains and the Great Smokies in the midst of the Appalachian Range. This is rugged country, much like some of the areas of the Far West, though the streams are much smaller. Good trout fishing can be had in spring, though much of it is put-and-take. Hiking for trout and camping out is the method, though much of the area is accessible by fair roads. Best bets are the Horsepasture, Toxaway and Whitewater Rivers where there's excellent dry fly fishing, reached by U.S. 64 between Highlands and Rosman, near the South Carolina border.

While you are in that corner of the state, don't fail to take a scenic boat trip across Lake Fontana, which you can reach via State Route 28 north from the intersection of State Route 28 and U.S. 64 in Highlands. If you like to hike and camp out, you can try a quartette of good streams, the Eagle, Forney, Noland and Hazel, feeding Fontana Lake from the north. They are all small but graced by gorgeous scenery and a good supply of breakfast-size trout. Here you'll find deep pools, fast runs—and challenging currents.

Taking it a bit easier, try the flatter streams from the Blue Ridge Parkway, which starts at Edmonds at the Virginia border and goes south through Asheville. You'll note that most of the streams are within wildlife management areas and special regulations apply. Some very good streams are limited to fly fishing only.

As to mountain lakes, this state also has them in abundance. I'd suggest the TVA system with its Fontana Lake in the southwest, where you'll find largemouth black bass with bream and crappie also. In the winter, at the mouths of the lake's tributaries, big rainbow trout up to 15 pounds are available. Fontana Village is the center of activity, and you can make it your base.

MAP 44

71

Going from the high areas to the best of the coastal lowlands, try famed Lake Mattamuskeet, north of Pamlico Sound, not too far from Greenville. The nearer you go toward the ocean the better the fishing, for the bass enter the brackish water and a mixed bag is guaranteed. It is ideal fishing with the fly rod or with plugs.

Since the fishing in this state is so varied, I suggest you send for the regulations and attractions amply set down for you by the Wildlife Resources Commission, 325 N. Salisbury St., Raleigh, N.C. 27611. Tell them you are taking your own boat and ask for their up-to-date list of marinas in the state.

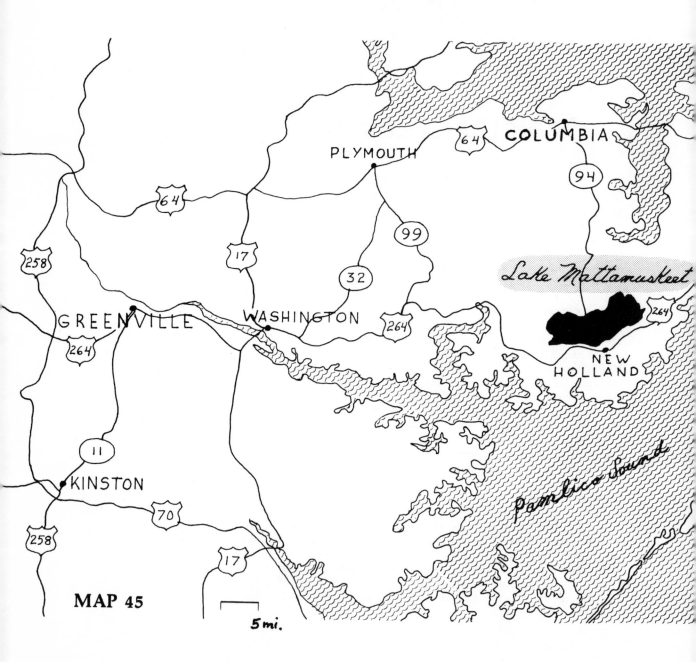

MAP 45

5 mi.

# SOUTH CAROLINA

Yes, there is some trout fishing in South Carolina, but it is limited to early spring and is found only in the upper areas of the northwest corner of the state in the Appalachian Range of mountains. The largest and best trout stream is the Chattooga River, which forms part of the Georgia border. It is reached by U.S. 76 between Clayton, Georgia, and Westminster, South Carolina, or from State Route 28 north from Walhalla, both of which roads cross the river. Fishing is largely put-and-take, but some fair-sized trout are taken each year. It is not heavily fished and is good wet fly water.

In the freshwater lakes department, the 170,000-acre Santee-Cooper Reservoir in the coastal area is famous. Actually it is made up of two very large reservoirs, Lake Moultrie on the Cooper and Lake Marion on the Santee. The two are joined by a quite narrow channel a bit south of the Santee Dam. Interstate 26 between Columbia and Charleston almost parallels the two lakes, and many state highways lead to the small towns on the shore. U.S. 301 and U.S. 15 offer quick access from the north and east, both crossing Lake Marion just west of Summerton, which is on I-95.

Many states boast that they are the bass capital of the world, and South Carolina is also guilty of this claim. It has been said that there are more big bass in the over-10-pound category in the Santee-Cooper waters than any lake in the United States. Okay. Prove it for yourself. You'll have fun trying and you'll catch at least some good "takers." The best months to fish this area are April and May and again in November and December.

Get a contour map, published by the Alexandria Drafting Company, 417 East Clifford Avenue, Alexandria, Va. 22305. The Map Atlas costs $5.50 at this writing. For more info on this water, write Dan Upton, Director, Santee-Cooper Country, P.O. Box 12, Santee, South Carolina 29142.

73

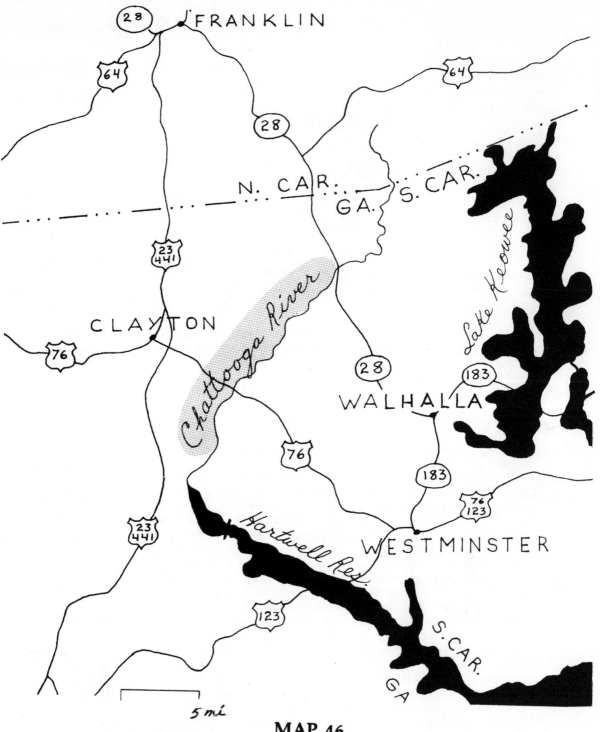

**MAP 46**

Another big attraction here in the reservoir is the landlocked striped bass. They currently average around 5 pounds but some over the 50-pound mark have been taken, so there's a prize for you to go after. I tried but failed, as I didn't have the time to really do it well. Largemouth bass, crappie and catfish are the mainstays. The largemouth bass fishing can be sensational in the spring, the peak of the season in this area.

There are lots of accommodations near Moultrie and Marion. The best stop is at Moncks Corner, where U.S. 52 crosses the southern tip of Moultrie.

This is a beautiful state to visit with the family. It is not crowded and the fishing can be most productive. For a detailed survey of the state, write the Wildlife Resources Dept., 1015 Main Street, Columbia, S.C. 29201.

MAP
47

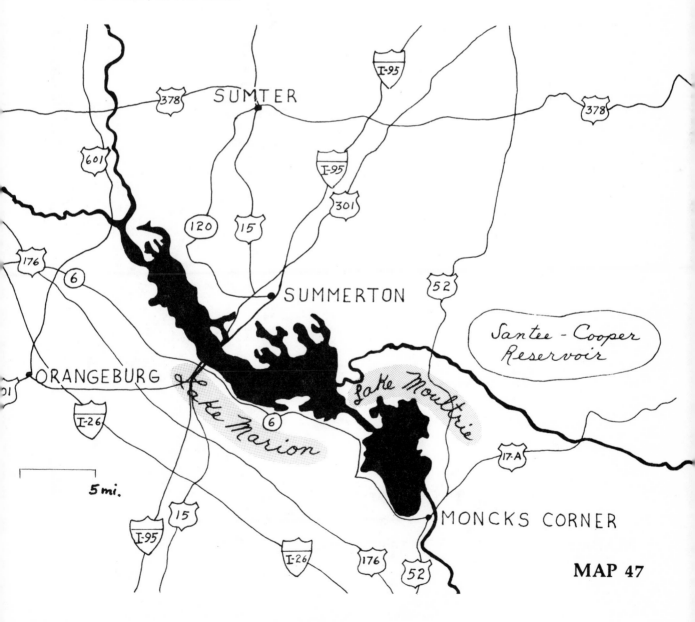

MAP 47

junction of U.S. 441 and State Routes 22 and 49. To the west on the Chattahoochee are Bartlett's Ferry (or Lake Harding) and just south of that, Goat Rock Reservoir and Oliver Lake. In southern Georgia, the Jim Woodruff Reservoir on Lake Seminole is known for its big strings of large bass.

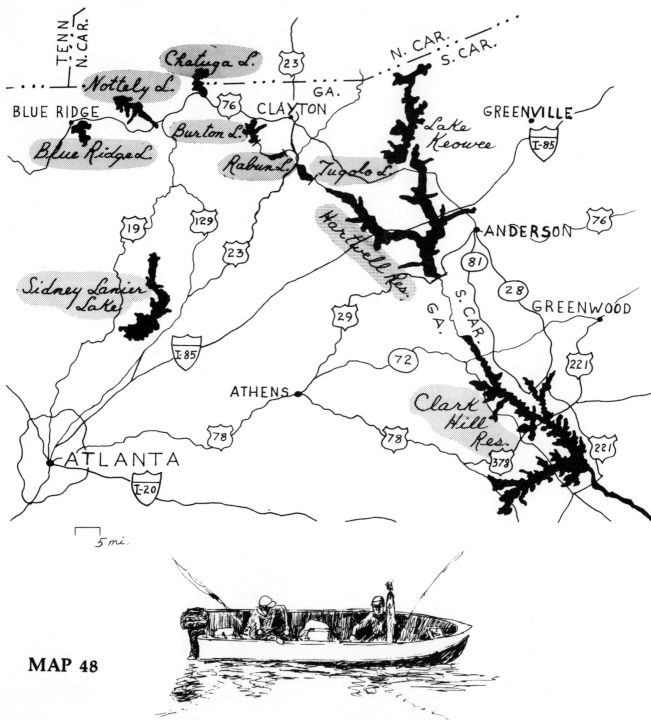

MAP 48

# The Southeastern States

# GEORGIA

Many people think that Georgia would not contain good trout fishing, being so far south. 'Tain't true! Brown, rainbow and brook trout abound in the mountainous area. Largemouth bass, spotted bass, white bass, yellow perch, crappie, bluegill, chain pickerel and big channel catfish are nevertheless the headliners. Look at the map and you'll see that Georgia also has a long coastline with all the big-name saltwater fish available.

Three watersheds drain the state: the Savannah, bordering South Carolina; The Altamaha, draining to the Atlantic in the center of the state's shoreline; and the Satilla farther south, along with the St. Mary's on the Florida border. The Chattahoochee system drains the western part of the state along the Alabama border to the Gulf. Up north, a few streams carry the water to the famed Tennessee River, which finds its way to the mighty Mississippi.

That's a lot of water to fish and it's all generally good, no matter where you go. Georgia is not a state that is heavily fished by out-of-staters.

Now, add to this the fifteen or more major reservoirs plus literally thousands of lakes and ponds, and you can be at a loss to know where to start. The famed ones, Clark Hill and Hartwell Reservoir about midway up the South Carolina boundary, are musts on the list. Tugolo, Rabun and Burton Lakes are just along the border in the same drainage system. There's good fishing in all three. In the north, you'll find Chatuga, near the North Carolina border. Nottely is slightly to the south of the border. Blue Ridge Lake, a beauty spot, lies to the west of that. In the north-central part of the state, north of Atlanta, Lake Sidney Lanier, a reservoir along the Chattahoochee system, is a popular spot for all species except trout. Central Georgia boasts the Sinclair Lake on the Oconee River, a branch of the Altamaha, near Milledgeville at the

MAP
48

MAP
48

MAP
49

77

The roads are generally good in Georgia, so don't be afraid to trailer your boat there. While there are lots of catering motels and sporting and boating marinas, it is best to stick close to the bigger towns for the best restaurants and motels.

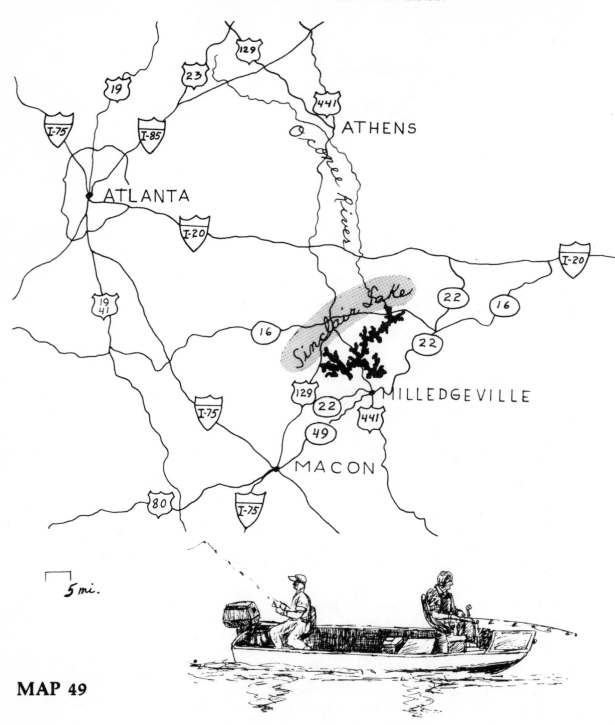

MAP 49

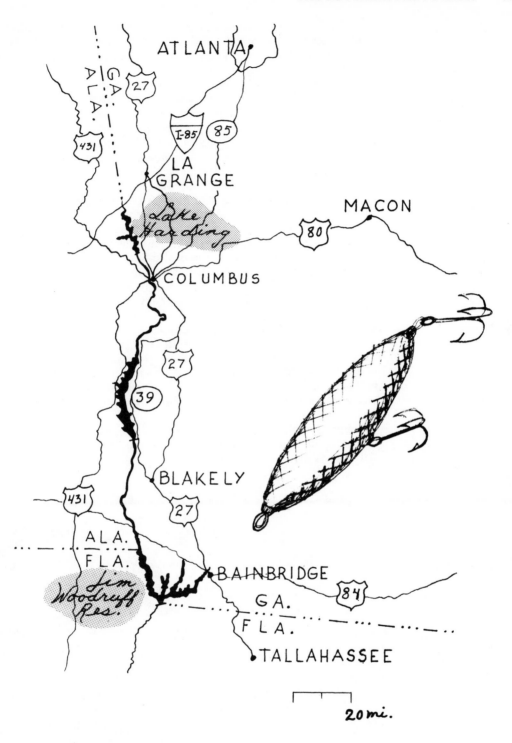

ATLANTA

ALA.
GA.
27

I-85    85

LA
GRANGE

MACON

Lake
Harding

80

COLUMBUS

27

39

BLAKELY

431

27

ALA.
FLA.

Jim
Woodruff
Res.

BAINBRIDGE

GA.
FLA.

84

TALLAHASSEE

20 mi.

**MAP 50**

Georgia is a big state, but there are a few good contacts to be made from the very good publication put out by the State Game and Fish Division, 270 Washington St., SW, Atlanta, Georgia 30334.

Trout fishing is limited to the very high elevations and very small brooks. It is best to concentrate on the lower reaches of these rivers and be content with bass and the other warm-water species. Among the better northern streams for spotted bass, redeyes, largemouth, crappie and bluegills is the Oostanaula, reached from Calhoun, on U.S. 41 south of Chattanooga. Walleyes and flathead catfish can be had in the lower reaches.

I like the Etowah River with its trout in the upper reaches near Rome, reached by U.S. 411 eastward from Rome. This is fast, tumbly water; beautiful country in the spring.

For my money, the Flint, which flows south from Atlanta to Lake Blackshear and then to Lake Seminole, should be rated the top stream in Georgia. It is classical mountain-type trout water.

Another favorite is the Ocmulgee, which carves a great circle southward from Jackson Lake, through Macon, and eventually joins the Altamaha to the east of Lumber City on U.S. 23 just south of McRae. An early world record 22-pound bass came out of it. Good for fly rod fishing with bugs.

That's quite a list to start on in Georgia, but I must add the bass waters of the Okefenokee Swamp in southeast Georgia, in which the famed Suwanee River has its source. Don't go near there without a guide because it is easy to become lost. But if you do go, you are in for the most varied wildlife and outdoor experience of your life.

For complete details on these and the state in general, I suggest you write to the State Game and Fish Commission in Atlanta, as mentioned earlier.

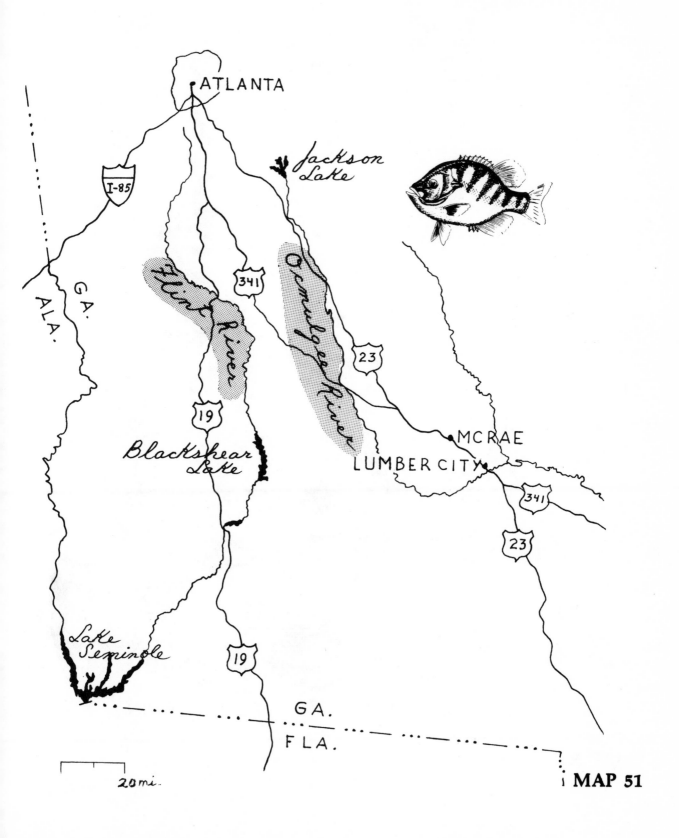

ATLANTA

Jackson Lake

I-85

GA.
ALA.

Flint River

Ocmulgee River

341

23

19

Blackshear Lake

MCRAE

LUMBER CITY

341

23

Lake Seminole

19

GA.
FLA.

20 mi.

**MAP 51**

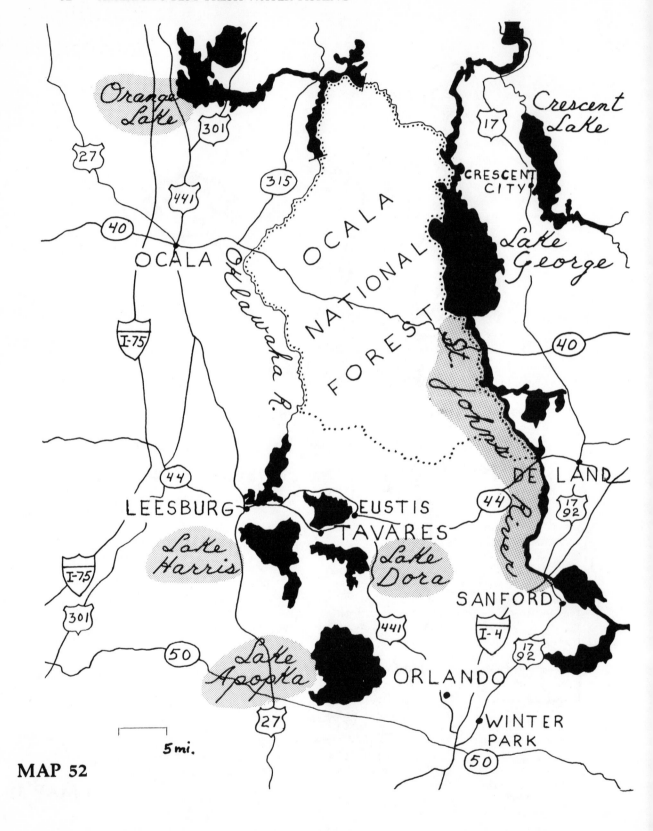

**MAP 52**

5 mi.

# The
# Southeastern
# States

# FLORIDA

Aside from the truly fabulous saltwater fishing to be found in this state, Florida is known as the bass capital of the world, and rightly so. Wherever there is water you can fish for bass, and virtually any river, creek, bayou, canal, pond or lake contains bass bigger than found in most other states. Along with the Florida black bass, the crappie, bluegill and striped bass offer good angling. Shad is also a specialty to a limited degree on the St. Johns River near Lemon Bluff, not far from DeLand, during January, February and March.

I have fished for bass in Florida for a period of over ten years, and despite the dreary reports of the supply of big bass, I never seem to be without some luck. Sure, the bass over the 10-pound mark are fewer, in the last decade or two. But, the odds are with you for landing a whopper at least once in a while.

Quite often when fishing rivers that empty into the Intracoastal Waterway or any coastal river where the saltwater blends into the fresh, I've been fishing for tarpon or sea trout or red bass and have taken some mighty fine black bass that have ventured down into the brackish water. These are surprise fish, however.

My favorite spots for bass fishing lie along the St. Johns River and its tributaries and lakes. This waterway extends from its outlet at Jacksonville a distance of 150 miles south to its source, Lake Helen Blazes. Below Mims (just north of Titusville) going upstream in a southerly direction, the river becomes lost in twisting channels and false rivers, and a guide is necessary to keep from getting lost. Some of the best duck hunting is found in this area, and many times after the sun was well up I'd change from the shotgun to the rod and reel and add bass, bream and white crappie to my bag for the Sunday dinner.

MAP
52

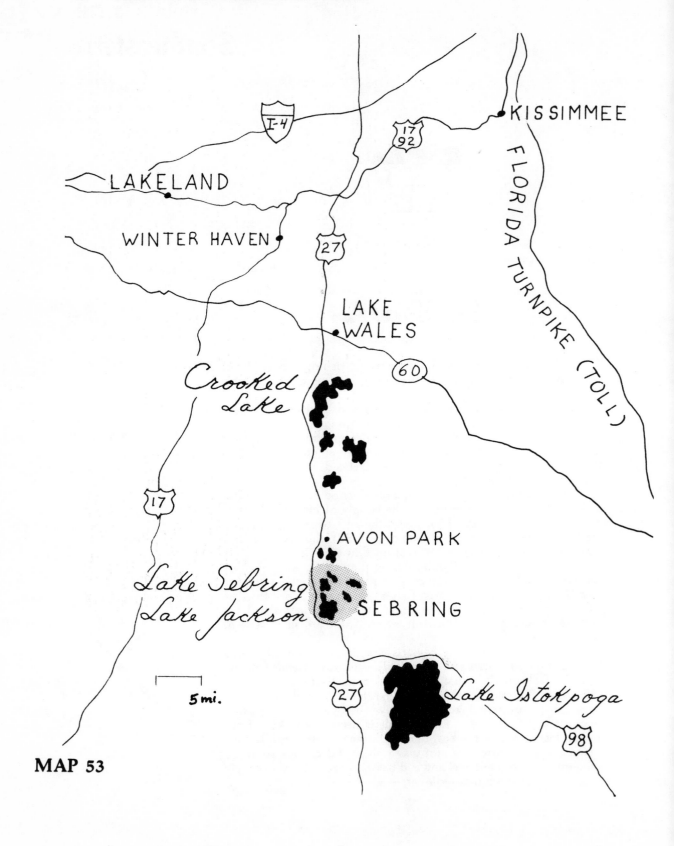

KISSIMMEE

I-4

17
92

LAKELAND

FLORIDA TURNPIKE (TOLL)

WINTER HAVEN

27

LAKE
WALES

60

Crooked
Lake

17

AVON PARK

Lake Sebring
Lake Jackson

SEBRING

5 mi.

27

Lake Istokpoga

98

MAP 53

While Lake Okeechobee is the most famous of the bass lakes, I have been skunked there more often than I've connected. This does not mean that the lake is not worth a try. For me, it is too vast a water, and finding the bass is a touchy proposition. When the winds are blowing (and they are most of the time) the lake becomes too rough for the delights of surface fishing and leisurely trolling. I prefer the smaller waters for my bassing. Lake George and Lake Crescent are large lakes in the northeast, both reached from Crescent City on U.S. 17. Try Lakes Harris, Dora or Orange, reached from Leesburg in the center of the state, on U.S. 27 and 441, or Tavares on U.S. 441. Lake Apopka in that area is another favorite of mine, right near Orlando. The bass supply has held up well despite the overdevelopment of this area. It is mostly shallow water, with grassy shoals fishing.

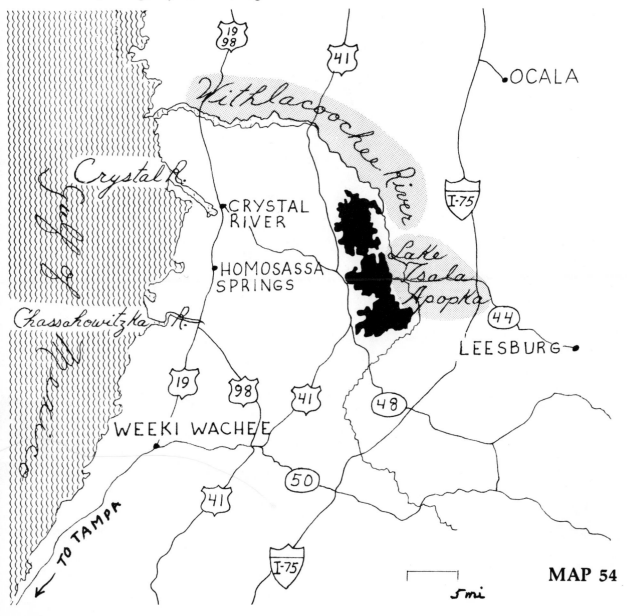

MAP 54

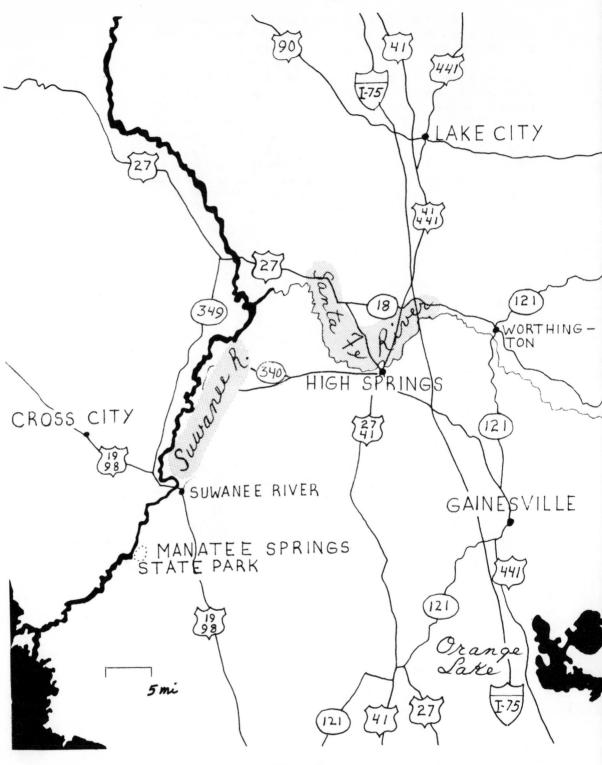

**MAP 55**

I've also connected with fine bass at Sebring, just off U.S. 27 south of Winterhaven. There's a fine group of lakes there, and details about them can be had from the Lake County Chamber of Commerce, Leesburg.

After you have finished in south Florida in Okeechobee, try the waters along the Tamiami Trail, U.S. 41. You'll likely bump into snook and tarpon at the same time.

Above St. Petersburg and Tampa, north on U.S. 41, you will find Lake Tsala Apopka, where there are bass, perch, bream and crappie of record size. Same with Withlacoochee, Crystal and Chassahowitzka Rivers near Homosassa Springs on U.S. 19 on Florida's west coast.

As you approach the Gulf Coast section of the state, fish and boat the Suwanee River. This can be float-fished for its entire length. Reserve a good two weeks for the pictorially beautiful run, plus some excellent fishing. Take your own boat or hire one with a guide. Go to Manatee Springs State Park at U.S. 19 and 98 near Cross City and follow up State Route 349 along the west shore of the southern part of the Suwanee. Further up the river along State Route 340 near High Springs at the intersection of U.S. 27, 41 and 441 just north of Gainesville, is the embarkation area for the Santa Fe River.

I've had outstanding luck at Lake Seminole, which was formed by the damming of the Apalachicola River on the Georgia-Florida-Alabama borders. It can be reached by U.S. 90 at Sneads, at the southern tip of the lake. Big bass here. Excellent surface plug and bug fishing.

If you plan to visit Florida, you'll undoubtedly run through the central part of the state at some time or other. Write to the three sources listed here for information: Wayne and Mike Buckley, Bass Haven Lodge, P.O. Box 147A, Welaka, Florida 32093; Hunting and Fishing Assoc., Dunnellon, Florida, 32630; the Fruitland Peninsula Sportsman's Assoc., 115 Summit Street, Crescent City, Florida, 32012.

For the overall picture, write to the Florida Game and Fresh Water Fish Commission, 620 South Mendian St., Tallahassee, Fla., 32304.

There is probably no other state that caters to tourism, especially fishermen, as does Florida. Everywhere you look there are excellent motels and guide services, places to store and ramp your boat, dealers who will care for and repair your rig. Good guides are easy to come by.

The weather is generally warm, but during the winter months when those northerlies break through the southern comfort, it can get cold and mighty windy, so at that season bring along the clothes you'd wear up north, and especially the rain gear. There are snakes and bugs and mosquitoes here, but reasonable precaution and bug dope will take care of them.

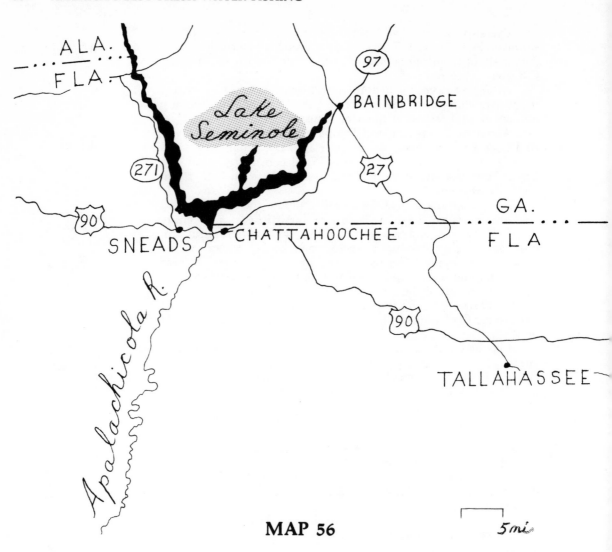

**MAP 56**

5 mi

# OHIO

# INDIANA

The same criteria apply here as for Virginia and West Virginia. They do contain some very good fishing but, again, the angler bent on big fish and the visiting of famed waters would tend to go elsewhere, such as Wisconsin and Michigan to the north or Tennessee, Kentucky or Arkansas to the south.

Despite the pollution, Lake Erie does produce for Ohio. Early in winter it begins to produce action in ice fishing for yellow perch, smelt and some walleyes near Port Clinton in western Ohio. Late in spring, the white bass and yellow perch start to run. Sandusky Bay is another hot spot. Leesville Reservoir, about 25 miles south of Canton on I-77 and east of New Philadelphia, boasts 1,000 acres of largemouth bass and crappie waters. It also is one of Ohio's best muskie waters.

Three excellent walleye lakes, Mosquito Creek Reservoir, Berlin Reservoir and Pymatuning Reservoir, all in northeastern Ohio, also contain bass and panfish.

One must not overlook the recent addition of the coho salmon to Indiana waters. At Michigan City the fishing for this species has been outstanding and may become the state's major push for celebrity. Peak months are April to June and then again in September and October. Lake trout are also on the list, along with brown trout and steelhead, another import supporting the attraction.

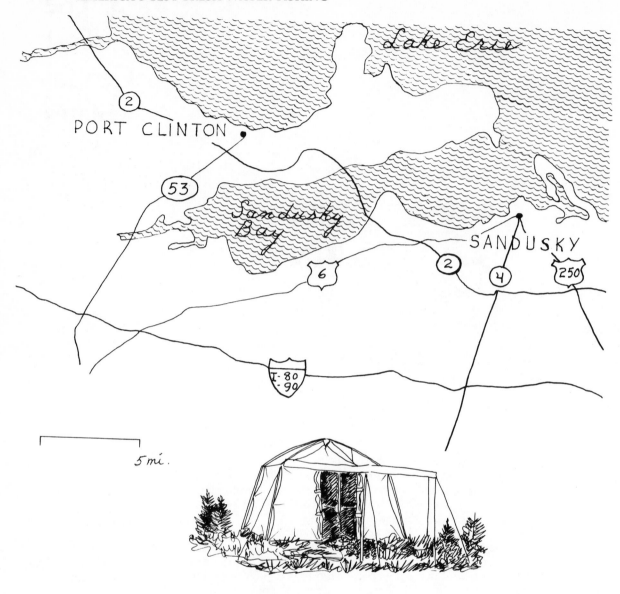

**MAP 57**

CANTON

30

MINERVA

43

183

MALVERN

WAYNESBURG

43

171

I-77

CARROLLTON

39

39

DELFRY

39

*Leesville Res.*

332

SHERRODSVILLE

LAMARTINE

NEW
PHILADELPHIA

212

250

39    LEESVILLE    164

5 mi.

**MAP 58**

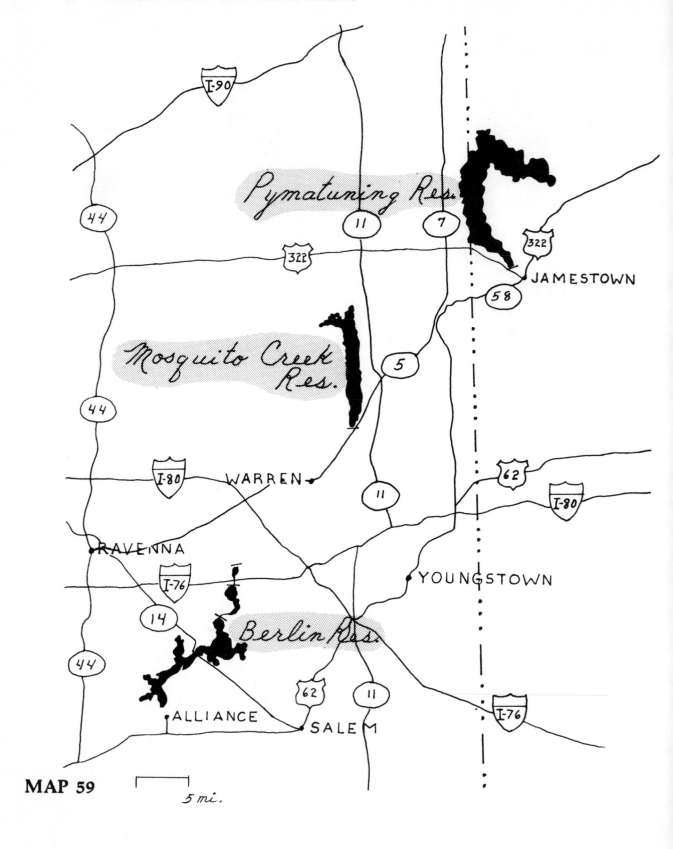

**MAP 59**

5 mi.

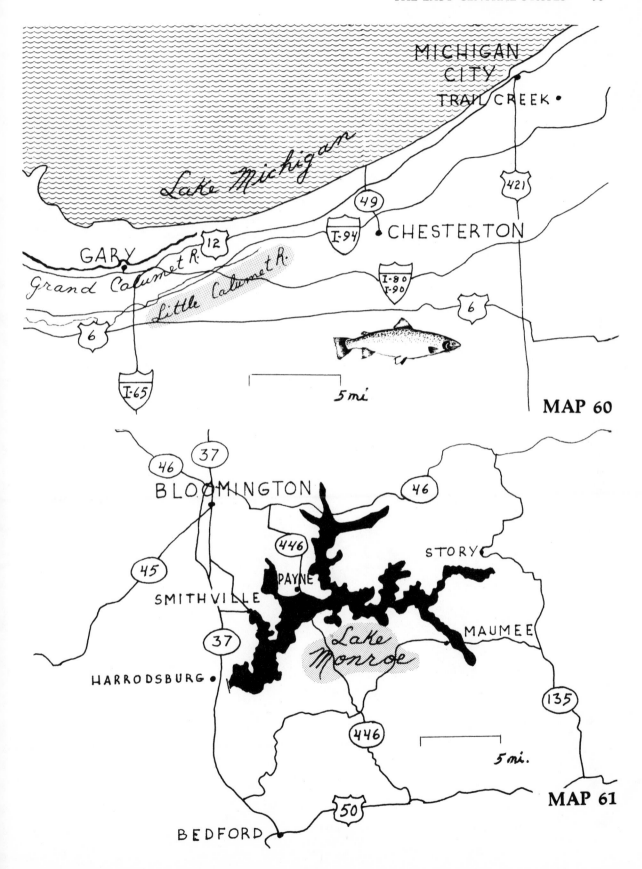

MAP 60

MAP 61

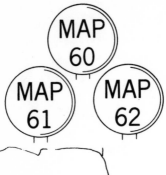

The Little Calumet River and Trail Creek (near Chesterton, east of Gary) are two good hotspots for salmon during the spawning run. Chinook is particularly strong now and getting better. For largemouth bass, Lake Monroe, south of Bloomington, is a major attraction, with excellent bluegill and crappie. Float-fishing is recommended, and one of the best and most famous is the Tippecanoe, Indiana's top-rated smallmouth bass river in the north-central part of the state, flowing southwest.

TO SOUTH BEND

6

31

30

TIPPECANOE

BASS LAKE

35

BEARDSTOWN

Tippecanoe R.

WINAMAC

35

MAP 62

BUFFALO

5 mi

# KENTUCKY

If you can stay away from the horses and bourbon in this state long enough to fish, you are in for some fine sport. The smallmouth bass is king here and is a fighter equal to its cousin way up in Maine or Minnesota. I got quite a surprise when I hooked my first few fish there. I supposed that Kentucky, being a Southern State and the water much warmer, would have bass that would be weak fighters. Not so. And the bass are big, too! The world record 11-pound 15-ounce fish came from Dale Hollow Lake, by far the most famed lake in the state.

Dale Hollow Lake is located on the Kentucky-Tennessee line and is easily reached from Burkesville at the intersection of State Route 61 (north-south) and State Route 90 (east-west). It has 4,000 acres of good water. State Route 52 at Celina, Tennessee, or State Route 42 at Byrdstown, Tennessee, are other accesses to this lake. The indented shoreline offers havens for bass and rainbow trout.

Kentucky Lake on the Tennessee River in western Kentucky boasts some 160,000 acres of reservoir. In April and May you can snag a large string of crappie, plus walleye and striped bass. The stripers run upwards of 20 pounds, and they fight! This is one of the world's biggest man made impoundments, and it would take a lifetime to learn how and when and where to fish it. Hire a guide—it will save you much time. There are lots of entry places for your boat, and rentals are available everywhere. Excellent local accommodations are available.

I've fished Herrington Lake in the spring for bass, especially the white bass. It's located near Danville, at the junction of U.S. 150 and U.S. 127 south of Lexington.

Farther south, toward the Tennessee border, is another topper, Lake Cumberland, with 50,000 acres of water. Deep areas provide havens for all species, and the Conservation Department

MAP 63

MAP 64

MAP 65

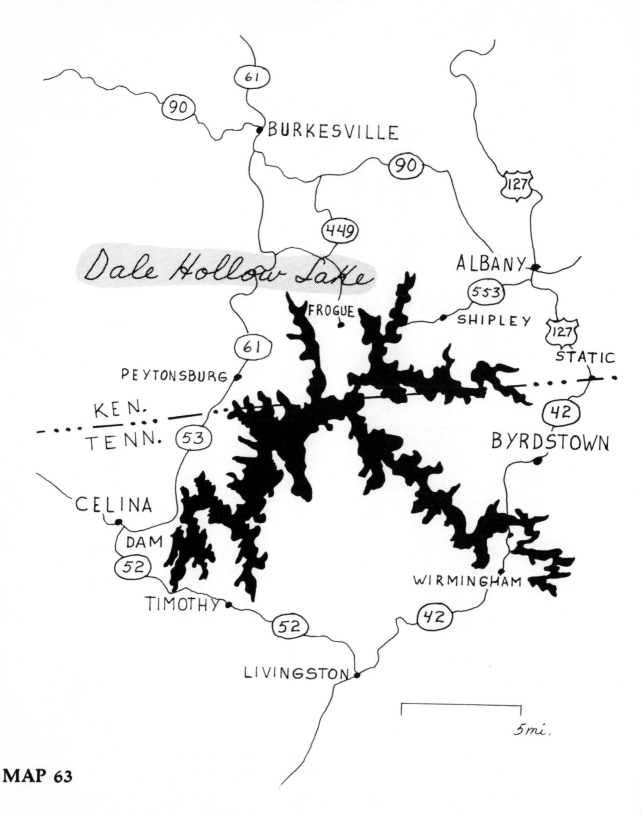

**MAP 63**

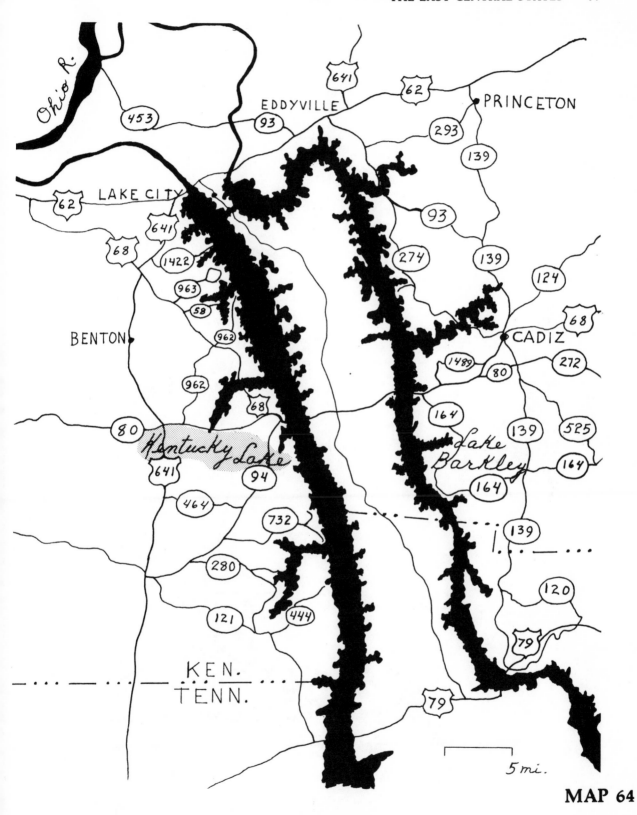

5 mi.

**MAP 64**

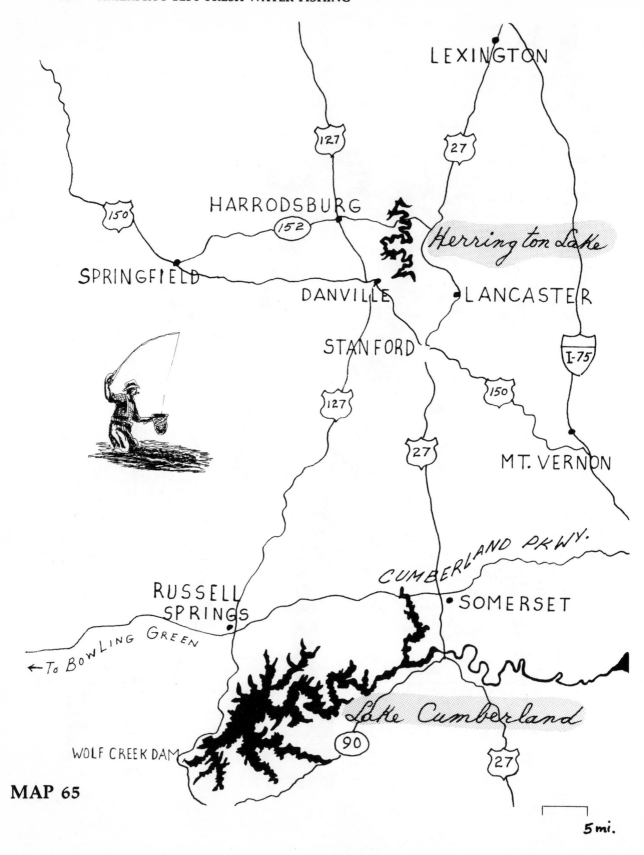

LEXINGTON

127

27

HARRODSBURG

152

150

*Herrington Lake*

SPRINGFIELD

DANVILLE

LANCASTER

STANFORD

I-75

127

150

27

MT. VERNON

CUMBERLAND PKWY.

RUSSELL
SPRINGS

SOMERSET

← To BOWLING GREEN

*Lake Cumberland*

90

WOLF CREEK DAM

27

**MAP 65**

5 mi.

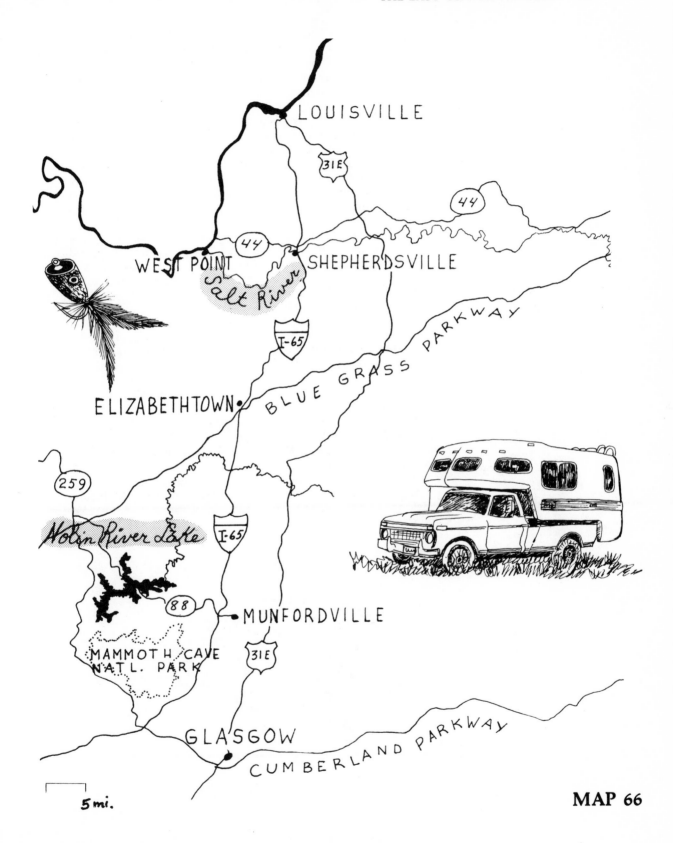

LOUISVILLE

31E

44

WEST POINT    44    SHEPHERDSVILLE

Salt River

BLUE GRASS PARKWAY

I-65

ELIZABETHTOWN

259

Nolin River Lake    I-65

88

MUNFORDVILLE

MAMMOTH CAVE
NATL. PARK

31E

GLASGOW

CUMBERLAND PARKWAY

5 mi.

**MAP 66**

boasts that there are more bass per acre here than in any lake in the world—smallmouths, largemouths, whites, walleyes, bream, catfish and channel cats of enormous size. The locals hit Wolf Creek Dam at the western end of the lake (U.S. 127, about 60 miles south of Danville) for the big rainbows in the spring. Good *night* fishing here.

Kentucky has its own brand of river float fishing, an experience you should not miss, whether you do it here or in Arkansas. There are at least twenty fine trout streams for rainbows, such as Sulphur and Lick Fork in Simpson County, south of Bowling Green, the Trammel in Allen County, southeast of Bowling Green, Big Brush in Green County, northeast of Bowling Green and east of I-65, and Mountain Forks in Harlan County, near the Virginia border.

Excellent smallmouth bass angling is at its finest from my records in Nolin River, while Salt River is a good one for spotted bass. The Salt River flows just south of Louisville, crossing I-65 at Shepherdsville and the town of Salt River, while the Nolin arises farther south of Louisville and south of the I-65 intersection with the Kentucky Blue Grass Parkway. It flows west and south to Nolin Lake, just north of Mammoth Cave National Park.

Another good one is the Cumberland River, the outlet of Lake Cumberland; and below the fast water beneath Wolf Creek Dam you can float for bass, walleyes and cats. U.S. 127 takes you to the dam.

And for scenery, you can't beat the Red River Gorge in the Lexington area.

It is a big state full of fish. For details, check the Department of Fish and Wildlife Resources, Capitol Plaza Tower, Frankfort, Kentucky 40601. Maps for Kentucky Lake, Lake Barkley and TVA Navigation Charts are available from the Maps and Engineering Department, Records Section, Knoxville, Tenn. 37902.

Also contact Irvine Moffet at Jamestown, or Andy McIntyre at Beaver Lodge, Monticello, for guide service for Lake Cumberland.

<br>

# The East Central States

# TENNESSEE

I had the opportunity to live and do extensive travel (and fishing) in this state. Being essentially a Northerner, I was surprised to find better trout fishing there than in many other highly thought of states.

Go east to the Appalachian Mountains for the trout. U.S. 411 from Johnson City near the North Carolina border runs parallel to the mountains for the full length of the state, and secondary roads take you to the best fishing. East of Johnson City you'll find Laurel Bloomery, Doe, Gentry and Upper Beaver Dam creeks. Good wet fly and nymph fishing. U.S. 19E leads you to Doe River and Stoney and Little Stoney—fine, small, rushing streams. These are good brown trout rivers with some rainbows. In the upper stretches you'll find small brook trout. One of the best can be reached from Erwin on U.S. 23. Check the Spivy, Granny, Rocky Fork . . . I took a limit there in an hour.

Scientifically and troutwise, I loved the Tellico, in the Tellico Wildlife Management Area on the North Carolina border east of Athens, Tennessee, which is near I-75, about midway between Chattanooga and Knoxville. There is gorgeous scenery, with lots of accommodations. Good brown, rainbow and brook trout fishing can be had with wet flies and nymphs.

The TVA Lakes are a vast chain too difficult to even approach in a few words. I will say, it is all good bass fishing and I'll leave it at that. Write to the Tennessee Wildlife Resources Agency, P.O. Box 40747, Nashville, Tennessee 37204, for their *Guide to Tennessee Fishing*. It is a volume well worth your study. It should keep you busy, because there is much to learn in connection with the year-round open season in this state.

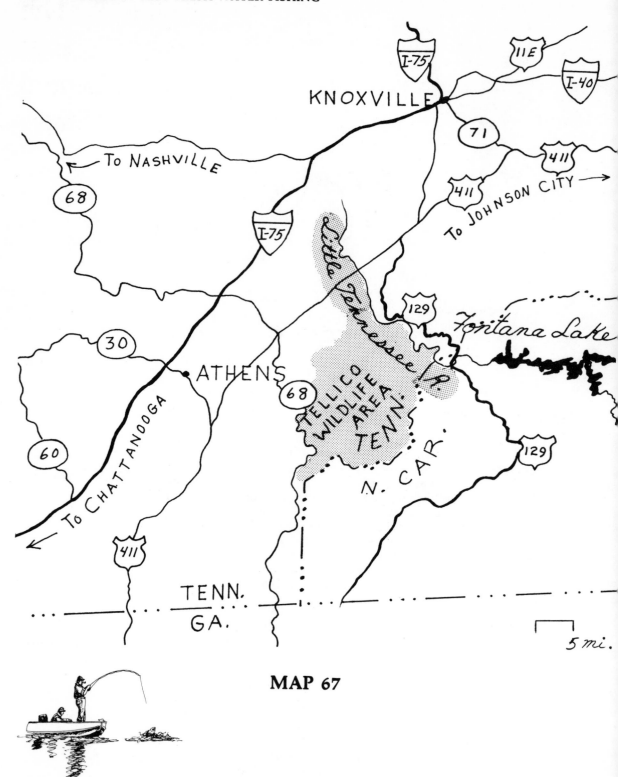

**MAP 67**

Tennessee is ready for you with on-location motels and marinas. Much of its is wild country, but it also offers all modern conveniences for its sizable tourist crowds.

Maps for Kentucky Lake, Lake Barkley and TVA Navigation Charts are available from the Maps and Engineering Department, Records Section, Knoxville, Tenn. 37902.

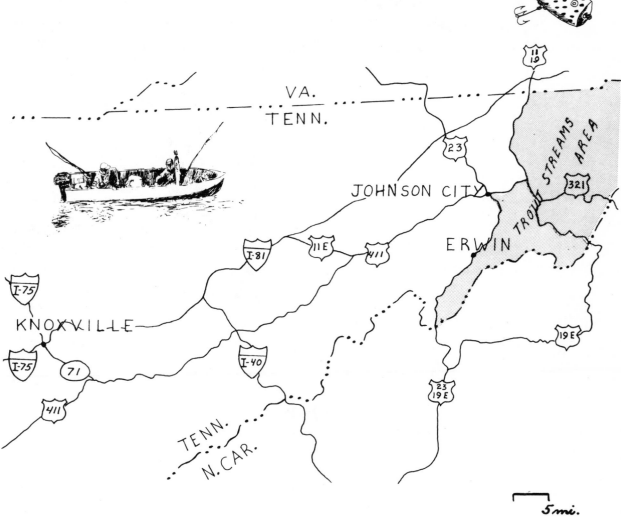

**MAP 68**

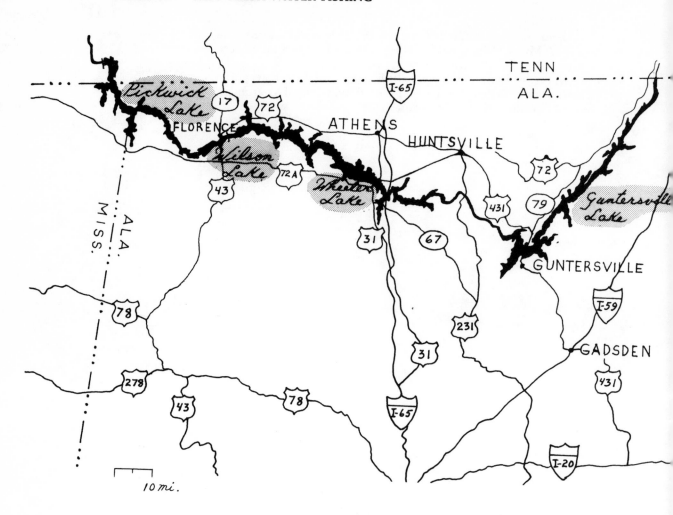

**MAP 69**

# ALABAMA

Largemouth bass, Kentucky bass, striped or white bass, crappie, shellcracker or redear sunfish, blue catfish and channel catfish —that's the angler's menu in this state.

Immediately, Tennessee River fishing comes to mind as the top attraction in Alabama, though there are other areas equally productive if not so famous. The Tennessee crosses the northern part of the state beginning in the west at Pickwick Lake, broadening into Wilson Lake, Wheeler Lake (south of Athens and southwest of Huntsville) and Guntersville Lake east of Huntsville. If you never fished another part of the state, you'd have your fill here. It is easily accessible by access points at many places off U.S. 72 to the north and U.S. Alternate 72 to the south, as well as U.S. 231 south from Huntsville and State Route 79, which follows the north shore of Guntersville Lake. Best accommodations, I've found, are at Huntsville east of I-65 at the junction of U.S. 231 and U.S. 72 and at Decatur on Wheeler Lake right on I-65 and U.S. Alternate 72. Before you visit the area, send for the very up-to-date and complete list of camps and boat liveries and launching ramps available from the Fisheries Section, Alabama Department of Conservation and Natural Resources, Montgomery, Ala. 36104.

I've fished Martin Lake in the central eastern part of the state, on the Tallapoosa River, reached from U.S. 280 between Opelika and Alexander City. This river runs from the Georgia border at U.S. 78, just north of I-20, southward. Secondary roads will take you to it. This is beautiful country with good fishing. Equally good is the Cahaba River toward the west, flowing from Birmingham to Selma. Take off from State Route 5 to the river, which is quite accessible. Lake Eufaula, known also as the Walter F. George Reservoir, contains some 45,000 acres of bass in southern Alabama. Maps are available from the Corps of Engineers, Walter F. George Reservoir, Eufaula, Alabama, 36027.

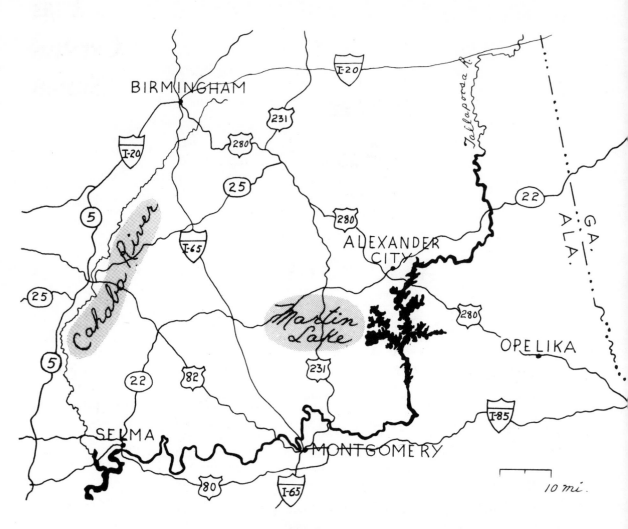

**MAP 70**

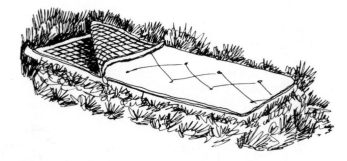

# MISSISSIPPI

Mississippi's best fishing is for the black bass found in the very large reservoirs and impoundments. Interstate 55 leads you to several of them, just south of Memphis: Sardis, Enid, Grenada, Arkabutla, and the Pickwick on the Mississippi-Alabama border. Also try the Ross Barnett, which lies above Jackson and the Okatibbee near Meridian; both contain bluegills, crappie, both black and white bass and, of course, the Southern specialty, catfish. Eat a meal of cats prepared at a local diner for a real taste treat. Makes a good breakfast.

Another set of lakes I've had good reports of are what are called the oxbows, tied into the Mississippi. The best ones are Eagle and Chotard, which are near Vicksburg on I-20, the Albemarle, not far from Woodville on U.S. 61, south of Natchez, and the Rodney up in Jefferson County, the next county north of Natchez. All of them are filled with good-sized largemouth bass plus crappie and cats.

For river fishing and the famed rubber raft and johnboat float trips that have made this portion of the country famous, the Tchoutacabouffa, located in the DeSoto National Forest north of Hattiesburg, is by far the best. The Jordan in Hancock County (a Gulf county next to the Louisiana border) is a good bet for bass and panfish.

One of the prime attractions of this state for the angler is the fact that it is not publicized as much as some of the others. This also means that there are far fewer motels and boat liveries. It is best to go equipped as if you were in a strange land. Stick to the towns for your overnight stays and meals.

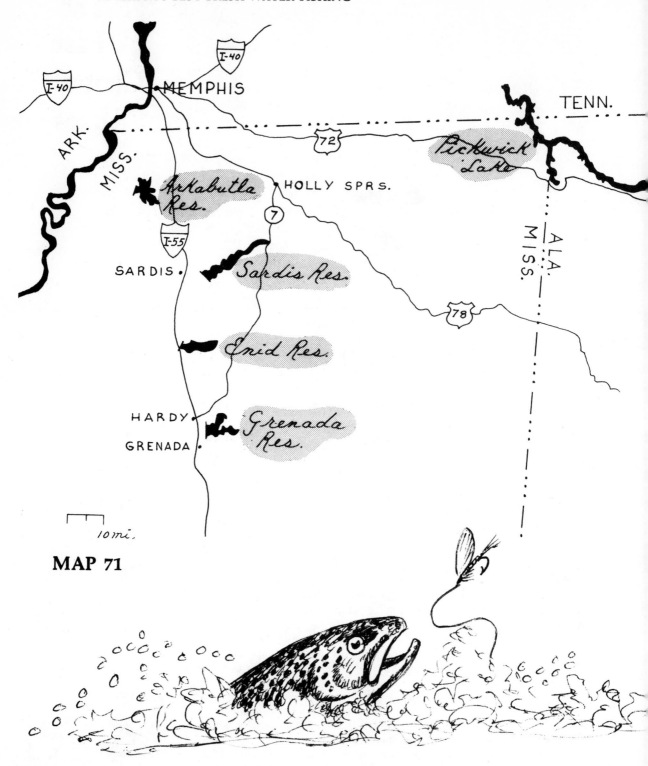

MAP 71

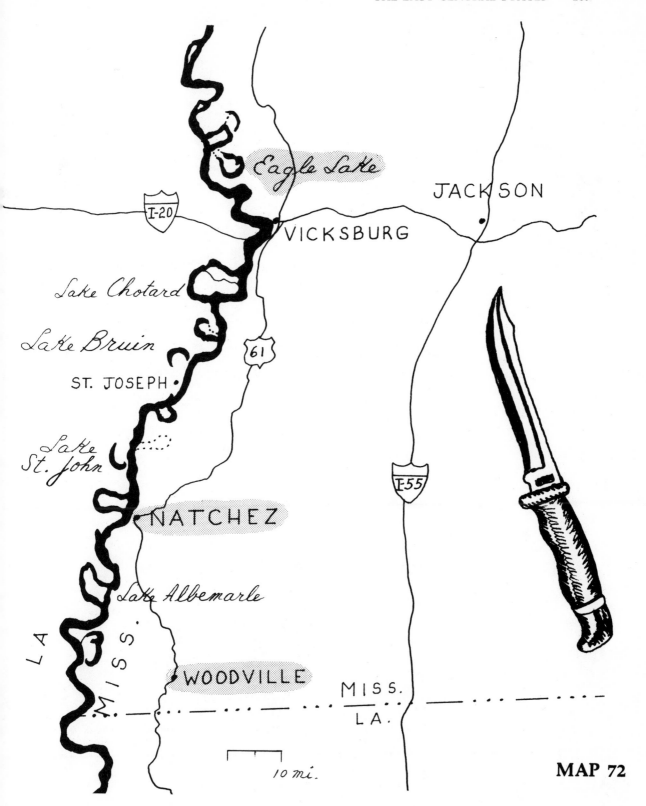

Eagle Lake

JACKSON

I-20

VICKSBURG

Lake Chotard

Lake Bruin

61

ST. JOSEPH

Lake
St. John

I-55

NATCHEZ

Lake Albemarle

LA.

MISS.

WOODVILLE

MISS.

LA.

10 mi.

**MAP 72**

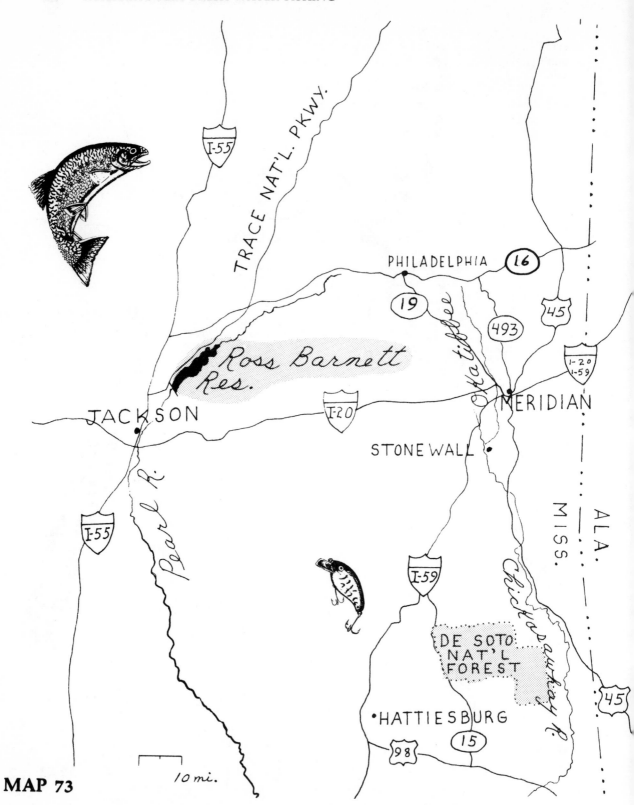

TRACE NAT'L. PKWY.

I-55

PHILADELPHIA    16

19

493

45

I-20
I-59

Ross Barnett
Res.

JACKSON

I-20

MERIDIAN

STONE WALL

Pearl R.

I-55

I-59

Okatibbee

Chickasawhay R.

ALA.
MISS.

DE SOTO
NAT'L
FOREST

45

•HATTIESBURG

98    15

**MAP 73**

*10 mi.*

It is pretty country, always green, with lots of foliage and scenic areas. It is warm all year long, and muggy and hot in the summer months. Light clothing is recommended except in the winter when cold waves do occur.

For more information, write the Game and Fish Commission, P.O. Box 451, Jackson, Miss. 39205.

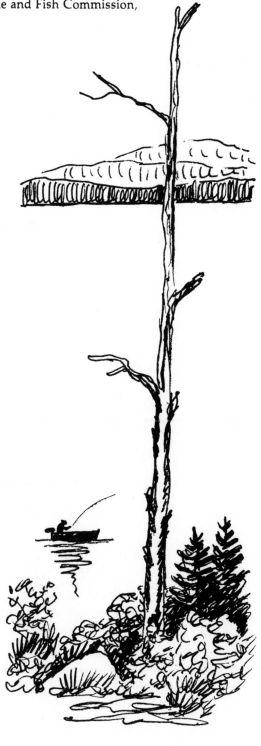

# 4. The Central States

# MICHIGAN

MAP 74

MAP 82

When you look at the fishing prospects in this state you are confounded by just too much good water: 11,000 lakes and 36,000 miles of rivers. The state is divided by water into two basic peninsulas. The Upper Peninsula pokes eastward from Wisconsin between Lake Superior on its north and Lakes Michigan and Huron on its south. The major portion of the state—the lower peninsula—extends northward from its borders with Indiana and Ohio, with Lake Michigan on its west and Lakes Huron and Erie on its east. It is large and lake-filled all the way from the western shore to famed Saginaw Bay on the east. All major species of fish are found here, including some excellent muskie fishing. This species is divided into two types. One resides in inland lakes and a slightly different type is caught in the Great Lakes. Only scientists know the difference. They'll go 40 pounds or more and that's enough identification for a fisherman.

Many of the muskie clan start out between Nine and Ten Mile Roads at St. Clair Shores, on State Route 29 north of Detroit. There are several good guides; the most highly recommended are Al Lesh Charter Boat Service, 3233 Los Angeles, Warren, Michigan 48089, and Homer Le Blanc, 23323 Liberty Street, St. Clair Shores, Michigan 48080. You'll need a guide to fish these famed waters since the area covers some 400 square miles in area.

To the north on Lake Huron is Saginaw Bay, one of the top spots for walleye fishing in the entire Midwest. It is also excellent for smallmouth bass.

My first experience fishing in this state was in the Grand Traverse area on the northwest shore of the lower peninsula. I was after the reputed monster smallmouth bass and accompanied a well-known sports writer on several outings. Best bet in this area is

MAP 74

Long Lake, reached by a secondary road southwest of Traverse City, and Little Glen Lake on State Route 22 northwest of Traverse. Grand Traverse Bay is best fished in July and August. I must also mention Crystal Lake near the shore of Lake Michigan on State Route 115, southwest from Traverse City by way of U.S. 31, and the Torch Chain of Lakes, reached by U.S. 31 to the north of Traverse City.

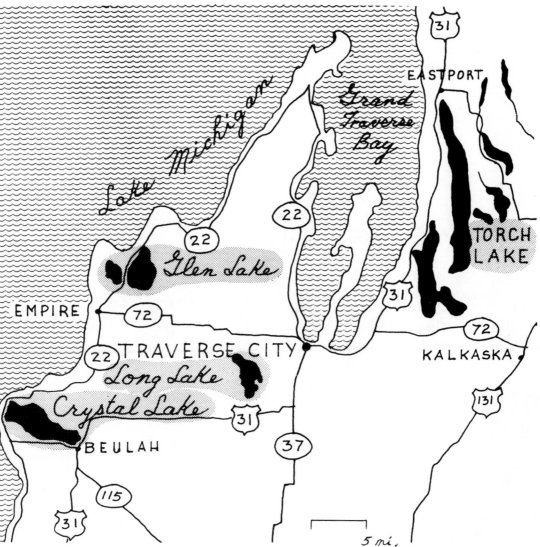

**MAP 74**

MAP
75

To the northeast is another system of lakes and streams mastered by the Cheboygan River System. For a precise description of the area write the Cheboygan Chamber of Commerce for their Sportsman's Guide to Cheboygan County. Campgrounds are available at the junction of U.S. 23 and State Route 27, accessible from Interstate 75 via the Topinabee interchange.

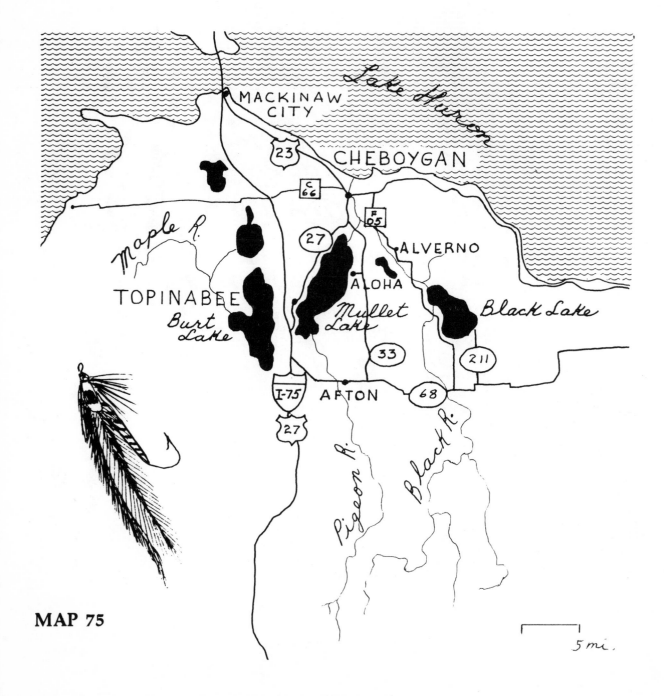

MAP 75

5 mi.

The Upper Peninsula country is made for canoe trips with fishing for all species, particularly trout. Remember that the Lake Michigan shore of the Upper Peninsula is noted for excellent walleye fishing. Escanaba and Manistique areas are particularly good. The shore is reached by U.S. 2, but there are only a few small towns and accommodations are somewhat limited.

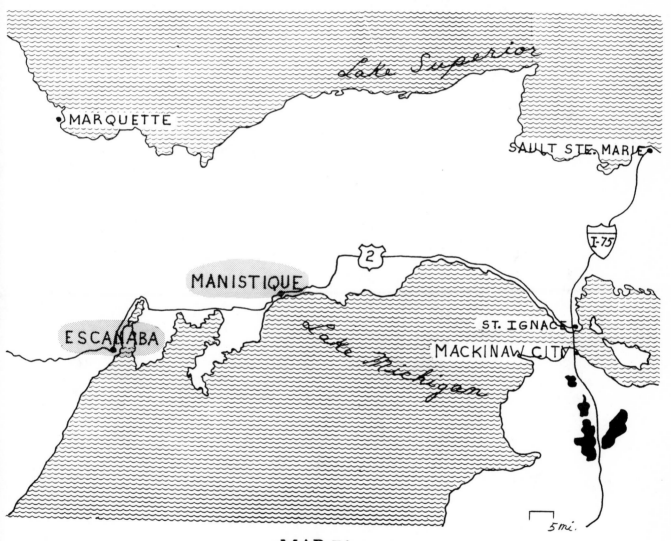

**MAP 76**

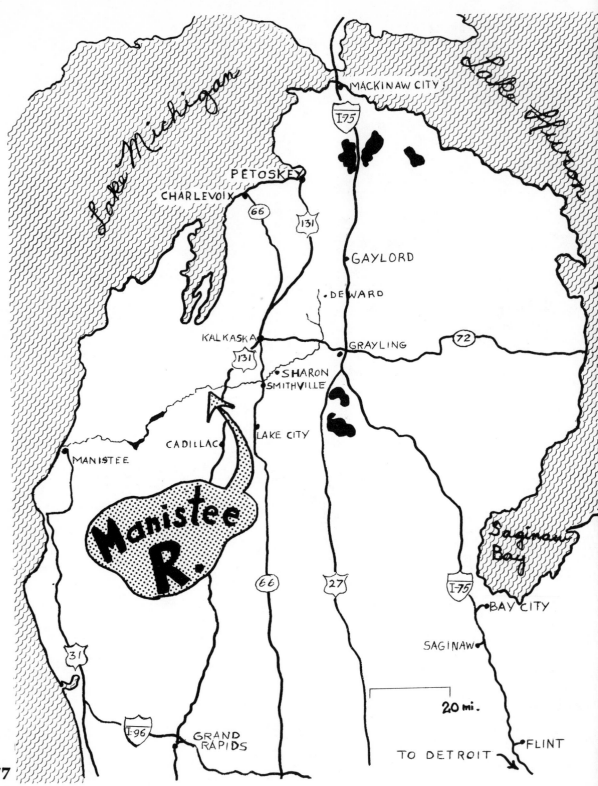

MAP 77

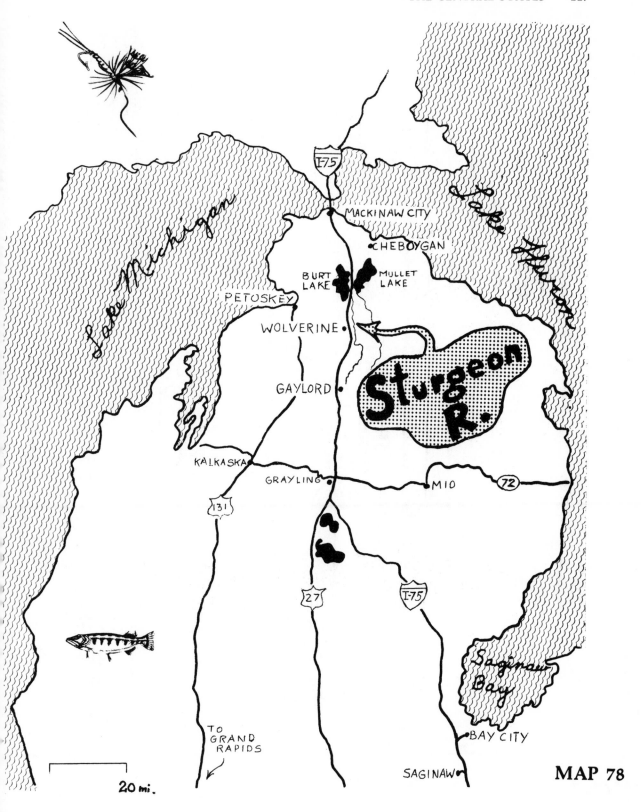

MAP 78

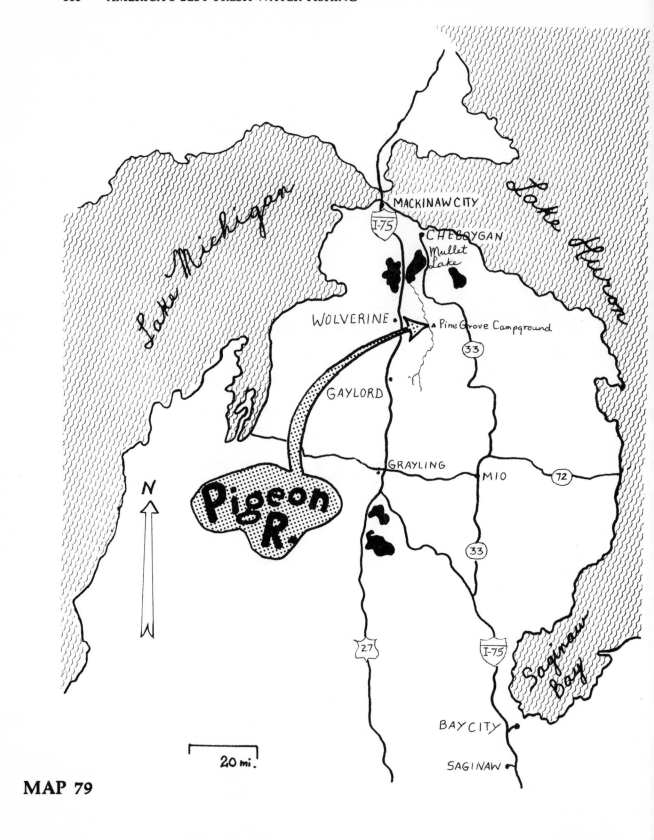

**MAP 79**

Since the seasons are so varied and the prime waters so broad in scope, I suggest you write to the Michigan Department of Natural Resources, Lansing, Michigan 48926, or the chambers of commerce of the towns and cities mentioned above.

Michigan boasts seven top trout streams, and I'm not going to select any one as best because I want to retain friendships among anglers in that state!

The Manistee is a magic word, particularly the upper river, upstream from the village of Smithville. It is also a canoeist's river in the lower sections where trout fishing is also very good. It flows through relatively wild country with few cabins and access roads to mar its natural wilderness aspect. Cabins and accommodations are more numerous near State Highway 72 west of Grayling and also at Sharon. The upper river has four excellent grounds for camping.

Starting out small, only a few feet wide at Deward, the Manistee widens to about 80 feet at State Highway 72 and some 200 feet at State Highway 66 at Smithville. It is generally less than 3 feet deep upstream from Highway 72 and 3 to 6 feet deep with even deeper holes and pools in the lower reaches. The bottom is mainly sand and gravel, with few large boulders. Banks are sandy and sometimes mucky, offering good grounds for the breeding of aquatic insects, notably the big Green Drake may fly. Reach this stream during a hatch and the flies literally cloud your vision. It is an easily wadable stream in the upper section, but like many of these Midwest streams, a canoe is a necessity in order to cover the water at all well. There are few, if any, really difficult rapids, but the stream flows fast enough to offer decent pocket water, white foamy stretches and long, slick glides for the fly fisherman. The stream has the atmosphere of the true north woods and is quite remote, considering the population of this state.

The Sturgeon, Pigeon and Black Rivers rise at the north edge of a prominent glacial moraine, just northeast of Gaylord. The Sturgeon is the one farthest west and flows northward from its source about 37 miles to its mouth at Burt Lake. Popularly and survey rated as excellent, it is a great stream for migrating, stocked steelhead downstream from Wolverine. The lower reaches are best fished from a canoe, and camping is popular at public-access sites during the steelhead runs.

It is a swift-flowing stream, generally less than 60 feet wide, usually less than 3 feet deep upstream from Wolverine. Below there, it has deep runs of 6 feet. The bottom is sandy gravel, similar to the Manistee. It is well banked, with overhanging trees and bushes, and boasts large hatches of aquatic insects such as caddis, stone and the big species of may flies. It, like the Manistee, is classed as near-wilderness, beautiful and solitary country in which to enjoy a fulfilling trouting vacation. The lower reaches are close to major highways, which aids in the convenience of fishing it.

All manner of tackle can be used on these rivers . . . bait, spinning gear and especially fly fishing with dry flies in June and into July.

The Pigeon River is a neighbor of the Sturgeon, rising in the same cedar swamp to flow generally northward for 43 miles, emptying into Mullet Lake. Regarded technically and esthetically as an

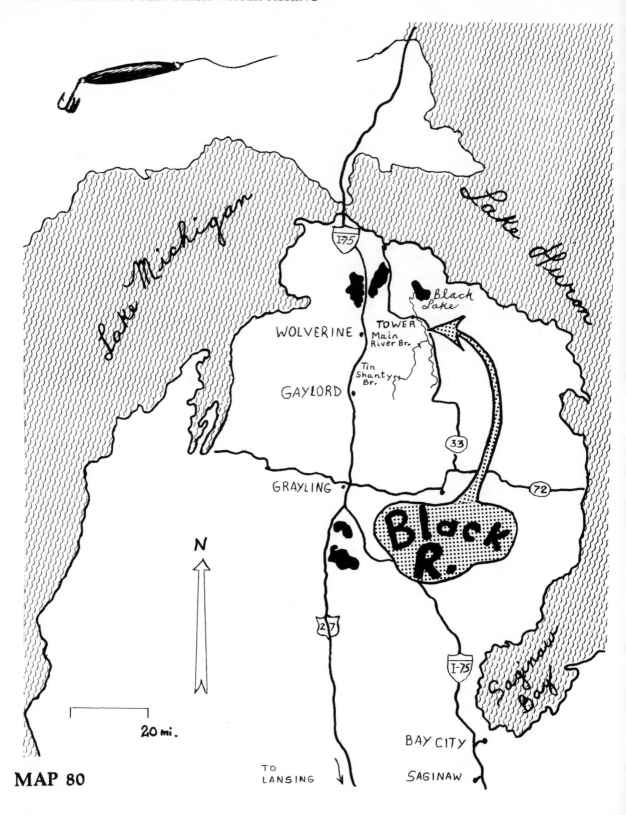

Lake Michigan

Lake Huron

I-75

Black Lake

WOLVERINE    TOWER
Main River Br.

Tin Shanty Br.

GAYLORD

33

GRAYLING    72

Black R.

N

27

I-75

Saginaw Bay

20 mi.

BAY CITY

**MAP 80**

TO LANSING

SAGINAW

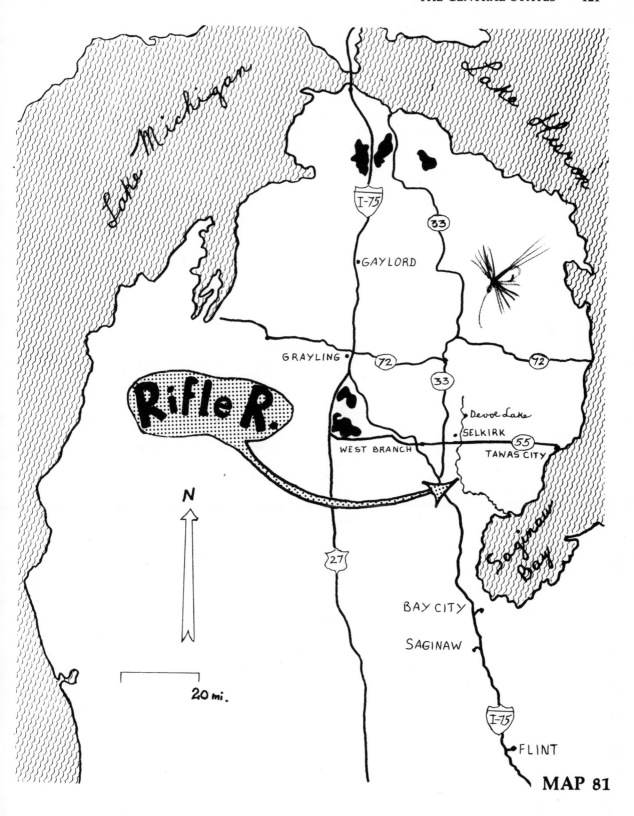

MAP 81

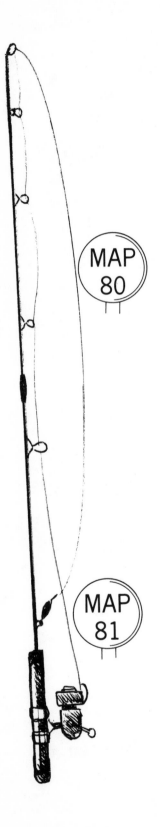

excellent trout stream, it is little used by canoeists. Much of the river is in state forest lands and so is protected from overdevelopment with but three state campgrounds. It is nicely remote and semi-wild, offering solitude and colorful scenery. The banks are indented, often fern- or moss-covered, with generous overhangs of trees and bushes. Much evergreen growth abounds along the course. Like all Michigan streams, the bottom is sandy, with some gravel and few big boulders. As such it is easily waded upstream from Pine Grove Campground, except in the lower reaches where it can be 3 to 6 feet deep. About half of the lower river is difficult, if not impossible, to wade to any extent and calls for a canoe. Brook, brown and rainbow trout abound in good size. Hatches are regular along its entire course, with big hatches of may flies and caddis from early June on through the summer season. Water flow is quite regular. Fish are full-colored and quite plump for their length.

The Black River is the easternmost of the three rivers that rise on the north slope of the moraine near Gaylord. I highly recommend the section above the village of Tower. This is true remote country well away from the traffic, and so is not overfished or overcamped or overcanoed. The angler-camper is encouraged to combine both.

Upstream from Black River Ranch, the Black is less than 50 feet wide and less than 3 feet deep in most stretches. In the lower reaches between Black River Ranch and Tower Pond, it is as wide as 100 feet and nearly 6 feet deep. It is easy to wade, though the current is steady and strong. It is very similar in make-up to the other rivers, with coves, tributaries, a well-broken shoreline with undercuts, mossy and fernlined shores, old windfalls and a generous collar of overhanging evergreens and hardwoods. High sandy banks border the river on both sides between Tin Shanty Bridge and Main River Bridge. Clay banks bound the river in places south of the village of Tower.

It is all good wading in most reaches upstream from Main River Bridge, but below the bridge it gets too deep and fast, with overhanging foliage that can make casting difficult. But the fish are there—big bright ones, brooks, browns and rainbows. Log jams, shoals and beaverdams in the upper river add to the challenge for fishing and raise the beauty count.

If you like to camp out, traveling light, you can have the stream mostly to yourself, a blessing in this part of the world.

Rifle River flows southeastward from Devoe Lake in Ogemaw County to Saginaw Bay. The best water is from Selkirk upstream. There is moderate canoe traffic and a canoe is recommended in the lower parts of the upper water. It is only 30 to 50 feet wide and generally less than 3 feet deep, making it an excellent stream for wading. Again, the bottom is sand and some gravel and few rocks, but the water is slick and fast, winding through thick swamps and forests, with a well-indented shoreline with undercuts and bars. Overhanging trees and bushes afford ample natural conditions for the very high quality of the insect hatches of aquatic species that comprise the trout's food. A good minnow supply is also present.

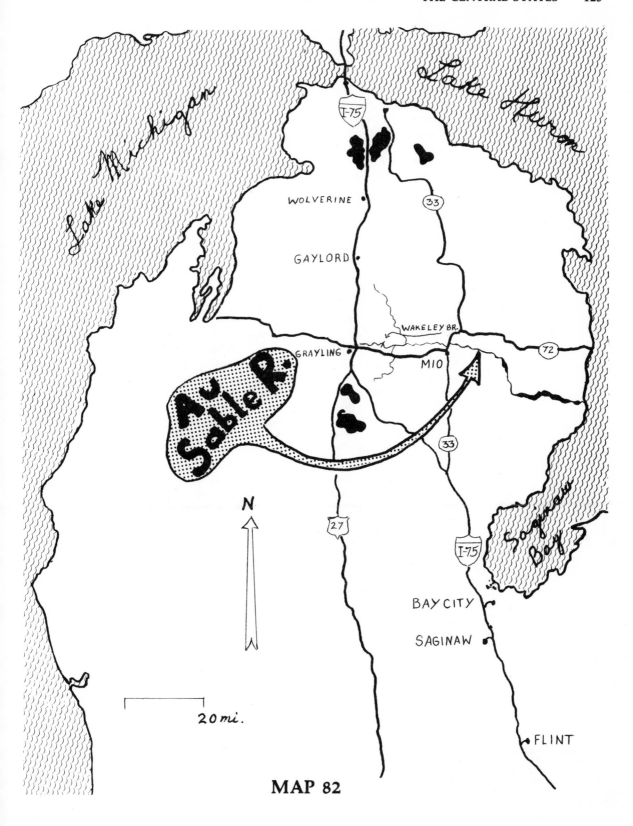

**MAP 82**

There are some paved roads and some farmland, so the atmosphere is pastoral rather than wild. It is less than an hour's drive from the well-populated Saginaw/Bay City area.

"... and the last may be first." The Au Sable is my personal favorite although it may lack the wilderness feeling experienced in some of the more remote streams of this state. It is famous, however, having been praised not only by anglers, but by philosophers, politicans and authors. It has also been well publicized, perhaps too well publicized, as the prime stream of the Midwest. Fifty years ago—even thirty years ago—it was comparatively wild, but today many homes, resorts, and much canoeing and boating have taken away the wild exclusiveness. Nonetheless, it still produces good fishing, perhaps even better since dedicated stream management has increased the trout population.

The Au Sable flows generally southward and eastward from its source near Grayling to Lake Huron. The section from Mio is considered choice. The river near Grayling is probably traveled more for outdoor recreation than any of the major rivers of the state. While trout fishing is there, it is not the best due to the human activity. The river has two state campgrounds and many camping areas, boat liveries and vacationing necessities.

Upstream from Grayling the Au Sable is less than 50 feet wide and an average of 3 feet deep. From Grayling to Wakeley Bridge it is 11 to 50 feet wide and as wide as 200 feet above Mio Pond. Upstream from Wakeley Bridge there are some deep dropoffs so, waders be warned. Shelving riffles, strong main currents of white water, long glides and glistening cross-currents make it a test for fly fishermen. Low banks of sand and muck carry much shoreline foliage and insect havens. Hatches of aquatic insects are steady and large, with the famed Michigan Green Drake may fly being the prime hatch of the season. Forested in evergreens, hardwoods and birch, it is a delight to fish and to float leisurely while casting. While it contains brook trout, these are sparse in comparison with the rainbows. Brown trout predominate and there are some big ones in that river, over the 5-pound mark.

The stream from Grayling up is not overworked and is recommended since it can be called relatively wild.

One in search of excellent Midwest fishing is urged to visit the Au Sable. Many fine rod makers of the Midwest have developed their wands on this water and many a famous fly tyer has cut his teeth on the selective trout that abound here. It is a famous river, and even though it has been highly developed, a point it shares with the streams of New York State and many other Eastern waters, it is a good producer and will remain for generations as a landmark.

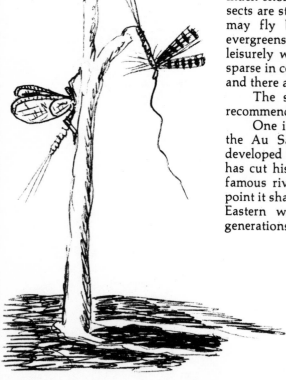

# WISCONSIN

In general terms, this state has three major areas of fishing. Lake Superior borders it on the extreme north with over 200 miles of shoreline, while Lake Michigan provides even more on the eastern border. Then, the northern section of the state is dotted with thousands of lakes and connecting streams. The St. Croix River, a tributary of the Mississippi, rounds out the attractions in the north. Muskellunge, large-mouth and small-mouth bass and northern pike are to be found almost everywhere and trout, including lake trout, are a main attraction.

The biggest muskellunge ever boated in this state weighed 69 pounds. It, and fish of like size, are available in three rivers in an east-west stretch of the state: the Chippewa, which joins the Mississippi below Eau Claire and flows out of the northern part of the state, the upper Wisconsin River toward the northeast, which runs from Rhinelander southward and turns west at Portage in order to reach the Mississippi, and the Amnicon River, which empties into Lake Superior east of Superior in the northwestern corner. Both U.S. 2 and U.S. 53 into Superior cross the Amnicon. The lower section of the Chippewa is available via State Route 85 south from Eau Claire and State Route 25 south of Durand. Visit above Chippewa Falls, for there are many rivers in that drainage that produce good-sized muskies.

Other hot spots are Escanaba and High Lakes in the Northern Highland State Forest just northeast of Boulder Junction. The Eagle Chain, a series of lakes near Eagle River at the junction of U.S. 45 and State Route 70, are also good bets.

MAP
83

MAP
84

MAP
85

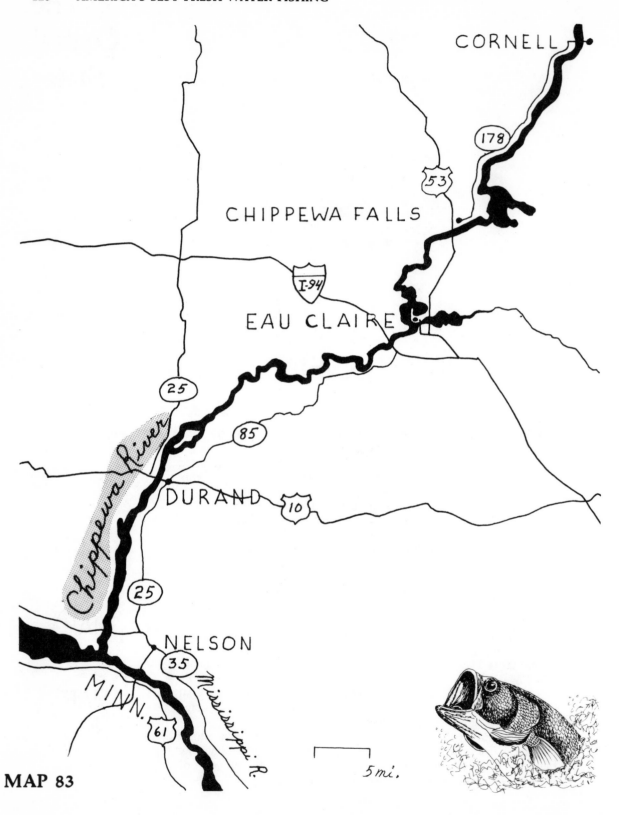

CORNELL

178

53

CHIPPEWA FALLS

I-94

EAU CLAIRE

25

85

DURAND

10

Chippewa River

25

NELSON

35

MINN.

Mississippi R.

61

5 mi.

**MAP 83**

The black bass angler had best try the Lac du Flambeau area with its hundreds of lakes. Walleye fishing is also good here. A little further west the Manitowish River and Manitowish Lake, plus the waters nearby, provide smallmouth bass fishing that is tops and quite famous.

**MAP 84**

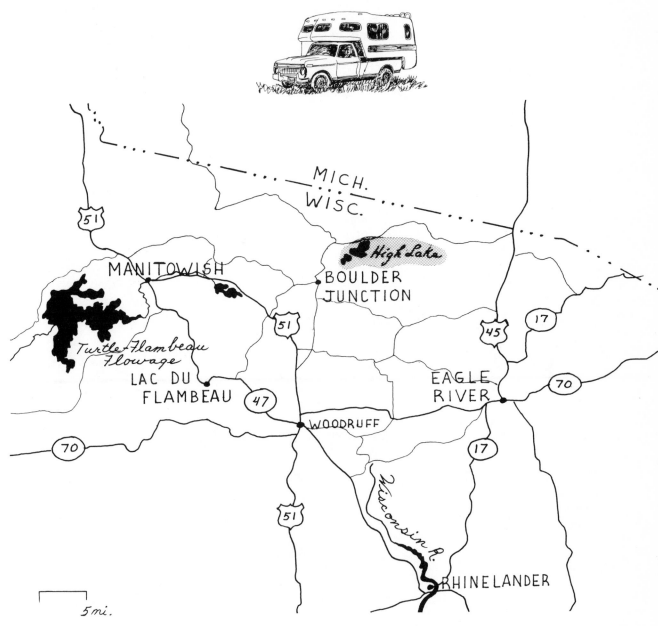

**MAP 84**

The tourist angler should try the Menominee on the border between Wisconsin and Michigan. This is a famed smallmouth river. Go south from the junction of U.S. 8 and U.S. 141 and then take off over country roads.

Another great bass river I can personally recommend is the Peshtigo to the south. U.S. 141 crosses it just south of Crivitz.

Excellent angling for walleyes can be had in the very well-respected Namekagon River. It follows along U.S. 63 south through Hayward and at Trego where U.S. 63 joins U.S. 53 it turns westerly to finally join the St. Croix.

There are transplanted Western steelhead in Wisconsin, and you can find them in good numbers and good size in the rivers along the shores of Lake Superior. Bois Brule, Iron and Flag Rivers are good samples. State Route 13 out of Superior, eastward, crosses all three.

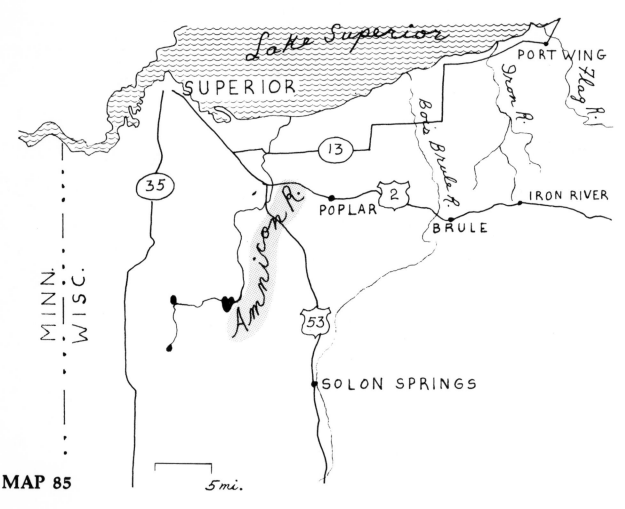

MAP 85

In the southern section of the state just below the Green Bay Peninsula is the famed and large Lake Winnebago, a traditional lake of the Midwest. It has excellent walleye fishing, shad, walleye pike and northern pike.

If you like big river fishing, try the Mississippi, which borders the west side of the state. Largemouth black bass are the attraction here, along with an endless variety of other species. There are about 225 miles of river to choose from and it's almost 2 miles wide in some places.

MAP 86

Since sport fishing is an important product here, accommodations are numerous and good. Boating ramps and marinas are also quite numerous and if you plan to bring your own boat, send for a list of boat launching places from the Recreational Publicity Section, Wisconsin Department of Natural Resources, at Madison, Wisc. 53701.

This whole state is just one big fishing hole and to really get to know it in advance you should contact several of the better known fishing resorts dedicated to the fisherman. For canoe and fishing trips, contact Armour Lake Canoe Outfitters, Presque Isle, Wisc. 54557, and for a vacation packet that describes some ten top lakes, especially about the muskie fishing, write Recreation Association, Hayward, Wisc. 54843. For another good bet for those intent on hooking their first muskie, I recommend Kings Lodge, Route 4, Hayward, Wisc. 54843. Also a must in your mailing is the Wisconsin Department of Natural Resources, P.O. Box 450, Madison, Wisc. 53701.

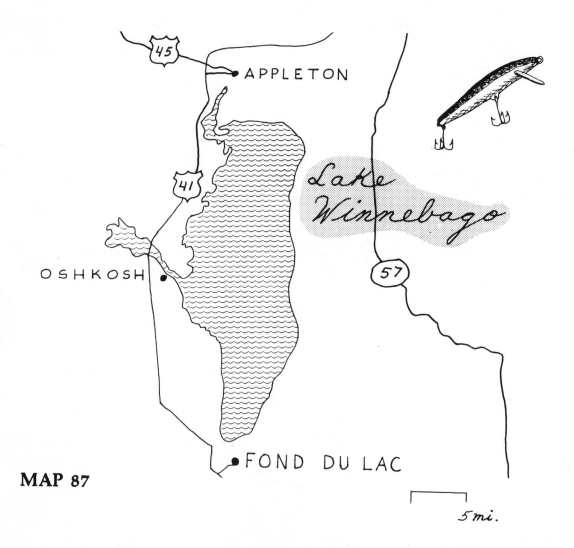

MAP 87

5 mi.

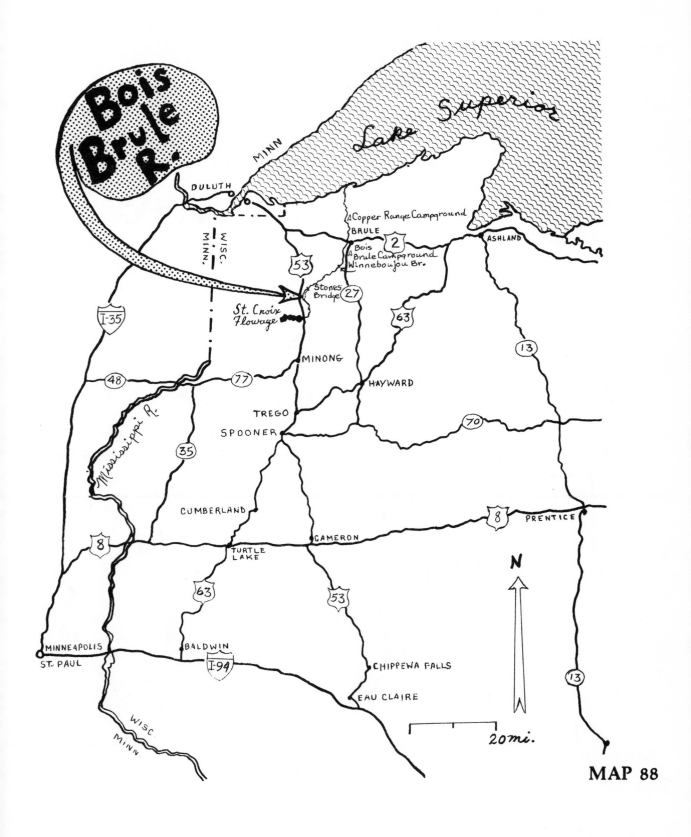

MAP 88

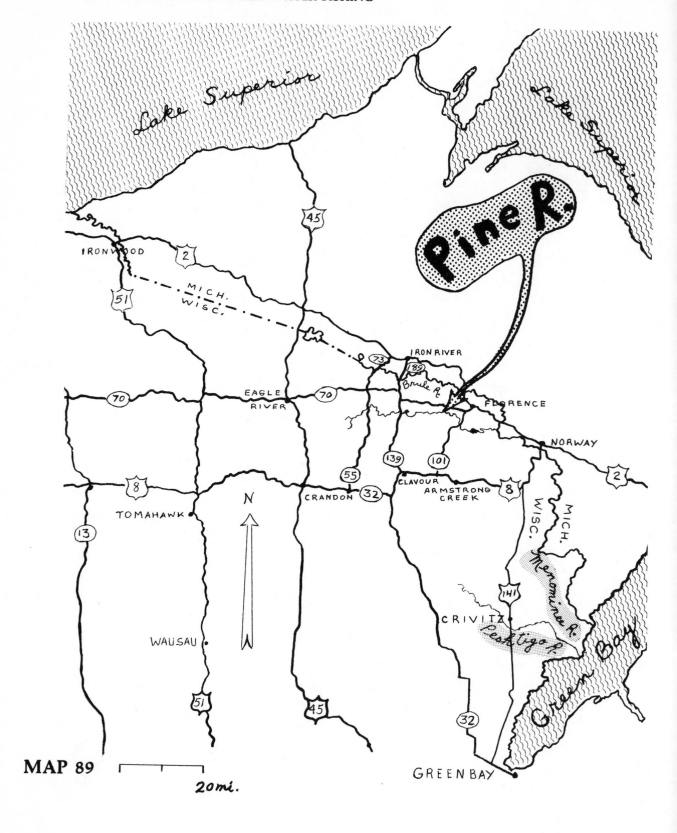

MAP 89    20mi.

Wisconsin anglers will argue over the best of the state's two prime trout streams, the Bois Brule and the Pine River. Visit them both and you won't go wrong. There are countless other fine streams in this state and many big trout have been taken in them. But there's always fame and popularity for these two.

The Brule is also a popular canoeing river and good fishing can be had from a canoe, drifting downstream or stopping at the heads of pools and rapids for wading. Best seasons are spring and fall when very large steelhead and brown trout ascend the river for spawning. Originating near the St. Croix Flowage in Douglas County in northwestern Wisconsin, the Brule flows generally north-northeast for about forty miles until it empties into Lake Superior. Most of the land along its erratic course is publicly-owned which guarantees that the river shore will not be overdeveloped. There are four campgrounds on the river, however. The one small village, Brule, provides accommodations for fishermen and canoeists. The river is crossed by U.S. 2 at the village of Brule, while several paved state and county roads cross the river above and below the village.

The Brule, from its origin to Stones Bridge is fairly narrow—generally less than 40 feet wide. For several miles downstream from Stones Bridge it widens into a series of elongated ponds or lakes that are several hundred feet wide. Just upstream from Winneboujou Bridge it narrows to about 70 feet. From here to Copper Range Campground, it ranges from about 40 to 80 feet. Average summer flow affords wading in about 3 feet of water, generally above the U.S. Highway 2 bridge (but holes of 5 to 6 feet are common). Below the highway bridge it deepens to 4 to 7 feet deep in the quieter sections, and less than 3 feet in the rapids. There are some mucky spots which can make wading somewhat hazardous. Wading is recommended in the upper reaches and a canoe can be used downstream.

Although crossed by several paved roads, the Brule has retained its semi-wilderness atmosphere, thanks to state ownership of its banks. The few riverfront homes and cabins do not detract from its beauty. The banks are thickly forested by coniferous swamps in the upper reaches, with mixed hardwood and evergreens in the lower section.

This is a very stable stream, and the headwaters drain out-wash deposits of sand and gravel that contribute a relatively large amount of groundwater runoff, resulting in stable stream levels throughout the year.

Hatches of caddis, stone and may flies are regular throughout the open season, and some of the hatches are classed as drove hatches. The stream also has a sizeable supply of varied minnows, offering plenty of forage for the fish to grow on to attain prodigious size. As mentioned, the river empties into Lake Superior, which is one reason for the large and tough fighting fish to be encountered, such as lake trout and white fish.

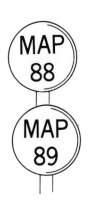

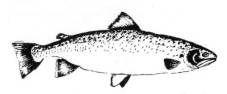

The Pine River was designated by the state in 1965 as a wild river, one of the first to be so designated, and is located in northeastern Wisconsin. Although it is not a popular canoe river, it is a good trout stream. In terms of remoteness and scenery, its location is protected within the boundaries of the Nicolet National Forest. It flows generally eastward from its source in extensive wetlands and lakes in northwestern Forest County to its junction with the Menominee River in eastern Florence County. It is crossed by several paved roads, but access points are several miles apart in some reaches.

The river, including the North Branch, is about 65 miles long and increases in width from a few feet at the headwaters to about 200 feet at its mouth. It varies in depth from a foot to 6 feet with many rapids, falls and shoals. Canoeing is recommended to the fishermen in the lower reaches. While most of the stream above is wadable, it is very fast, treacherous and deep. The Pine has only one developed campground, but many camping sites are available.

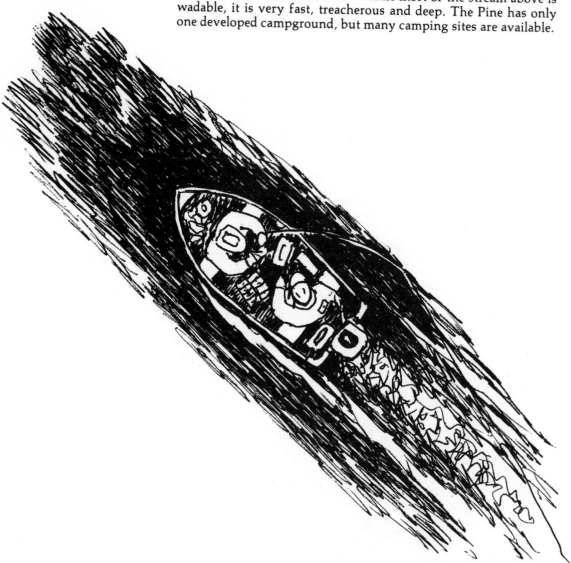

# MINNESOTA

Now, here's a state to visit, no matter how far you have to drive your car or tote your boat. With over 14,000 lakes to choose from it is difficult to single out any top waters. But they are all excellent. The game fish list is large, including largemouth and smallmouth bass, walleyes, northern pike, muskellunge, bluegill, black and white crappie, lake trout, brown trout, rainbow trout and some brook trout and landlocked salmon. There are also what are called "managed lakes" for trout fishing centered in three areas, one near Bemidji, U.S. 2 and 71; one near Brainerd, State Route 210 and State Route 371; and one in the northeast above Gran Marais on the Lake Superior shore on U.S. 61.

Several regions are naturally evident in terms of watersheds. I've fished the famed Arrowhead Country, jutting out in a point between Lake Superior and Canada. It is highly developed for sure, but once off U.S. 61 along the Superior shore, you are in for excellent wilderness angling. There is some lake trout fishing along Lake Superior, but better fishing for lakers can be had in the interior lakes. Also in Arrowhead Country I liked Greenwood Lake, east from the Gunflint Trail, which offers landlocked salmon, brook, brown and rainbow trout plus walleyes, northern pike and bass.

Along the Canadian border the smallmouth bass waters include Basswood Lake, a portion of it in the Quetico Provincial Park in Ontario . . . and I'd put this one as the top smallmouth lake in the United States, rivaling the Grand Lake Stream area of Maine.

For wilderness angling in northern Minnesota, go via U.S. 53 north of Duluth and northeast on State Routes 169 and 1 to Ely.

**MAP
90**

**MAP
92**

135

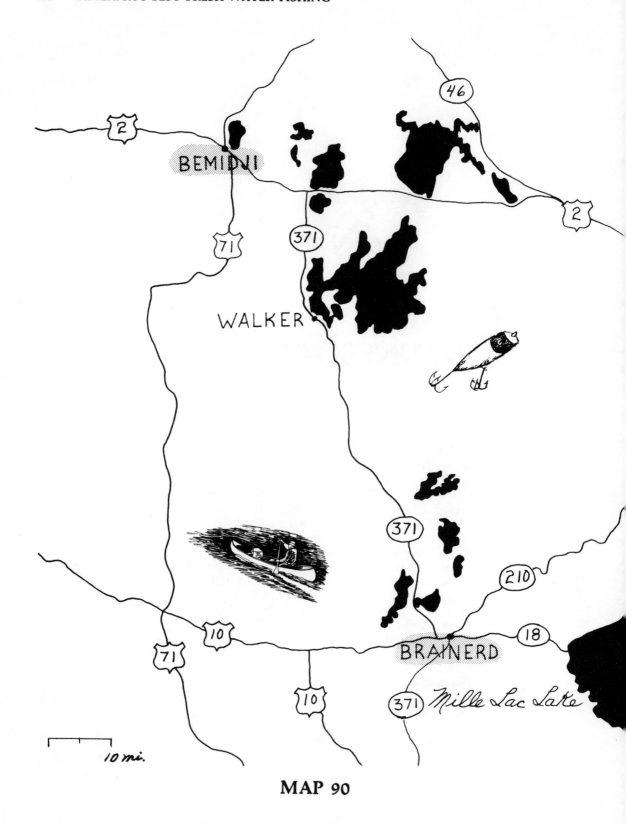

**MAP 90**

Contact Bill Rom or Wilderness Outfitters, in Ely. Cliff Wold, at Bovey on U.S. 169 west of Hibbing, can also set you up for a wilderness canoe excursion.

The most famous lake in the state is Rainy Lake, the largest along the chain between Ontario and Minnesota. Record smallmouth bass are here. Contact the Chamber of Commerce at International Falls, Minn. Good short- or long-term outings can be arranged for you, plus fly-in trips to more remote fishing lakes.

Those who like float trips can find what they are looking for on the Big Fork River southwest of International Falls, accessible from U.S. 71. The Lake Of The Woods is known worldwide for its excellent fishing, reached by State Routes 72 and 11.

MAP
91

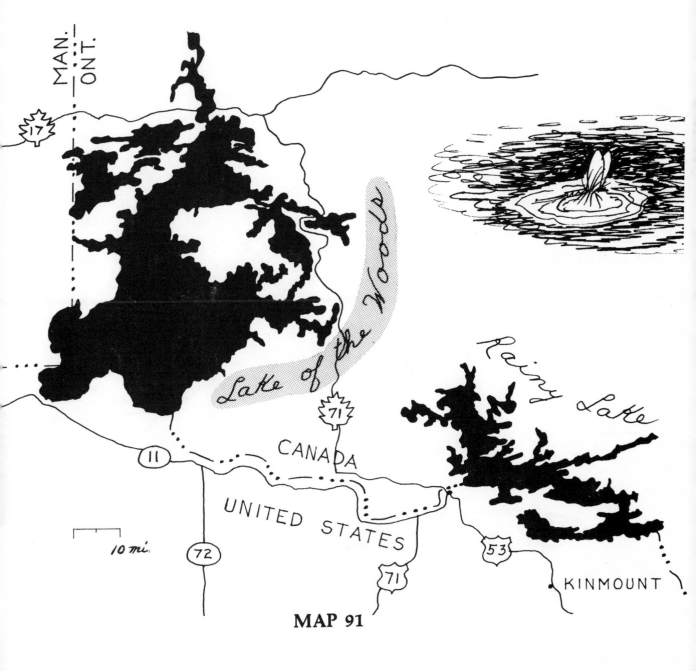

**MAP 91**

Fish the mentioned waters because of their fame, but remember there are thousands of other chances if you have the time and are willing to get off the beaten path. Stay to the north, however, for the best angling. For regulations and maps, write the Department of Natural Resources, 300 Centennial Building, 658 Cedar St., St. Paul, Minnesota 55101.

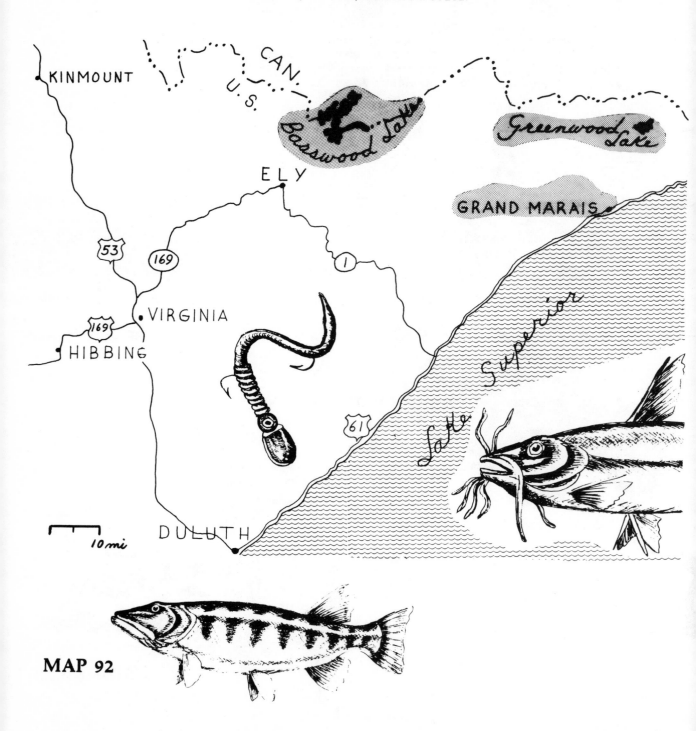

MAP 92

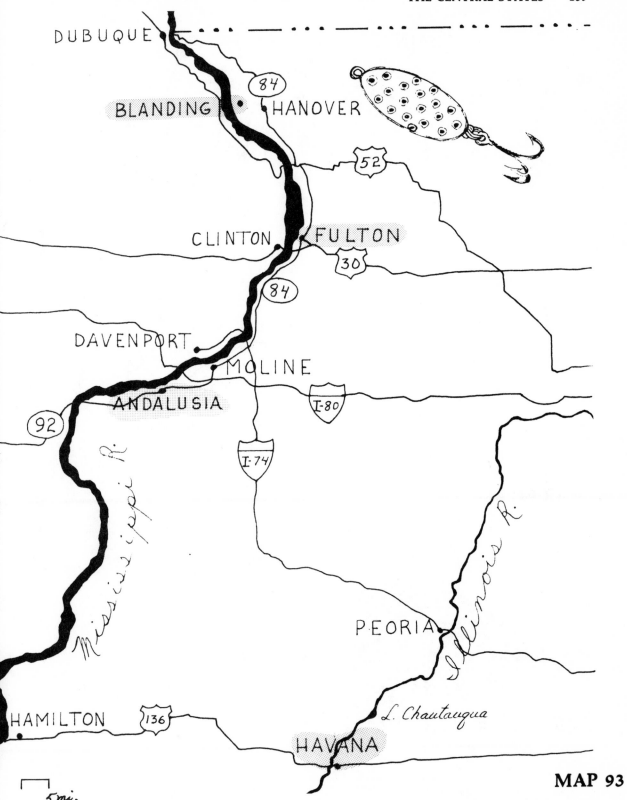

DUBUQUE

84

BLANDING HANOVER

52

CLINTON FULTON

30

84

DAVENPORT

MOLINE

ANDALUSIA

I-80

92

I-74

Mississippi R.

Illinois R.

PEORIA

L. Chautauqua

HAMILTON 136

HAVANA

5 mi.

**MAP 93**

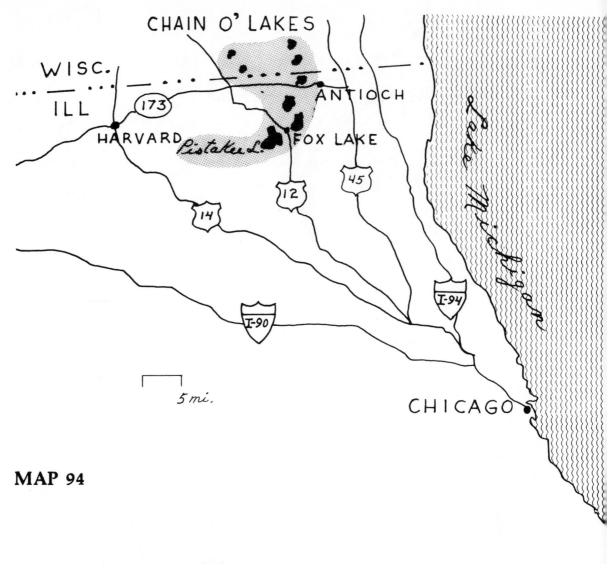

CHAIN O' LAKES

WISC.

ILL

173

HARVARD

*Pistakee L.*

ANTIOCH

FOX LAKE

45

12

14

I-94

I-90

*Lake Michigan*

5 mi.

CHICAGO

**MAP 94**

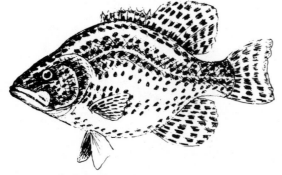

# ILLINOIS

# IOWA

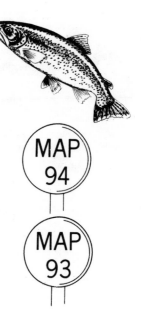

Perch are the big attraction in Illinois where the state borders on Lake Michigan, but the best natural lake fishing for bass and panfish is in the Chain-o-Lakes region in the northeastern section of the state. Try your luck at Channel Lake, Katherine and Marin, Bluff Lake and Pistakee.

Lake Chautauqua at Havana on the Illinois River south of Peoria is a good bass water reached by U.S. 136 where it crosses the lake. It's heavily fished.

Fish the Mississippi at Blanding in the northwest corner off U.S. 52 near Hanover. Go to Fulton where U.S. 30 crosses the river to Clinton, Iowa, and try at Andalusia on State Route 92 west of Moline. You'll find bass, panfish and catfish.

While the fishing is good in this state, generally, it is because of the out-of-the-way lakes and creeks that only the locals know, but none of them are considered in the context of this book as "famous." For a listing of up-to-date conditions, write the Illinois Department of Conservation, 605 State Office Building, Springfield, Illinois 62706.

Some good fishing can be found in Iowa, but the famed fishing waters are in the states that border it.

MAP
94

MAP
93

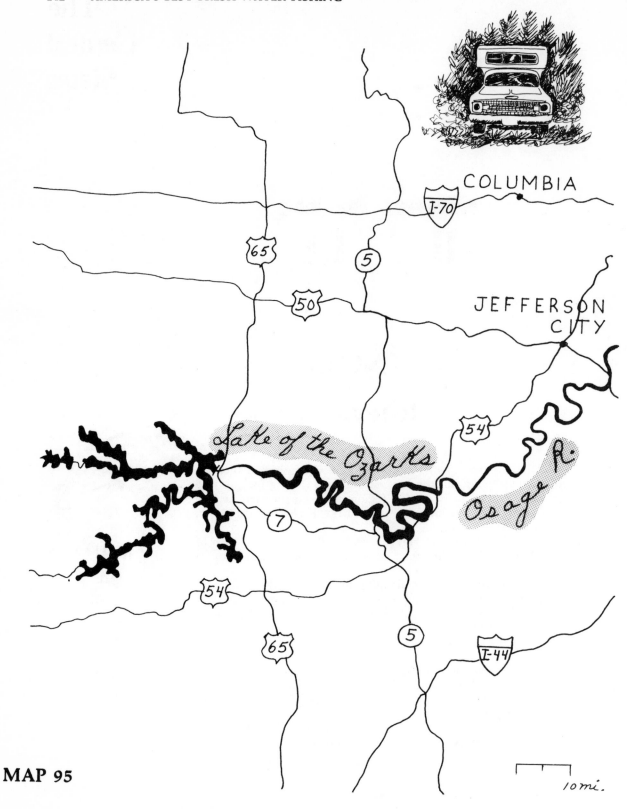

COLUMBIA

I-70

65

5

50

JEFFERSON
CITY

54

*Lake of the Ozarks*

*Osage R.*

7

54

65

5

I-44

**MAP 95**

10 mi.

# The Central States

# MISSOURI

MAP 95

MAP 96

Graced by two great rivers, the Missouri forming the western border, and the Mississippi forming the eastern, this state has a variety of good river and stream fishing. It also has many lakes, mostly man-made, that offer fine angling. Walleyes, bass and panfish are the staples, with some new trout waters where they have been introduced into streams flowing from the giant reservoirs. A few of the springs and lakes also have trout planted in them and the fishing is fine. Some good remote fishing is available, but most of the better waters are easily accessible.

Lake fishing is tops in the Lake of the Ozarks right in the center of the state. This lake, formed by a dam on the Osage River, a tributary of the Missouri, can be reached by U.S. 54 and U.S. 65 at the east and west ends of the lake respectively, while State Route 5 crosses the lake from north to south and State Route 7 roughly skirts the south shore at a distance of about five miles. It is highly developed along its 1,400 miles of shoreline. This is a good place to take your own craft, with many launching sites and resorts.

A recent addition is Table Rock Reservoir south of Springfield on the southwestern border between Missouri and Arkansas. The cold water below the dam running into Taneycomo Lake at Branson produces good trouting as well as all species of bass and panfish, including walleyes. My friend Bob Bright, Baxter Boat Dock, Table Rock Lake, Lampe, Missouri, 65681, is the one to contact for this fishing.

A section of Bull Shoals Lake (actually formed in Arkansas) comes into Missouri just east of Taneycomo and is good for all

143

species. It can be reached from Lutie or Isabella on U.S. 160, with food resorts nearby.

Float fishing rivals that of Arkansas since it is typical Ozark country. Largemouth and smallmouth bass, walleye and some trout are available on at least fifteen rivers, among them the White. My best results have been on the Gasconade, north of Mansfield on U.S. 60, past Hazelgreen on I-44, through Mt. Sterling, U.S. 50, and entering the Missouri River at Gasconade, and also Jacks Fork and Eleven Point near the Arkansas border.

Write to the Department of Conservation, P.O. Box 630, Jefferson City, Missouri 65101, for their booklets on the best fishing spots.

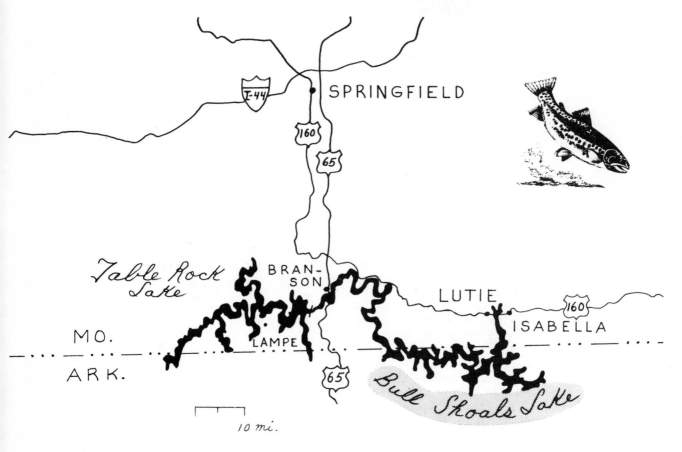

**MAP 96**

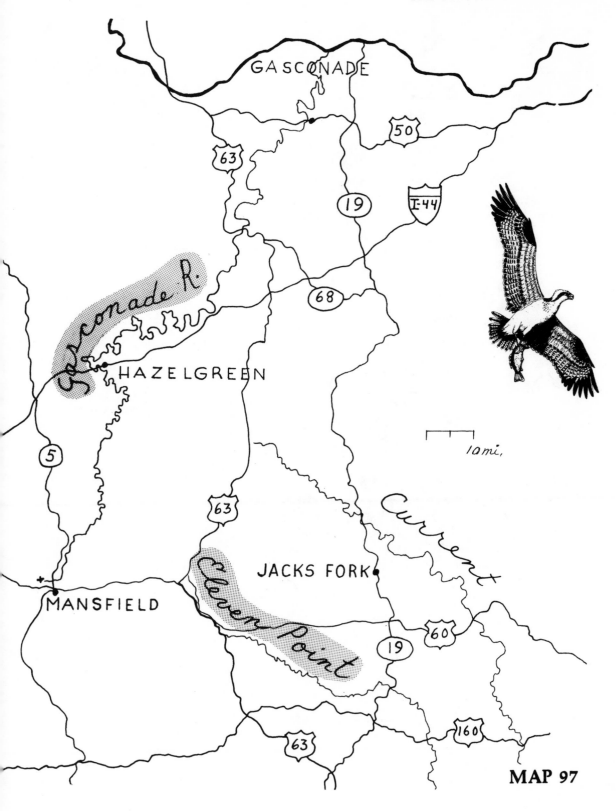

GASCONADE

50

63

19

I-44

Gasconade R.

68

HAZELGREEN

5

10 mi.

63

Current

JACKS FORK

Eleven Point

MANSFIELD

19

60

63

160

**MAP 97**

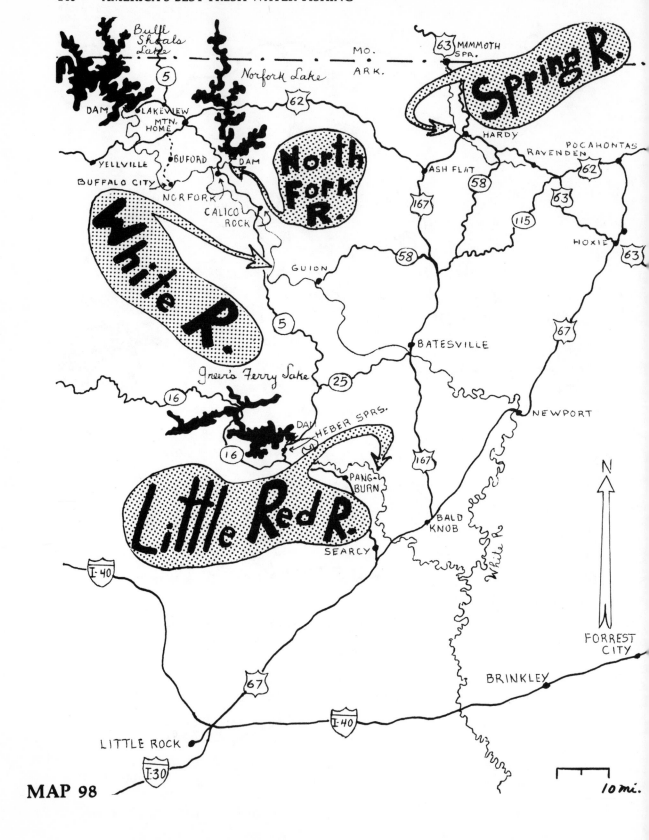

**MAP 98**

# ARKANSAS

Except for the recently discovered "two-story" lakes in Arkansas, which maintain trout at depths below 20 feet and several warmer water species about that level, Arkansas' trout fishing is mostly limited to "tailwater fishing" in the cold waters below the large hydroelectric dams. This trout-supporting water is released from the bottom layers of the impounded reservoir and is, therefore, an artificial situation directly dependent on routine water releases. Only the water quality and available food favor the trout; suitable habitat for natural reproduction and survival of the young does not exist in this man-made situation. Consequently when the trout program in Arkansas was initiated it was conceded that it would be a put-and-take type fishery. This is, nevertheless, good fishing, with the White River as an example.

Fish management such as this, to be practical, requires that 75% or more of the trout stocked must be harvested each year. The small percent which elude the angler the first few weeks grow very fast, often as much as one inch per month. If only a small percentage of the fish are harvested, competition among remaining trout and among these and other species present in the stream at the time of stocking will suppress the growth of the trout. Therefore, it is obvious that a closed season would present a situation of slow growing fish and would deprive the fishermen of catching good sized fish, because many of the fish would die "naturally" before the season is opened.

The establishment of a minimum size limit on certain species of fish has been found to be beneficial only in permitting these

fishes to reach a spawning size. The smaller trout which are hooked and handled by the angler may not survive after being released. Trout programs on the North Fork River below Norfork Dam and on the White River below Bull Shoals Dam are in full swing and are paying off dividends.

Trout for all of these programs in Arkansas are supplied at the present time by the federal trout hatchery below Norfork Dam. Top priority is given to the White and North Fork Rivers and Bull Shoals Lake. This is due to the past success of these areas, the short hauling distance from state hatcheries and the similarity of water quality between the waters in which the trout are raised and the waters in which they are stocked. At the present time, the Blakely Mountain Dam and the Narrows Dam tailwaters do not offer these advantages. However, when the Greers Ferry Trout Hatchery reaches full production, trout programs in these areas can be enlarged as environmental conditions are suitable.

The trout area begins at the base of Bull Shoals Dam and flows for 105 miles to Batesville. The area between Buffalo City and the dam is the No. 1 area of the river and the stretch from Buffalo City to just below Norfork is the second best area. The portion from Calico Rock to Batesville is not the same quality water as that upstream, but many fishermen will argue with you on this point. However, the quality catches are most often reported in the No. 1 area.

When the Commission first began stocking the river, it used brown trout. Two years later this was switched to rainbow trout. Since that time (mid-50's) no brown trout have been released, and yet each year quite a few brown trout ranging from 10 pounds to 30 pounds have been caught. I feel there appears to be reproduction of brown trout in order for the fish to sustain itself. Since it has been over 20 years since small ones have been released, any catch of a brown trout in the 6- to 10-pound class has to indicate reproductivity. The brown trout is found nowhere else in Arkansas.

Although stocking totals vary from year to year, the Commission stocks 1 million to 1½ million rainbows (and rainbows only) in the White River.

There is quite a variety of winged aquatic insects, as well as aquatic "bug" life, although not in the same quantity as found in the Little Red River trout area. Lack of vegetation in the river has reduced some insect life and availability. Recently floods have scoured out many of the weed beds, and since the White River (like all Arkansas trout streams) has a rock bed bottom, the vegetation suffers during floods.

There are nearly 30 trout docks on the White/North Fork combined, and access points are far too numerous to mention. As for state records, the White/North Fork has set all but one.

Out of all the 9,000 miles of fishing streams in Arkansas, there's a unique lunker hole about two miles long on the upper White River trout area. It's recognized as the home of America's largest brown trout. The record catch was made on May 24, 1972, by Troy Lackey of Lakeview while fishing with a live crawfish. The trout was netted after a struggle that lasted over an hour, and its weight was 47 pounds, 4 ounces.

The catch set several marks:

(1) The largest brown trout ever taken on the North American continent in either stream or lake on hand-held sport tackle;

(2) second only to the international record that has withstood all assault since 1866;

(3) largest brown trout ever taken on line in the 12-pound test classification; and

(4) the new Arkansas state record.

The famed hole, which begins at the lower end of the first island in the river below Bull Shoals Dam and extends beyond the curve of the river just past Bruce Creek, is known locally as the Dew Spring hole. Brown trout taken from this stretch of water hold three spinfishing records that are based upon the size of line used to catch big browns. Lackey's catch is tops in the open class, lines of 12-pound test or higher; Dr. Louis McFarland of Hot Springs holds the record in the 8-pound class with a 28-pound 3-ounce brown; and John Lanza of Lakeview is the new holder of the 6-pound-test class by catching a 19-pound 15-ounce brown. All three of the spin fishing record catches were made within one-half mile of each other.

Several other large brown trout have come out of the hole, including a 23-pounder that was caught by Dr. Dan Matthews of Little Rock. His catch ranked tops in the 8-pound test bracket until Dr. McFarland caught his huge brown.

How did these lunker browns happen to be found in the White River? When the river was plugged in the late 1940's with a slug of concrete known as Bull Shoals dam, the river below the dam was deemed suitable for trout. In 1952 brown trout were introduced from below the dam to Cotter. All of the 1,800 in the initial release were from 6 to 8 inches in length. Rainbow trout were jointly stocked, but at a lesser rate since biologists felt the river to be most suitable for browns.

Commission records reflect that about 20,000 brown trout

were first introduced prior to halting the program. Since the fish has extremely limited reproduction, any brown trout caught in the famed hole of water just about *has* to be one of the stockers planted over 20 years ago. Occasionally a fisherman will land a small brown trout, and it is believed that the fish is one that has been naturally spawned. There's little else to believe since the brown stocking halted in 1953.

Located near Heber Spring, Arkansas, the Little Red River flows from the base of Greers Ferry Dam to below Pangburn, 25-plus miles. The floating portion from the dam to the Winkley area, also known as the Swinging Bridge area, is the best. There are several good shoals where nice fish have been caught (John's Pocket is especially good).

For some unknown reason, the fish don't run as large as those in the White. There have been many 5- to 7-pounders caught, but very few over 10 pounds. Yet, the average stringer of trout of the Little Red will run fish in the 1-pound class, and quite often there will be a couple or so in the 2- to 4-pound class mixed.

The river is very thick with moss beds. The dam was completed in the mid-'60's, and trout were introduced in about 1968. Prior to trout stocking, the stream had not yet converted to coldwater stream (from the previous warm-water situation). To speed up the conversion process and to assure food for new fish, biologists with the Arkansas Game & Fish Commission planted coon tail moss and other vegetation from Spring River (another trout stream). As a result, the moss is solidly embedded and is absolutely teeming with sowbugs, which make up 90% of the winter diet of trout, according to a recent study. Probably there is a greater, wider variety of winged insect life than on any other trout stream in the state.

Spring River, which runs from Mammoth Springs to Hardy, Arkansas, is the nearest thing to a natural trout stream, since it is fed by a huge spring at Mammoth Spring, has a very static water flow and level and the temperature is 58-60 degrees year around. As a result there is (by state standards) good reproduction . . . but not enough to maintain itself.

This river is extremely limited in access, and thus very, very low fishing pressure occurs except at public launch areas. These are located below Dam 3, Bayou Access about half way to Many Islands, and also Many Islands. There is no take-out point for boats at the end of the trout waters. Myatt Creek warms up the water sufficiently so that trout are not to be found there. Upon leaving Many Islands, the next take-out point is either Kierl Camp (outside Hardy) or the Hardy public swimming beach.

Unlike other trout streams, the Spring has a good population of walleye and smallmouth bass associated with trout.

Due to lack of moss beds, there is abundance only of may flies, shrimp and hellgrammites. Caddis fly, stone fly, etc., seem to be absent. Huge numbers and species of fish life and crawfish exist here. Trout feed heavily year around on crawfish. As a result of the lack of winged insects, trout in spring are rarely seen dimpling or surface feeding.

This river is apt to be rude to fly fishermen . . . but it is the most scenic of Arkansas' trout streams!

The trout in the North Fork River range from 2 to 10 pounds. The trout area begins from below Norfork Dam and runs only 5 miles to its merger with the White River at the town of Norfork.

The river has a very heavy hatch of winged insects, and thus is a favorite with many fly fishermen who know both the White and the North Fork.

Note: The river is North Fork but the town is NORFORK (not Norfolk) and the dam is NORFORK . . . a situation apt to be confusing.

A survey by university scientists has turned up a very heavy population of spotted salamanders, which the trout feed upon largely. Below the dam the stream is very small, shallow and dotted with small islands. A large number of private homes are on the north bank, and about 5 or 6 docks are also situated in less than a mile of river. As a result, fishing is poor in that area due to pressure.

Note: There is a feeder stream coming in from the north directly below the dam. This stream stems from the federal fish hatchery and is CLOSED TO FISHING . . . the only closed area on either the White or the North Fork.

Access to the river is available at a public launch ramp below the dam and adjacent to the hatchery. The only other access, other than via the docks, is another public ramp at the town of Norfork at the White River junction.

The stream can be waded during the nominal flow periods, when there is about 1 to 3 feet of water in the stream. During the peak generation periods, the river rises up to 8 feet, and is extremely swift and dangerous.

Many bait shops, grocery stores, motels, etc., flourish in the area of Norfork on Highway 5 leading to Mountain Home, some 15 miles north.

This is the Arkansas story, and it is all of recent development. In the old days, trout fishing was a relatively minor sport since the bass is king in this state, or was.

But since the building of big dams and their resultant lakes, Arkansas is a world-beater for trouting. True, most of it is of an entirely different nature than the classical miles of winding natural trout streams. The "new" trout streams created by dams are sensational, and I use that word as an understatement. They are also producing excellent bass fishing.

For more information, write the Arkansas Game and Fish Commission. Capitol Mall, Little Rock, Ark. 72201.

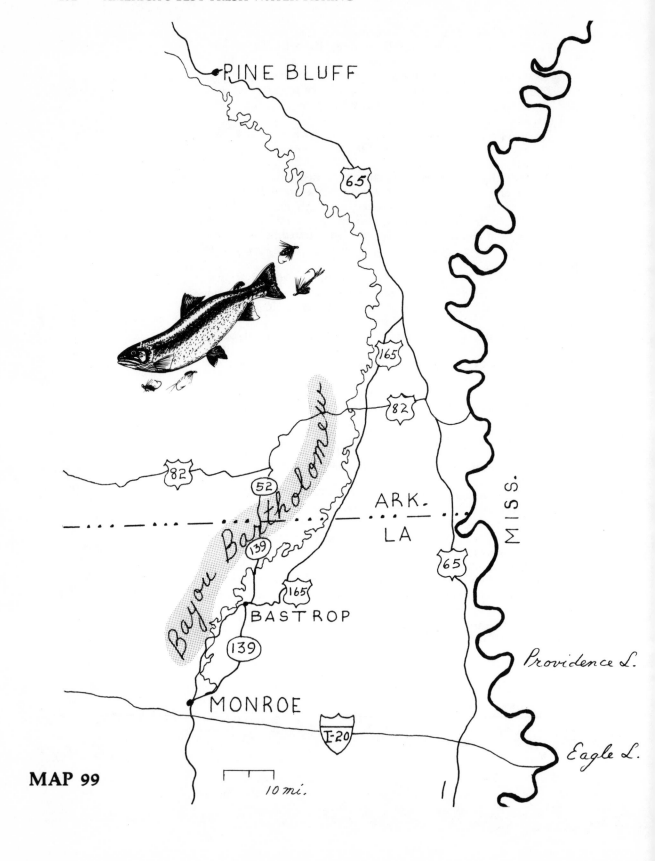

MAP 99

10 mi.

# LOUISIANA

Deep South, Suh! There's plenty of largemouth bass here along with catfish and panfish, in a string of lakes along the great Mississippi. Lake Providence and Eagle, just north of I-20, and Yucatan, Bruin and St. Joseph offer a choice just south of I-20. Resorts are easily available. These would be my choice of lakes for good bassing. The rivers are often broad and muddy, augmented by bayous and ponds that are for catfish lovers as well as bassers. The smaller and faster streams are in the northeast; the Bayou Bartholomew is supposed to be the best in the state, winding down from Arkansas toward the town of Monroe and reached by U.S. 165 and State Route 139. The Little River in the hilly area near Lake Catahoula, north of Alexandria, is reached from White Sulphur Springs or Fishville on State Route 8. Close to Baton Rouge is the Atchafalaya running alongside the Mississippi, west of it. It is reached by State Route 105 off U.S. 190, west of Baton Rouge.

For complete regulations, write the Wild Life and Fisheries Commission, 400 Royal Street, New Orleans, La. 70130.

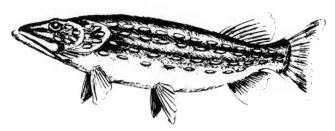

153

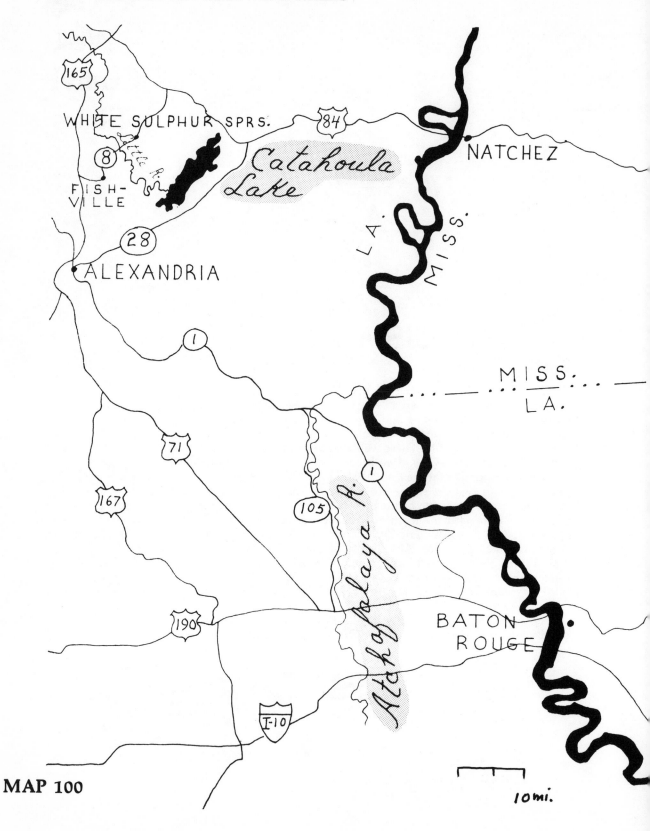

MAP 100

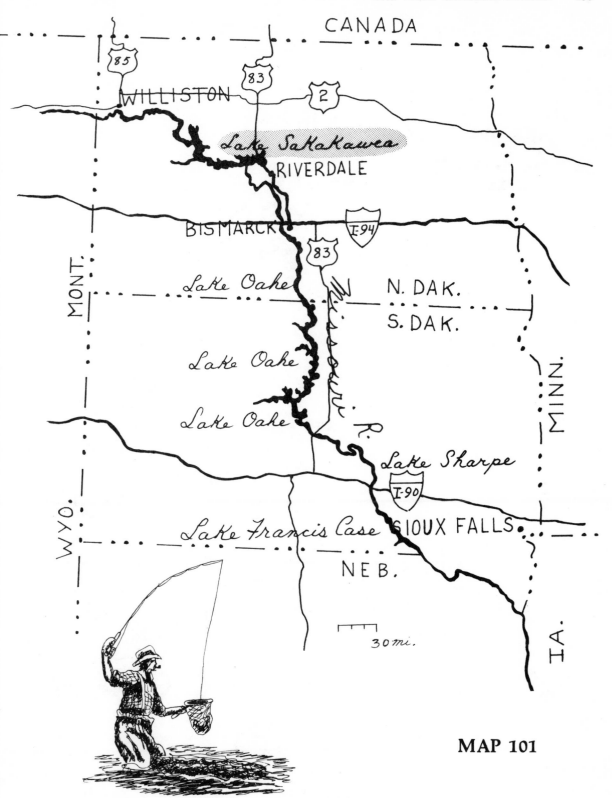

CANADA

WILLISTON

Lake Sakakawea

RIVERDALE

BISMARCK

MONT.

Lake Oahe

N. DAK.

S. DAK.

Lake Oahe

Lake Oahe

MINN.

Lake Sharpe

WYO.

Lake Francis Case SIOUX FALLS

NEB.

IA.

30 mi.

MAP 101

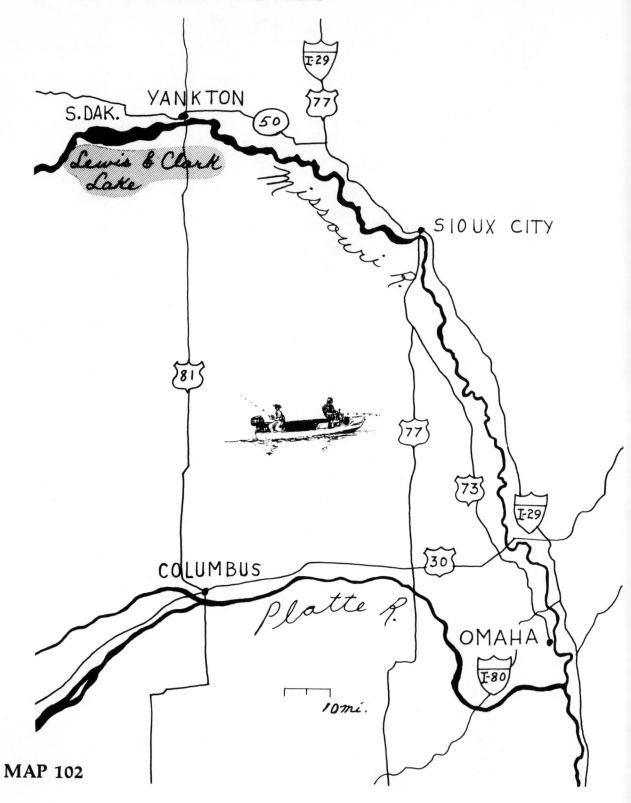

MAP 102

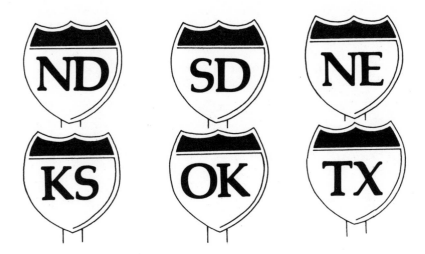

# NORTH DAKOTA

# SOUTH DAKOTA

# NEBRASKA · KANSAS

# OKLAHOMA · TEXAS

This state has a series of reservoirs on the Missouri River that run from north to south. The northernmost is Lake Sakakawea formed by the Garrison Dam at Riverdale and extending to the town of Williston on the Montana border.

There are some rainbow trout, but it is mainly walleyes, pike and panfish for sport. This state is known for its hunting rather than its fishing. Write the State Game and Fish Dept., 2121 Lovett Ave., Bismarck, North Dakota, 58505.

MAP
101

The Missouri River traverses the center of the state and the main fish is the walleye, with panfish as second best.

Write the Department of Game Fish and Parks, Sigurd Anderson Building, Pierre, South Dakota 57501.

Lewis and Clark Lake in the northeastern corner on the Missouri is good walleye water. The tributaries that feed the Missouri and the North Platte Rivers are the main waterways. Not too much here.

For more information, write Nebraska Game and Parks Commission, 2200 N. 33rd St., Lincoln, Neb. 68503.

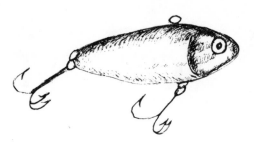

Some good fishing can be found in all these states, but again, residents can go elsewhere in search of famed and top waters, either to the north or south, as was suggested for the residents of Ohio, Indiana, Virginia and West Virginia.

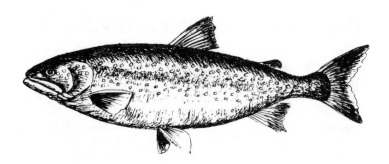

The casual observer or the intent driver bent on rapid travel through Texas whisks through the state seeing very little other than desert or flat farming lands. But a closer look finds this state bordered by magnificent and large river systems, and in these systems are found large reservoirs and impounds which were nonexistent fifty years ago. A network of excellent highways provide access to these waters. But one word of warning here. When you see a highway sign ahead of you that says "DIP," respect it, especially on secondary roads. It means what it says. The road dips, sometimes quite fast, into a gully or wash, or for a brook or stream, or even a dry brook that is only a wash in time of rain. Slow down, *really* slow down, especially if you are toting a trailer or if your car is heavily loaded. If you don't, you are liable to wreck or, at the least, bust a spring. Loose and straying cattle are another hazard, especially in the remote areas.

Now, to the fishing. Texas rivers are numerous. The Rio Grande carves the western border of the state from El Paso to Brownsville on the Gulf. The famed Red River divides Texas and Oklahoma on the north border. The Sabine marks the Louisiana border on the east. Right down central Texas, the Colorado enters the Gulf at Matagorda, midway between Galveston and Corpus Christi. In addition to these streams, all of which are tops and contain bass and panfish and big catfish, are the Trinity—draining central Texas and making a turn southward at the Dallas-Fort Worth area—and the Brazos, in the east-central section of Texas near Abilene. Excellent float trips and much good fishing can be had all along these rivers, so it is just a matter of picking out an area to concentrate on.

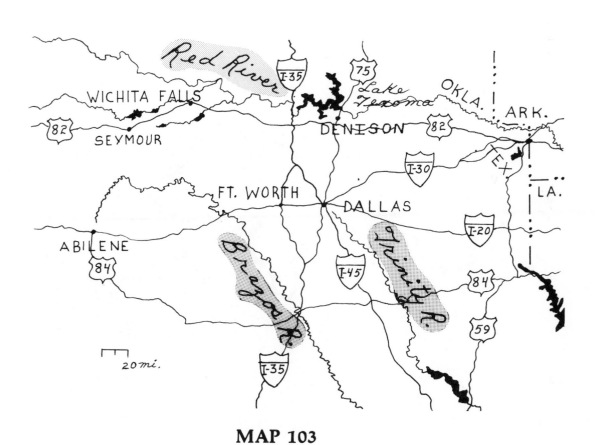

**MAP 103**

But to my mind, the lakes are what really offer the best angling, especially for largemouth bass, panfish and enormous catfish. Lake Texoma on the Red River north of the Dallas-Fort Worth area is a case in point, one of the largest bodies of water in the state. The town of Denison, on U.S. 75, touches the southeast corner of the lake. Good accommodations and boat ramps are available. Going west, there is a cluster of lakes formed by dams on the Wichita, a tributary of the Red River. Lake Kemp and Diversion Lake are tops as are Kickapoo Lake and Lake Arrowhead, all between Wichita Falls and Seymour.

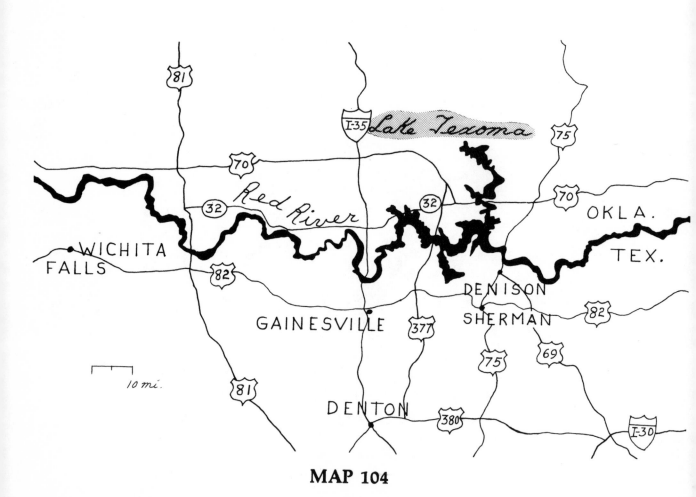

**MAP 104**

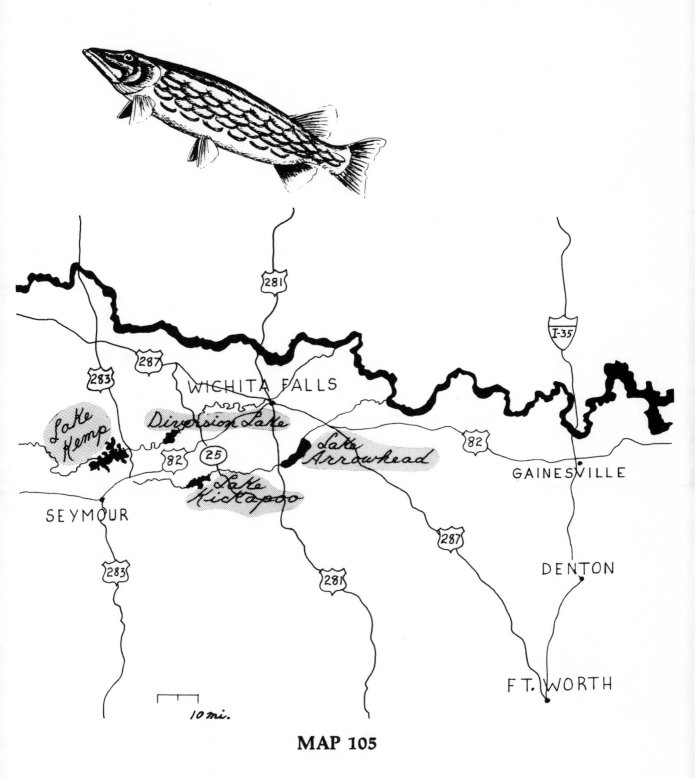

**MAP 105**

Lake Texarkana is famous in the northeast corner, coming from Sulphur River, another tributary of the Red. Find it 9 miles from the town of Texarkana on U.S. 67 or U.S. 59.

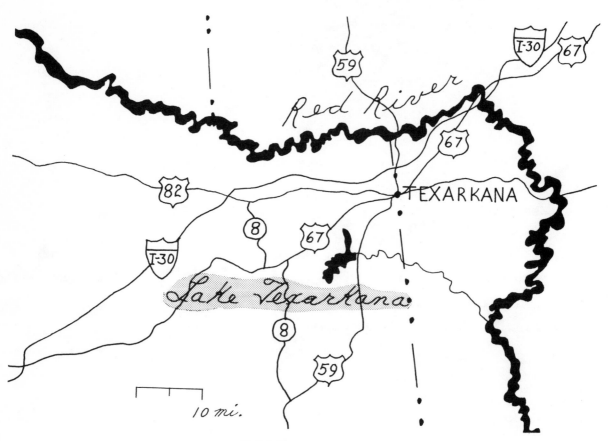

## MAP 106

While there are countless others that produce all season long, the above are my recommendations as top waters.

Although I would not necessarily leave my Florida home and arbitrarily decide to go to Texas for its fishing, it can be rated as one of the top states. Being a big area, it draws many sportsmen to its remote waters, while anglers from the big cities of Texas need not venture beyond the borders of the "Texas Kingdom" to find excellent fishing for themselves.

For more information and regulations, write the Texas Parks and Wildlife Dept., Austin, Texas 78701. Maps are available. You can order Toledo Bend Lake maps with fishing regulations from Texas Parks and Wildlife Department, Austin, Texas 78701.

# MONTANA

Montana is big country, high and mighty in nature's bounties. Everything is on a grand scale and trout fishing is no exception. When it came time to measure the attributes of the streams of this state, it seemed impossible to put one before the other.

The Big Hole is not only a trout stream, it is a monument in the history of America and a tradition among trouters. It is romantic and as highly charged in the angler's heart as it is in excellent fishing. To the Easterner used to fishing a bare few miles of, say, the Beaverkill, here are over a hundred miles of productive water that would take the angler at least a hundred days of constant fishing in order to merely cover once!

And big fish? A certainty. Yes, you and I have struck out many times, something that happens to all of us. But grand and glorious days do occur when the fish just seem to leap up at us no matter what we do. And what a setting! What scenery!

On the map, the Big Hole heads from the Continental Divide south and west of Jackson, Montana, and twists and slithers its way south for a hundred miles, seeking out the crags, cliffs, gorges and open country before it joins the Beaverhead and Ruby Rivers near Twin Bridges. There it enters the Jefferson. It is fast, hard, slow, broken, deep, shapely, and contains all the elements that make it the complete trout stream. Big boulders break its course. Gravel bars accent the pocket water and separate the depths from the shallows. There are long riffles and long oily-smooth glides and pools where the water seems to stop momentarily for the dry fly fisherman.

163

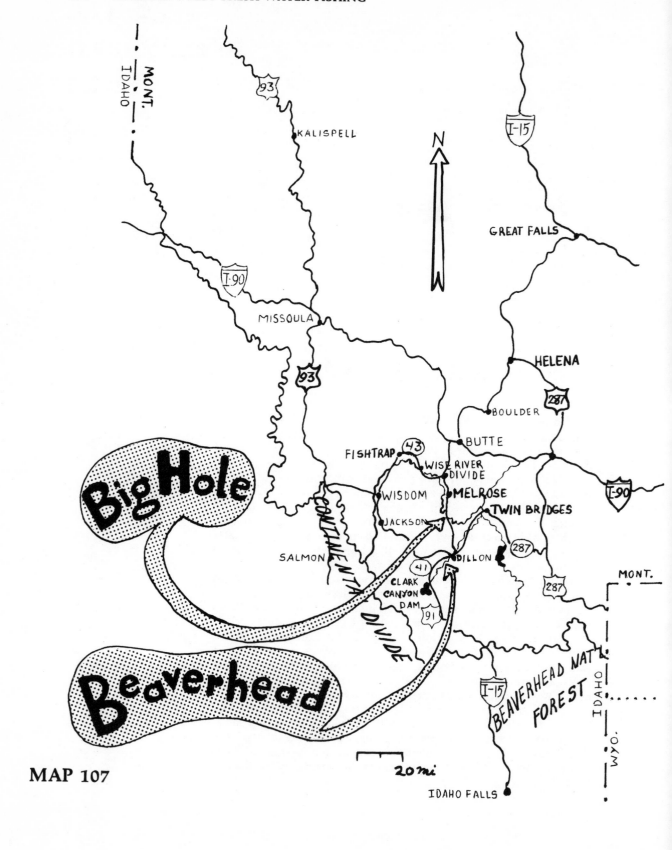

MAP 107

Montana, generally, has a short summer season. Once the ice is out and the temperature is warm, the season lasts from the middle of July on into the early weeks of September; not much time to fish, but every moment is loaded with thrills. And the fish are big. Dangerous to wade until the end of the spring runoff, the river is wadable until October, except in the deeps. Good boats and guides are available all along its course. Montana streams are noted for the best fly activity during the salmon fly hatch, which usually comes off during June. Rainbows and browns predominate, and if you are luckier than I have been, you can hook into trout up to 10 pounds that will rival any Atlantic salmon grilse. This is cold, clear water and the fish are firm and stiff.

If you fish the upper reaches of the stream near Wise River, you'll possibly encounter Montana grayling, a gem of a fish that will run to about a foot in length. They will be taken in company with cutthroat and the pinkest rainbows you've ever seen. Dropping in farther upstream near Wisdom, the water is wadable earlier and is a trifle easier than further down. There are some big fish in there that come to big, fluffy, dry flies during the hatches. Where the Big Hole joins the Wise River, it's big and voluptuous and will produce rainbows and browns from 4 to 10 pounds. This is water for streamers and bucktails, or weighted nymphs allowed to settle in the depths.

Fly fishing is at its prime on the big water from the last week in July through September and, weather permitting, into October. Naturally the stream is lower and clearer in the fall and the biggest and deepest stretches can be waded. This is water for the experts, for trout can be spooked easily on the open stretches by a mere wave of the rod. Long leaders over the 10-foot length are a must, and selective casting is the rule. Small flies do the trick and big trout will come to the sparse-tied twenties. Best water is in the Beaverhead National Forest. There are also many private ranches dotting the valley where you can enter with permission.

From Divide to Wisdom, a paved highway (No. 43) meanders along the river for about 50 miles. There is a good gravel road past Jackson for about 20 miles and then smaller dirt roads. Paved highway I-15 south of Divide stretches for about 25 miles along the Big Hole. From Twin Bridges south there are campsites north of Wise River. Many good accommodations are available at Wisdom, Wise River, Divide, Melrose and Twin Bridges and adequate supplies can be bought locally. I recommend the Sportsman's Lodge at Melrose, and Stardust and Big Sky Motels at Twin Bridges. For a local information check, try Dan Pendergraft at Melrose and also Frank's Sport Shop at Twin Bridges.

Remember to bring the mosquito lotion. Indian Summer brings them out in full strength.

## Beaverhead

After you have fished the Big Hole, Madison and Yellowstone Rivers, try the Beaverhead. That's the advice I followed and what I found there puts the river in this book despite its relatively low public profile. The Montana Conservation Department was

amazed when it found, by the technique of electro-shocking, that there were nearly 300 pounds of catchable trout per 1000 feet of stream, with most of the fish ranging near the 5-pound mark. This is like fishing in a hatchery, but a natural hatchery to boot, since almost all of the trout are wild, stream-bred fish. It has been more than ten years since the stream has been stocked with browns and rainbows. So when you connect with a whopper it will be a tackle killer—nothing soft about these big-sky trout!

This stream does not receive the constant tourist pounding that the big name rivers get. Limits of trout averaging over 2 pounds are taken by rank amateurs, so the expert can be expected to top this average. The season is at its best from mid-July on into September and October. All through those weeks good fly hatches keep the trout active.

The most productive section of the stream is between Clark Canyon dam downstream for 36 miles, although for 8 miles of that stretch below the town of Dillon the stream level fluctuates a good deal during the irrigation season. The levels do not always interfere with wading, but it is a good idea to know the water release schedule or to keep alert for rising or falling levels so that you will not get hung out on a shelf with no way back to safety if the water level rises. A good float stretch exists from Clark Canyon, 11 miles downstream to Barrett's Diversion Dam. Boat access points are obvious below the dam at Pipe Organ Lodge as well as at Barrett's.

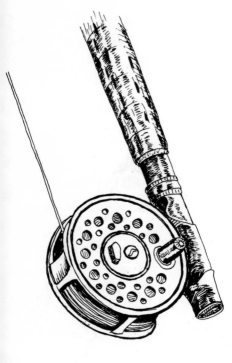

Looking at the map, the Beaverhead is seen to flow in a northerly direction for 28 miles from the 4,000-acre Clark Canyon Reservoir to Dillon, with Highway 91 following alongside. A stretch of 30 miles from Dillon to Twin Bridges is paralleled by Route 41. From here the river winds a slow and curvy course through a broad valley where agriculture predominates. Scenically, it is another version of this big-sky country with its endlessly rolling hills and jutting buttes, with the always present snow-capped peaks as the picturesque backdrop. Open casting is possible along the shore, but there are stretches where excessively thick brush laces the stream edges. Big trout can be taken in the stretches along these foliaged banks, for it is there that the water is shaded and the insects drop in to feed the big fish that lurk under them. A great deal of private land borders this stream, but if the angler is gracious in his asking, permission is usually granted to fish the water. Private ranch roads lead to good access points along the river.

Near Twin Bridges the Beaverhead is joined by the Ruby River and Big Hole River to form the mighty Jefferson. There are some small tributary streams which can afford a welcome respite from the big water angling. They supply trout that are sometimes bigger than the ones taken in the big open stream. These tributaries are loaded with good fish, since they are bypassed by most visiting anglers. Try Poindexter Slough upstream from Dillon, for example. Browns in there will reach the 5-pound weight and can be taken on wet flies and streamers.

As a change from the rapid roaring of the bigger waters, the Beaverhead is of moderate current and ranges from 30 to 50 feet across. Glassy flats should be sought out, and if the timing is right

for the twilight rise, good and big fish can be enticed to small dry
flies. Cast on long, light leaders. A few swift riffles and dropoffs
afford good wet fly fishing, and wading is easy over the gravelly
bottom which does not contain dangerous holes and slippery
rocks. It is a potent stream because of the abundance of underwater plants that create ideal conditions for aquatic insects such
as may flies, caddis and stone flies. Imitations of sculpins and minnows should also be in the tackle box.

Contact Hobart Sneed of Sneed's Sporting Goods in Dillon.
He knows the river like the back of his hand and from the tackle
counter you'll be exposed to his favorite patterns for this river.
Nearby are enough stores for accessories and supplies.

There are several motels in Dillon and a state-operated camp
at Barrett's Diversion Dam south of Dillon on U.S. 91. For the
camping angler there are also improved public campgrounds and a
recreation area for the family near Clark Canyon Reservoir, with
good food available at the marina.

A multitude of adjectives falls far short of describing the
Flathead River and its three major tributary streams; the North,
Middle Fork and South Fork. Here, the Dolly Varden trout can be
added to the list of natives such as the rainbow and cutthroat, and
there are some big Dollies in there just waiting. Add to this the little Kokanee salmon and the variety is considerable. These come up
from Flathead Lake, and with the combination of a good lake for
growth and lots of virgin country to spawn in, fishing for good
solid fish is as productive as it is exhilarating.

All three forks of the river start their life in the mountains in
the western and southern sections of Glacier National Park. The
South and Middle Forks flow through the enormous Bob Marshall
Wilderness Area. Outside of the official wilderness, however, this
country is being gradually scuttled to the real estate brokers, the
lumbermen and coal strip-miners, so every trout fisherman should
get behind the efforts of Trout Unlimited and the Federation of Fly
Fishermen, who are trying to achieve wild river status for these
waters.

All three tributaries and the main river can be reached from
Kalispell where U.S. Highways 2 and 93 meet. Several secondary
roads offer easy access to many of the better sections of the river.

Your fishing here will have wide variety but your wading will
have to be good and steady, for the stream hosts big boulders
which means deep holes, a lot of shifty gravel and uncertain underwater contours that can fool the unsteady wader. Riffles, big
and long pools, and broken white water offer possibilities for the
use of everything from nymphs to tiny dry flies that must be used
if the very small may flies and minute caddis and land-bred insects
are to be duplicated *au naturel.* The opposite, those big Royal
Coachman and other puff-ball flies, will sometimes bring up the
big ones at twilight or early in the morning. The lower reaches can
be floated if not waded, but chest high waders are necessary as are
the long rods and extra long casts if one needs to reach a particular
run on the other side.

The spring runoff begins in the middle of May, and the water
is very high and dangerous until late in June, a prime time here for

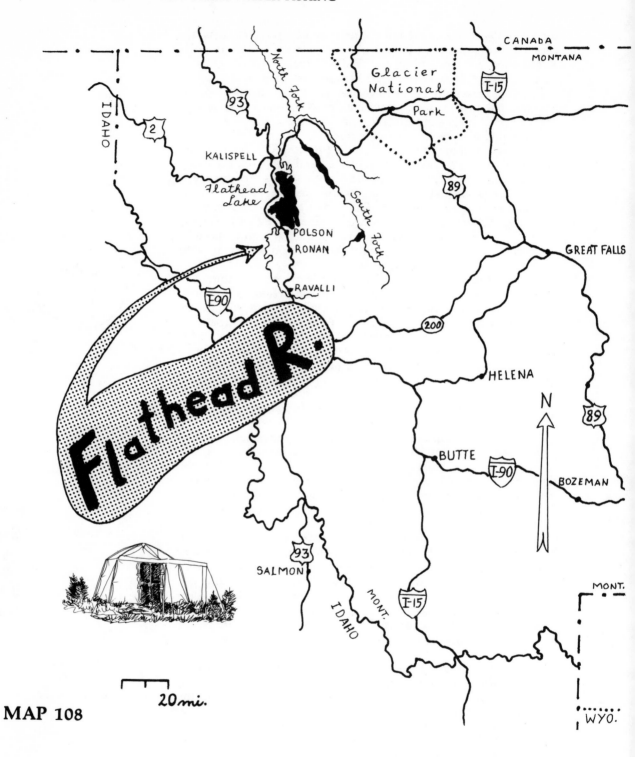

MAP 108

20 mi.

spin fishermen. July to October is ideal time for fly casting, if you can arrange it. After September the crowds are gone, leaving the streams almost bare of anglers.

Good prizes here in cutthroats up to 16 and 18 inches. Dolly Varden must be 18 inches to be legal takers. A 10- to 15-pound Dolly is a keeper to write home about. Dollies can be taken on big flies, but the spinning fraternity get in their best work before the water drops its high level and begins to clear.

For more information contact the Montana Fish and Game Department at Kalispell or any one of the sporting goods stores in the neighborhood. Good accommodations of various styles and varieties are near at hand.

## Boulder River

MAP 109

We have run out of adjectives for Montana trout streams and when I see the Boulder River near the bottom of the book, I feel as if I am underrating it. Not so. Page One has to be Page One in a book. Fish the Boulder if you are in the neighborhood. In fact, it would be my recommendation that you head for it directly.

Boulder River is a river aptly named. The Creator liked boulders when he built this one and the trout like them too. That's why an unbelievable concentration of big trout is found here.

The Boulder begins as a trickle of icewater from the high plateau country marked by the boundaries of the Absaroka Primitive Area at a mere 12,000 feet. It is located near the Montana-Wyoming lines at Yellowstone Park. It then takes off in a northerly direction for about 50 miles to enter the famed Yellowstone at Big Timber, where it is now traveling fast at an elevation of some 4,000 feet.

In its upper reaches it wastes no time in cutting its way with dramatic slices and thrashings through crevasses, timbered draws and cavities that must have amused the Divine Dentist. Big rocks, slabs of cliffs, boulders the size of a big car, downed trees and a mixture of rocks and spray characterize the area. The water is clear after the runoff, and wading can be tricky.

This wild river runs for about 25 miles and then goes underground for about 200 feet and into a falls for another 400 feet. From here on downstream it has suddenly become a full-fledged river with a completely different mood; bordered by meadows, fields, farms and ranches, it is pastoral and handsome, with its banks cushioned with everything from cottonwoods to rose bushes. It is a fly fisherman's heaven, since the trout feed on aquatic and landbred insects. The stream supports a vast lineup of good trout feed, and the fish are plump, well-fed and very selective. It is the kind of water that you can't wait to wade into and start casting. July, August and September are the best months.

The big browns dominate the scene in the lower stretches and they are found in some 25 miles of water before the river changes its name. The brown trout cannot migrate above the falls, so are content to just stay down and grow bigger and bigger. The Yellowstone River below sends many of its browns into this water

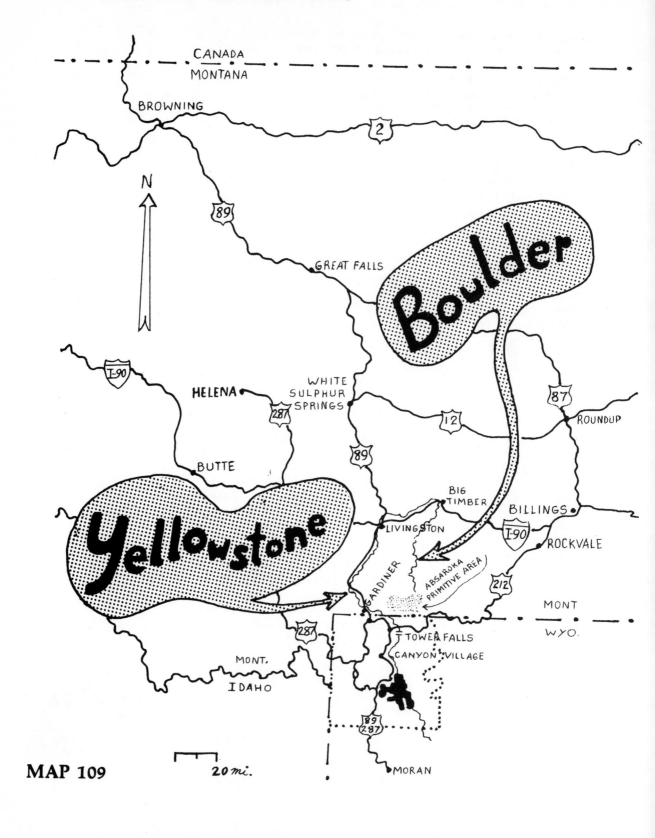

MAP 109

20 mi.

in September to spawn and some of them are almost too big to tangle with.

On the map, spot the Boulder near Big Timber, Montana, on Interstate 90, 35 miles east of Livingston.

My friend Dan Bailey, who owns a fly shop in Big Timber, is the best source of angling knowledge and equipment in this area. He's one of the best fly tyers in the West and you should not visit the area without shaking hands with him. If you can get him out from behind the tackle counter, he might even fish with you. He'll show you where record breakers hang out and you can tempt them with some of his special fly patterns.

There are several big motels at Big Timber, plus KOA and Forest Service campgrounds along the river. Boulder River Ranch and Lion Head Ranch are good check-in points.

A good road runs along the stream from Big Timber. For about 15 miles it is paved and then it turns to dirt and gravel all the way to the ghost town of Independence. The Boulder splits into two main branches some 15 miles up from Big Timber. Fish 'em both. Balmy days and chilly nights are the rule, and are perfect for pup-tenting if you like to camp.

## Upper Yellowstone

Why the Upper Yellowstone with a choice of fishing Armstrong Creek, Boulder River, the famed Gallatin, the various forks of the Madison, the Bitterroot, and the Beaverhead, Jefferson, Clark and Rock Creeks? Yes, the choice is tough! My advice: Fish 'em all!

The Upper Yellowstone, recommended by many, is a river never to be forgotten, and one to be saved from the ravages of progress and small down-payment retirement sites!

And the fishing . . . marvelous! The scenery is equal to anywhere on the globe. Bring the family along to enjoy Yellowstone Park and combine a wondrous early fall vacation with superb fly fishing.

This is possibly the most glamorous stream in the U.S. It has been praised by the top outdoor writers, and an expert graduates to angling sainthood when he has taken trout in this water.

It is about the largest trout stream in the U.S., in length as well as width. It is a real river containing all the elements from the fast and turbulent stretches to the more placid, almost lake-like sections. Different species of trout inhabit the special sections of the watercourse. Some parts are fairly easy to fish; others demand the astute wader. Long rods, strong arms and lots of power are needed in order to bring out the best results. Fortunately, all the waters of the park are limited to flies and lures.

One section, possibly the most popular, is that between Yellowstone Lake and the Yellowstone canyon because it is easy to fish and wade. A good gravel road with several pullouts and places to park parallels the course. While slow pools are few and far between, the runs and riffles afford much studied angling. During the hatches the pools produce most action, and at other times the riffles and broken waters offer good wet fly fishing. One method is

that of walking along the shoreline gravel and casting to the bars and dropoffs, allowing the flies to dangle and sink into the deeper lanes of current. When a particularly tricky set of currents converges near a cluster of rocks or drops off into a deep hole, more time can be spent sinking the nymphs. For the most part the water current is steady and fast. Morning and evening should be reserved for the dry fly. Here the cutthroat is supreme and ranges from 12 to 16 inches.

More rugged and more dramatic fishing is encountered after the river slips into the canyon and down past Tower Falls. Access also becomes a bit more complicated. Don't try to pick your way through the almost vertical rocks and snags, but stick to an established trail.

More tributary water enters the Yellowstone as the course heads for the Montana border. It is a veritable highway of water when it reaches the neighborhood of Gardiner. It also starts to slow down in its tumbling and some long, glassy stretches lure the dry fly angler to try for really big trout. Imagine a stream 200 to 300 feet across and nothing but record fish under your cast. The bottom is basically large rocks, making wading hazardous, so much fishing is done from the gravelly edges. Long casts are necessary to really get the flies out there where they can drift.

From Gardiner along Highway 89 you have some 50 heavenly miles to indulge in before arriving at Livingston, considered to be the trout fishing capital of the world. Numerous public access points allow stream entry, and even the posted water can be fished with permission. Many ranchers cater to angling parties and so reserve the water for them.

It is in this lower section that the monster brown trout are found. Hard to entice, just enough of them are taken each year to whet the appetite of the novice as well as the expert.

For local information contact Bud Lilly's Trout Shop in West Yellowstone, Dan Bailey's Fly Shop in Livingston, and Merton Parks' Fly Shop in Gardiner. These are the big league guides, fly tyers and fishing experts, who have known the water since their birth. Guides are available from them as are tackle, specially tied flies and other tackle, plus, of course, a myriad of supplies and accessories.

Good motels in West Yellowstone, Gardiner and Livingston and the lodges and campgrounds in Yellowstone National Park provide ample accommodation.

The best season for trouting is in the latter days of September and on into October when you'll find the stream lower, less crowded and crystal clear. But the trout are spookier, having been fished over by tourists all summer. Clear and low water argue for extreme caution if a big fish is to be taken.

The Upper Yellowstone continues to get better with time, especially since the addition of the Yellowstone cutthroat trout. These grow big and the water can sustain a bunch of them. They are also fairly easy to outwit; they are a far cry from the brownies in this respect. Check tackle regulations . . . they vary from year to year. Most, if not all, of the water is only open to fly fishing, thanks in large part to the efforts of Jack Anderson, a recent superintendent of Yellowstone National Park.

# COLORADO

### Gunnison River

Colorado's Gunnison River is another one of those "you-aren't-a-complete-angler-unless-you-have-fished-it" type streams. You'll never make status in fishing bull sessions until you've wet your line here and been almost dragged by a Gunnison native trout.

Fish the Animas, the Pine, the Conejos, the East, the Taylor, Upper Rio Grande, Upper Arkansas, Frying Pan, Roaring Fork, White and the Yampa . . . but don't miss the Gunnison.

Browns, brook trout, rainbows, Kokanee salmon and cutthroats are the varied fare of the region in both lakes and streams.

The Gunnison is a vast watershed, as you'll see from the map, and the Lake Fork River offers much variety in fishing water types. Its starting point is the high ice water of Hinsdale County in southwestern Colorado.

The Blue Mesa Reservoir area is another great spot and offers some 50 miles of top fishing. This is medium-sized water, and fairly long casts are necessary. Along its course is a natural lake, Lake San Cristobal, comprising some 300 acres in good trout fishing. From here the river drops down 400 or so feet in elevation over another 50 miles of good fishing water amid some very spectacular waterfalls. There are some remote and hard-to-reach canyon stretches that you'll like. It takes effort to walk down and back up, but the trout will be well worth that effort. Too much trouting these days is made too easy for the casual angler. It is great sport to work a bit for your rewards. Most people skip these areas; that's why they are great. There are the quieter stretches, however, where the river weaves a slower course through meadows and plains.

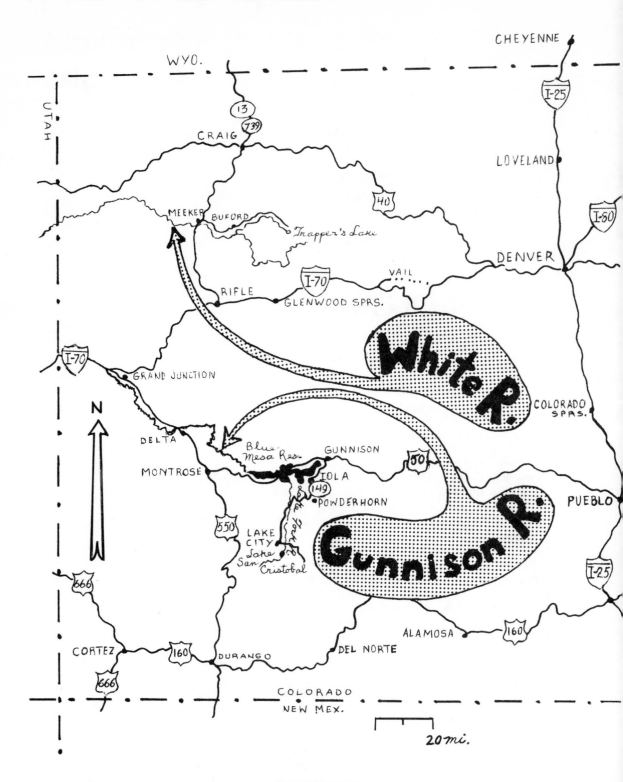

**MAP 110**

I've taken some mighty fine strings of brook trout from this water and I must say they are far superior to most of the natives I've creeled in Maine. They grow big and fat and their colors are sensational. You have to see these beauties to realize their coloration.

For those Easterners who like to fly fish for the big brown trout, the Gunnison serves up a portion of this fish that is a trial for the most astute angler. They are found, naturally, in the lower water and wider stretches and pools. Some of them written up in the local papers will clock in over the 10-pound mark—quite a challenge with flies.

Visit this country after the middle of June and you'll find fly fishing on the upswing through July and well into August, with possibly two good weeks in September. The tourists have left by Labor Day. The water is lower and more clear then and the fish are ready. Combine bird hunting with your trouting at this time. Many of the landowners restrict fishing on their water to the fly and that's one reason why the river remains so exceptional. A small tributary, the Henson Creek, is restricted to fly only for an 8-mile stretch.

Phillip Mason will fill you in on details at Lake City, Colorado, and you'll find accommodations in the form of dude ranches (many of which have posted waters), resorts, motels, camps and campgrounds. Try a letter to the Hinsdale Chamber of Commerce for complete reservation listings. The area can be reached by State Highway 149, with Lake City some fifty miles south of Gunnison.

## White River

A few years ago when I was bugging Duncan Campbell to collect his travels over the entire West into one book about his trout fishing experiences (which appeared as *88 Top Trout Streams of the West*, a publication I strongly recommend for anyone visiting the West), I asked him, confidentially, to name his favorite state for trout fishing. He answered that Colorado was the fisherman's dream state, with over 8,000 miles of flowing streams averaging from 50 to 150 feet wide. He added that Colorado ranks first place in stocked trout, with 22 streams presently set aside as Quality Fishing Waters, and with 12 sections where fly fishing only is available. He assured me that fishing pressure on these streams is lighter than in most states. This was enough answer for me.

In my travels, I've fished a number of Colorado's best spots. Trying to recall them all is almost impossible.

The White River is one of my favorites, and judging from my correspondence, the favorite of many anglers. It contains everything from a small rushing mountain stream, in the heart of the Rockies, to a big water where it joins the Green River. I like it best from the town of Meeker and its 6,000 foot altitude, up to the headwaters at 10,000 feet, because of the hard-bodied rainbows and "native" brook trout found in this 50-mile stretch.

MAP 110

Some 200 miles from Meeker, in a westerly direction, rainbows and browns are found in abundance along with bonetail and squawfish, offering their pleasant diversion. I'd recommend you hit this water after the spring runoff in late June. The water is clear then and fishing requires long, thin leaders and smallish flies. The trout are not big, but they are brightly and deeply colored and native born. I've caught a four-pound brown there, but that was an exception.

Another choice stretch is on the South Fork east of Meeker, since it is set aside as Quality Fishing Water with restrictions. There are over 30 miles of river through National Forest lands plus nearly 20 miles, through private land, where you can get permission to enter and use the access roads and trails. This is boulder-strewn water with dramatic current changes and an ever-switching course through steadily falling terrain, offering tantalizing riffles, pools and glassy water. Large brook, brown and rainbow trout offer variety. The brookies are the easiest to catch, with the browns being the toughest adversaries.

The width of the stream varies from a small mountain brook to pools over 200 feet across. The general type of water is fast and broken with a width of from 30 to 50 feet. Most of it is wadable where there are long gravel bars or shallow shelves along the riffles. Fish it from June until November, weather permitting. It gets pretty cold after September 20 or so, and the action falls off in late October, due to the high altitude and sudden cold blasts.

Twenty miles above Meeker the White divides at Buford into the North and South Fork. I like the South Fork because it courses through the Flat Top Wilderness area and is uncrowded. This is not carside trouting. You can either hike in or use a horse rented from local outfitters.

The North Fork is equally good fishing, starting as it does out of Trapper's Lake, which also borders the Flat Top Wilderness Area. This stream is bordered by a gravel road. Pinpoint the White on the map at Meeker on Highway 789, 100 miles north and east of Grand Junction and 67 miles northwest of Glenwood Springs.

Places to stay are generous though simple in the back country. Numerous lodges, cabins and resorts are scattered throughout the area and pack trips and guides are available. You can get adequate directions, reservations and equipment and needs at Gambles Store in Meeker.

Bring plenty of film. The first time I visited this section of Colorado, I spent more time behind the lens than I did with rod in hand. This is truly God's country, but again, outside the formally protected wilderness areas, it is being invaded and destroyed by real estate developers who are in the lucrative but unfair business of providing second homes for the wealthy at the expense of the landscape and those of us who like the outdoors decorated with trees and not with A-Frames.

# The Intermountain States

# WYOMING

There are almost too many great streams in Wyoming. Like its neighbors, Colorado and Montana, this state boasts trout stream runoffs from the Rockies that are uncountable. If a man were to fish a lifetime in this one state, fishing one stream at a time, he'd be an old man before he finished the list. But he'd be a happy one!

There are 20,000 miles of good rated trout streams in the state and some 5,000 good lakes, and this includes the waters of Yellowstone and Grand Teton National Parks, the latter being the most spectacular in terms of scenics because of Jackson Hole. There is a considerable number of fly-fishing-only waters and others with catch-and-release regulations.

This unforgettable rainbow and cutthroat stream begins near the Togowotee Pass of the Continental Divide some 35 miles east of Jackson Lake in the Grand Teton National Park. From there it descends in mad rushes and deep gorges in a southeasterly direction past Dubois and on to Riverton, where it turns in a northerly direction into Boysen Reservoir, finally dropping down into Wind River Canyon. This trip, if you were to follow its every foot, would involve dramatic changes in both scenery and fishing.

Most of the river is paralleled by U.S. 26 and 287, with the upper 80 miles considered the best fishing for rainbows, cutthroats and whitefish. There are few monster trout, but the numbers of fat trout up to 14 and 16 inches makes the trip well worth it. Despite the difficult terrain and sometimes hazardous conditions, the access to the upper regions is not too difficult, since there are many road pullouts and numerous side roads leading to the large percentage of unposted stretches.

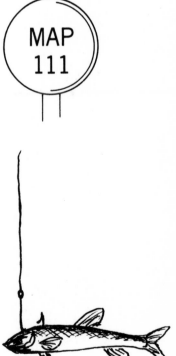

MAP
111

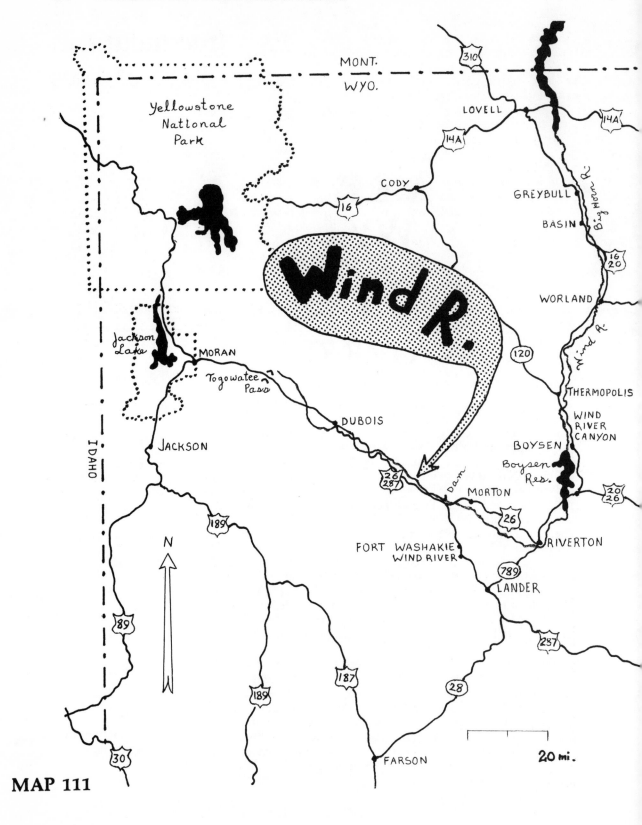

MAP 111

Downriver, near Dubois, much of the land is privately owned, but as usual in this state, if you are courteous and ask permission, you have little trouble gaining access. Below Dubois where the water is larger, so are the trout, with even better fly fishing—particularly with the dry fly. Public fishing sites also provide easy access.

About 10 miles below Dubois the Wind River Indian Reservation has much good water for those who will obtain a special permit which costs $5.00 and can be purchased at the reservation headquarters at Fort Washakie, situated on U.S. 287 a few miles from Lander.

I prefer the upper Wind, for it is a typical mountain stream with riffles, runs, some deep pocket waters and quick-change variety. It is a dramatic river with surprise challenges all along the way. The best time to visit is in late summer and early fall, which is typical of Rocky Mountain trouting. The water is clear; long leaders and a minimum of sloppy casting and wading are required if you want to catch fish of the size the promotion folders show. It is good dry fly water all the way and you won't find better scenery anywhere. With the forward march of progress this stream, like all good places on earth, is in danger of encroachment from the 100-foot plot investors.

There are sporting goods stores and guides in Dubois, where you'll also find good motels and nearby public campgrounds. W.R. (Dick) Titerington is among those who guide and arrange pack trips into the fabulous Dinwoodie Glacier area, a good suggestion for a combined back country and trouting trip.

Much of the scenery is broad and open, with the mesas predominating along the sections where the stream gorges its way through sandstone and majestic rock formations. Bring the camera and use it.

While Wyoming has hundreds of good trout lakes, the fabulous fishing is in its streams, so following the context of this book, the lakes are not detailed.

MAP
112

## Yellowstone Park

Yellowstone National Park's three major trout streams, the Firehole, Gibbons and Madison Rivers, have been specially reserved for fly fishing only and serve as an example of what purist fly fishing stands for. These streams produce the results that can be had from restrictive fishing. They should be thought of as an ideal trio of trout angling waters.

Each is wadable and each can easily be crossed at almost any spot. The Firehole and Gibbons each have about 15 miles of fishable water before they join the Madison, which flows another 15 miles filled with delightful pools, riffles and runs. There is much underwater growth which affords good habitat for the varied fare of insects such as may flies, caddis and stones. The better water is in the lower section where the current fans out into broad pools. These streams vary from 30 to 50 feet in width. Fish the short rod and small flies—big tackle is not really necessary. Wade quietly to the fish instead of strong-arming them.

**MAP 112**

No fishing license is required within the Park, and the rewards of browns and rainbows up to 17 and 18 inches and brookies up to the foot mark make it remarkable fishing regardless of the constant pounding these streams take in vacation time. The best fishing, however, is in June before the vacationers reach the park, and in September when the colder weather revives the water from the hot summer doldrums. I've fished it in July and had to work awfully hard for my rewards, but I had good results in early morning with wet flies and in the evening with small dry flies on very long leaders. If you can work some of the spring holes that enter the river as tributaries, you can scare up some lunkers that hide out in the brushy creeks until summer is over.

Look at the map and you'll find these streams on the western edge of the Park. The nearest town is West Yellowstone, Montana, which is 95 miles south of Bozeman, Montana, and some 70 miles north of Ashton, Idaho, on Highway 191. Good places to stay are at Old Faithful Inn, and at the park campgrounds. West Yellowstone provides many motel and hotel facilities with good restaurants, stores and guide services. Pat Barnes' Tackle Shop in West Yellowstone, is a good contact.

On the Madison you can strike it rich if you happen to find yourself in the middle of a spawning run of brown trout en route from Hebgen Lake. Experts enjoy this water, but those interested in simply introducing the family to the park should also visit these pretty waters. They are convenient, not too strong of current, not difficult to wade, and they contain fish of sizeable proportions to whet the appetite. And the scenery . . . yes, it's grand.

The Madison produces trout of 4 to 6 pounds and larger, especially to the bucktails and larger varieties of standard wet flies. Sunken nymphs, especially during the bright light of day, will entice lunkers from the hideaways. With much food available and summer-warm water flowing past their gills, these trout are not going mad to strike everyone's offerings. They are touchy, persnickity and highly selective, but once on the hook, you'll know you are into something that you won't forget for a long time.

There might be more sensational streams in the area, but this trio bears inspection and some good solid angling. When you are fishing, the scenery may include a steaming hot geyser somewhere in the background. Big game such as elk or bison may watch you from afar, and you are sure to see a bear or two. Not bad extras, but keep your distance from all big wild animals.

My favorite section is where the Madison goes through the town of Ennis to Ennis Lake. As it approaches the lake there is a kind of fingered delta area called the Channels. Ed Maynard has a ranch there and owns much of it, but you can fish it for a price. There are all kinds of little islands as the river breaks into six little ones, each from 25 to 40 feet across. You are fishing big water in small packages, for big fish.

Dan Bailey's Tackle Shop in Livingston, Montana, is one of the best sources of information on all this trout fishing country.

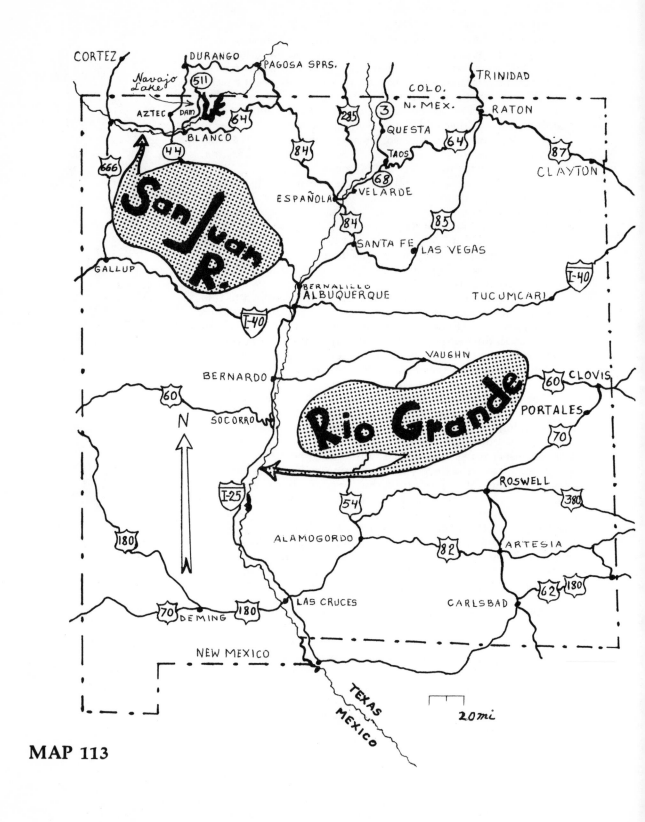

**MAP 113**

# NEW MEXICO

When one looks at the map of New Mexico or drives through this state casually, it would take much imagination to consider any possibilities of good trout waters in all that desert landscape. But trout are there, and so are trout streams that defy description. They are backdropped by some of the grandest and most varied scenery that one would wish for. Along with the San Juan River, there is the Rio de los Pinos, the Chama, on which I've had much memorable trouting, and the Rio Grande and its glorious upper tributaries in the Indian reservation country.

Lying in the northwestern part of the state where the mountains are high with timbered ridges, the San Juan starts in the Rocky Mountains of southern Colorado, cutting its dramatic way through 140 miles of New Mexico before threading back into Colorado in the vicinity of the Four Corners area where Utah, New Mexico, Arizona and Colorado meet.

At this writing there are no improved camping facilities on the river but there are numerous camping areas. This is good, since it discourages too much casual tourist traffic. The improved campgrounds are all located in the vicinity of Navajo Lake where you'll find trout and bass. Most of the lower and larger parts of the stream flow through what can be called semi-desert. One wonders how good trout fishing can be had under the blistering heat where the water should come almost to a boil, despite the relatively high altitude. There is little foliage along the river to afford a cooling shadow, but the trout grow prodigiously. The water temperature stays below 70° and that's the saving grace.

The Navajo Dam was completed back in 1962 a few miles south of the Colorado line and about 12 miles north of Blanco. Since then, its some 16,000 surface acres have made it a prime trout fishing attraction.

It is on the San Juan below the dam, along state road #511 to Blanco, that the fishing is almost unbelievable due to the cold flow from the portal, affording cool water all season long. In the miles of water below the dam, the living and growing conditions and more than ample insect life produce big trout. The temperature of the water is a constant 42° below the dam, gradually warming as it flows downriver. To start the fish ball rolling, the state planted a 15-mile stretch of the river with some 400,000 rainbow and brown trout fingerlings a few years ago and, according to conservation department estimates, the survival rate has been good to excellent. With these trout growing about 7 inches a year, a 5-pound trout is not the exception. Some anglers report having taken trout of 10 pounds from this water on flies. The best water is from the dam downstream for about 15 or 18 miles. The first 3 miles are classified as quality water, where only artificial lures and flies may be used. The limit is also set annually below the regulation state limits with a minimum size of 15 inches to be taken. The fishermen who like to catch and release their fish have a real time here. The entire area is controlled by the New Mexico Department of Game and Fish. Only a small portion of the river is privately owned. Thankfully, the water flow from the dam is regulated so as to maintain constant stream conditions, but the release does vary from time to time, freshening the stream and stimulating the fish into a feeding mood.

The entire spectrum of fly fishing can be enjoyed at one time or another during the long, open season on this river. The insect ecology is building up bigger hatches in these new conditions due to the dam. Also, the streambed is beginning to form a defined pattern, since it is not now subject to sudden washouts and floods. There are excellent flat stretches of dry fly water and at very few places will really fast, mountain-stream type of thundering rush-water be encountered. There are bubbly stretches and many split and broken riffles, undercut banks and deep centerline troughs. The stream bottom is nearly all gravel and medium-sized rocks, with a few boulders to hold back the main current, affording resting places for big trout. The water is clear most of the time, with long casts the rule, using long leaders and smallish flies.

There is a great variety of insect life, both aquatic and land-bred, making the choice of fly a tough assignment if one wishes to try and match the insects on the water. Fortunately the trout do not read the experts on such subjects and they seem to take almost any pattern of fly one minute, only to become excessively shy and selective a moment later.

Most of the time it is warm-water fishing and if you are wading, it is a pleasure to dip down deep in the waters in order to cool off during the midday. The air can become suddenly cool and even cold just the minute the sun sets behind the nearby hills.

## Rio Grande

Thirty years ago while studying the Indians of the Southwest, I spent many a day on the hard-to-reach and hard-to-fish Rio

Grande River. The rewards were great and I'm told that even today brown and rainbow trout are there, just as plentiful and just as big or bigger than they were then. Not too many amateurs fish the Rio Grande in New Mexico despite the fact that the experts rate it as one of the best in the West. It boasts some 70 miles of unposted water and excellent angling throughout the year. This persistent stream has been carving its course steadily through the eons, chipping away at the ancient lava mesa to a depth of nearly a thousand feet at some points and you often have to make a rigorous climb down to the river to get to the finned gold to be found there. Naturally where the climb is the hardest, well away from any easy access by rough gravel roads, the fishing is at its best. You'll be rewarded some times with brown trout that top the 8- and 10-pound mark. Rainbows vie for size and make up a possible shorter length by their aerial antics. Many good fish are taken on big bucktails and hopper or stonefly imitations. The Muddler Minnow, too, is a good taker. Spinners, spoons, all manner of hardware are used to attempt to snake out the cannibals, but enough of them remain to lure treasure hunters able and willing to make the trek down and then back up.

At the beginning of the fishing year, the spring runoff of melting ice water from the northern Rocky tributaries makes the river quite dangerous to wade, so cast it from the bank or wade in very cautiously in a backwater. During the first week in July the water simmers down and clears a bit, offering the first real fly fishing opportunity. Since there is little or no foliage cover to hold back sudden rain water, the river quickly clouds during a downpour but clears again in a short while. The stream bottom is tricky. A staff is a must here, and don't fish alone.

Some of my best fishing was done from Velarde north and upstream to the Colorado border, which allowed a generous 70 miles to work over. Highway 64 from Velarde to the Taos Junction bridge offers good access. The Rio Grande State Park borders parts of the river, and good camping facilities are nearby. Turn off State Road 3 some 4 or 5 miles north of Questa and then 5 miles west to the Rim of the Rio Grande Box. Many motels, lodges and sporting goods stores are here.

And, while you are there, do visit the little and exotic town of Taos and see the Indian pueblo. There are some great stores on the square and they can offer good advice about the Rio.

While in Taos, contact Carl Berghofer, the Taos Conservation officer for New Mexico Department of Game and Fish. Maybe he'll take you fishing with him.

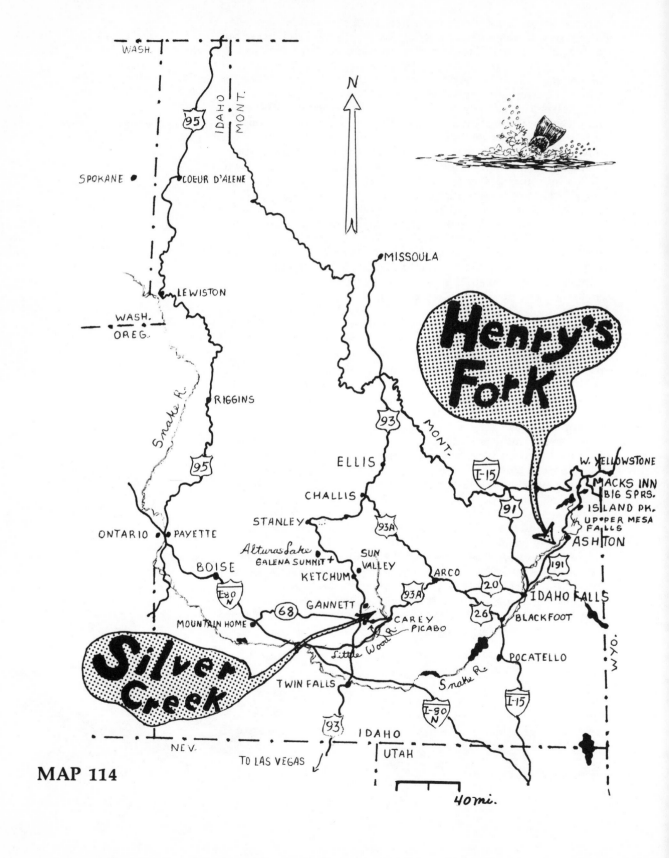

**MAP 114**

# IDAHO

### Henry's Fork

A top-rated stream of Idaho, the Henry's Fork is also known as the North Fork (of the Snake River). Superlatives are in order, for this is really a phenomenal stream in a four-seasons center of outdoor recreation.

It begins its flow at Big Springs, Idaho, several miles east of Macks Inn on U.S. 191. At Big Springs, gin-clear water boils out of the ground and flows about 15 miles west to Island Park Reservoir. The river flows in smooth glides for about 10 miles before it turns into surging rapids and shelving riffles at upper and lower Coffee Pot Rapids and then courses into the impoundment. All manner of fishing is done along this stretch, but fly fishing can be tops in the hatching periods. At other times, steady and slow nymph fishing with flies on the very bottom will produce action from big 10-pound fish. Long casts are in order. Due to the flat and glassy surface, care should be taken and casting should be held to a minimum; trout that are big will be scared down by sloppy rod work. Access during the dry weather is by numerous, unmarked dirt roads. These can mire in minutes during a downpour.

Most anglers consider the famed Box Canyon of the Snake to have top angling. This canyon is located below Island Park Dam. Flowing for some 4 miles through a picturesque and dramatic steep-walled gorge, the river becomes flat and smooth for the float

fisherman as it progresses on through the Harriman Ranch and on down to Riverside. It picks up momentum as it pounds down on Sheep Falls near the approach to the 108-foot Upper Mesa Falls. It gains more speed now, bringing on treacherous wading for big fish in deep runs and torrents as it bashes over Lower Mesa Falls and on to Ashton, where it rests momentarily and affords easy wading and some excellent dry fly fishing.

Every expert who has worked this famous Box Canyon extols its virtues, for it represents the best dry fly water for rainbow trout in the entire West. It is a wonder that the stream has not been fished out or that there is room enough in the prime times to work it properly. One can fish this water for an entire season until the snow drives you away and not really get to know it. The fly hatches are unorthodox, hardly timed in sequence. One day might produce a horde of flies and the next day or days, nothing. Action too, is unpredictable. A big hatch can come off on the silverly late afternoon blaze, and not a trout will be seen active. Much of the river can be fished by floating. It's easier than wading this particularly rocky and unsteady bottom. The currents are not only strong but sudden and harsh, and there are holes that could give you a sudden bath. Use your wading staff, and don't wade it alone.

A big moment in this area is the tremendous salmon fly hatch that is scheduled for the first week in June. Off and on, this same insect type hatches for about three weeks and if you time it right you can enjoy some of the best fly fishing and catching on this globe.

The rainbows will weigh in at from 4 to 10 pounds, but the usual run is around 2 or 3 pounds. Even the smaller ones give a tough account of themselves due to the excellent feed and cold, clear water. Big, fluffy dry flies are the medicine when the trout are popping those hatched naturals as they drift enticingly in the glistening silvered currents. In the dead spots between hatches, a brace of medium-sized dark or brownish wet flies or nymphs can take trout if fished well under the surface and allowed to swing across the currents or dabble in the dropoffs.

Some memorable may fly hatches occur during the latter days of June, through July and into August, temperature permitting. These are at their prime on the smooth water of the Railroad Ranch stretch just south of Last Chance. This is a series hatch. It is advisable to match the insects as best as you can, having stocked your fly box with every color and size available. Local fly tyers and tackle stores carry the patterns that seem to be the best local attractions. Fishing in the company of several anglers, I've seen times when the trout, big ones of up to 10 pounds, have taken artificials ranging from sixes and eights to minute little twenties. It is a matter of tying into the appetite of the trout at the exact moment.

A surprise brook trout or cutthroat will chomp on your fly to offer a diversion.

Looking at the map, the Henry's Fork is located at Last Chance, 17 miles north of Ashton on Highway 191. The Island Park area is some 25 miles south of West Yellowstone, Montana, on Highway 191. Will Godfrey, a famous trout buff, is based at Last Chance, and you should make it a point to check in with him at Ashton. There are good motel accommodations at Last Chance, with many campgrounds and two trailer parks situated within easy access of the river.

This is a big-water stream and one which bears many returns over the years until you can really get to know it. During the summer there is much camping and vacationing going on, but it does not seem to interrupt the fine fishing.

Last Chance is a frightening name for the area, but given the way the vacation home developers are proceeding, it may not be a misnomer. Such good water may not be with us in the next generation unless we band together to combat the way real estate developers are intruding upon the wilderness waterways of Idaho.

## Silver Creek

Idaho's Silver Creek is a shrine river, one for the dedicated fly fisherman who can really appreciate beautiful water that contains all the necessities for excellent trout growth. In part, this is because in its best stretch it is limited to fly fishing only, with catch-and-release also being encouraged. It may seem that this kind of angling is artificial in a way, but this opinion will vanish once the angler wets his line and hooks into a beautiful rod-bending trout taken on a dry fly, nymph or streamer.

This is the haven for experts, the famed fishermen from all over the world. It has been heralded as the finest water in North America. As long as it is owned and controlled by the Sun Valley Ranch it will remain a model of trout fishing that could well be copied in other parts of the country. Silver Creek is, in fact, very short, about 15 miles. It is formed where Stoker and Groves Creeks join south of Gannett. It winds its way slowly and deliberately in a southeasterly direction to where it combines with the Little Wood, south of Cary.

A prime attribute of the stream, guaranteeing a steady flow of cool water, are its many natural springs and underground waters that enter it from various irrigation projects. The flow and temperature of the water during the summer and early fall months produce insect hatches: may flies, caddis and stone, as well as many others that offer superb fly fishing for nymphers and top-water addicts. A regular series of hatches can be catalogued, and they run on a very even schedule, somewhat like the hatches on many Eastern waters such as the Beaverkill in New York. Fish Silver Creek from June through September and into October, depending on the weather.

The creek bottom is easy to wade, since there are no really fast or deep stretches. The water is mostly smooth, requiring long casts. Careful fly delivery is a must if the bigger fish are to be enticed. Despite the relatively heavy pressure, the water in the ranch area can support as many as thirty fly fishermen without over-crowding. The fish seem to stay out in the open unless poor wading and casting drives them under cover. Very tiny flies seem to be better than the larger sizes due to the latter's splash and water disturbance. Trout of three to six pounds are regular fare, but a

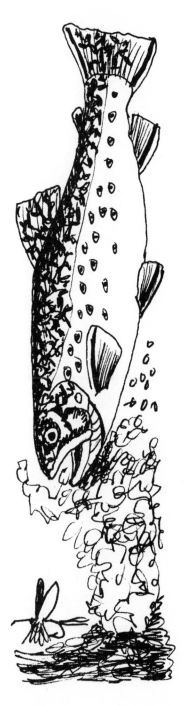

take of two-pounders is about average for the casual angler not used to the techniques needed here.

The section of the stream from Kilpatrick Bridge to the highway west of Picabo is surrounded by private property, but it can be fished. Below this the Idaho Fish and Game Department controls the land and assures access to well over a mile of this golden water.

Obtain more information on Silver Creek from the sports director at Sun Valley Resort. Dick Alf's Fly Shop in Ketchum is also a good information source.

Make reservations early and try to hit this water in the latter weeks of September or the first two weeks in October.

## Upper Salmon

MAP
115

Unquestionably, I'd select the Upper Salmon River system and specifically its best tributaries, the Upper or Middle Fork. Of course, they are all tops, but one has to have a preference which is usually guided by experience. It is pure Idaho, and that means that it is world-famous merely because it is top water. This one comparatively small state in the big block of Western states more than makes up for its lack of size due to the particularly dramatic Rocky Mountain panorama of peaks and gorges and timbered lands. Idaho has more miles of trout water flowing through wilderness area than any other state. At least 50% of this is in National Forest lands.

At one time this was a guarantee that it would remain forever the property of the American public and the taxpayers. Unfortunately such is not the case today. As a result, much destruction is taking place due to increased lumbering and other drains on the natural resources. Much inroading is whittling away at this wilderness. The real estaters are draining off much of the lumberlands and selling it out in retirement lots, each of which must have road access, and roads bring dramatic changes to the ecology and the water flows. They cause unruly damage to streambeds and bring excessive runoffs, bogs and floods. Watch this section of the country. It hasn't got long to survive if the plunderers continue to have their way.

Try the Upper Salmon River for its fine scenery as well as for its trout. It drains near the Stanley Basin Recreation area, very high up in the Challis National Forest. Salmon and steelhead are the first call, but rainbows and some big Dolly Varden augment the list. Resident wild trout are joined with generous plantings of rainbows all along the upper tributaries.

It is impossible to fish this water until the spring runoffs subside, and that means summer. Good fly fishing is rare before the middle of July. Four to 6-pounders are common with smaller trout in large numbers. They like all flies, particularly the small bucktails and Muddler Minnows. In the dry fly book try the Royal Coachman dry. Puffball that it is, it will snake out those natives when many of the more subtle flies die on the vine. These trout up here seem to like a whitewinged fly.

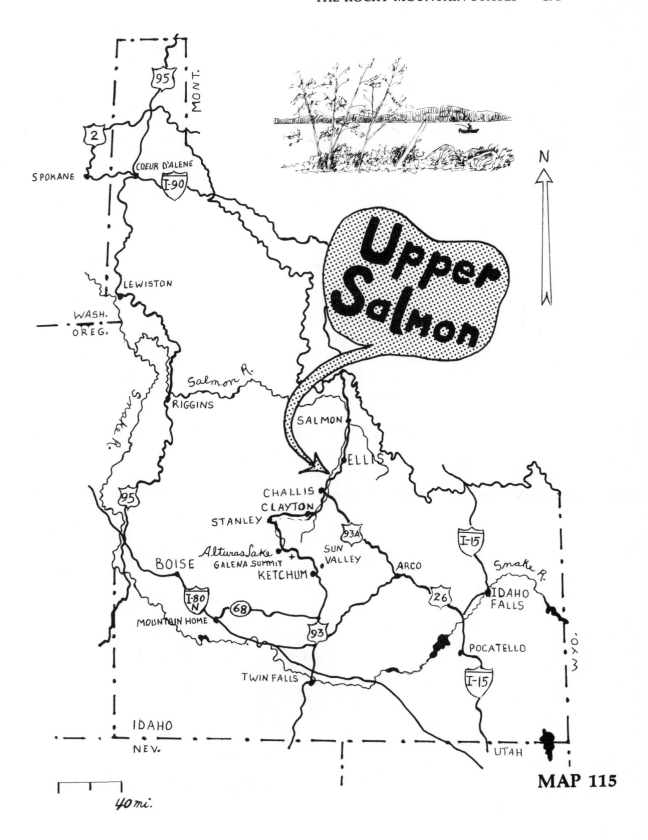

MAP 115

The main river begins just below Galena Summit near Alturas Lake, some 35 miles northwest of Sun Valley. It then turns northward to Stanley, then east northeast to Challis, and on past Salmon, Idaho, offering some 150 miles of priceless angling. U.S. Highway 93 parallels the course and good access points are to be had near most good runs. Look at the map and the entire Salmon River drainage system.

Cold waters keep the Upper Salmon alive, and they originate in the Stanley Basin Lakes ice packs. The upper 35 miles is most wadable, with varied, pleasant and comparatively easy fishing. That's where you'll find me. Numerous shelving riffles with their long gravel bars offer easy wading to the hot spots where flies can be cast for a perfect drift. There is not too much interference from bushes and snags along the banks, so casting is a dream. The upper water narrows down to from 12 to 25 feet in width, and the small rod and tiny flies will bring up some good-sized trout.

If you like to explore, there are some interesting tributaries such as the East Fork entering the Salmon 5 miles east of Clayton and the Pohsimeroi River that joins at the little town of Ellis, some 18 miles downstream from Challis. Working down, the stream becomes bigger and so do the trout. It doesn't take long for the river to widen to 150 feet. This is glorious big water and larger tackle is needed, plus of course the chest waders and wading staff. It's fast, too, and full of boulders. Float trips of varying lengths of time and distance can be arranged, with excellent guides. While some tourists and vacationers do clutter up the landscape, the upper water is left largely to itself and the enterprising angler, one used to hiking in and camping overnight or for a week, or more. Many of the resorts afford good fishing for brook trout of the eastern strain and it is all beautiful and photogenic country.

Contact Dick Alf's Fly Shop in Ketchum, Sun Valley, and ask for Frank Stahl. Or contact the Idaho Fish and Game Department at Ellis, Idaho.

This is not country for the neophyte. It is big and vast and before you venture out you had better know what you are up against and where the best fishing is to be had along with the techniques to be used. Make local inquiries, and follow directions of the resident anglers.

# UTAH

This intermountain state boasts two major rivers, the Colorado and the Green. These are mainly for bass and panfishing. You have to trek into the mountains for trout.

The famed Logan River is the best of the larger trout streams where a 37-pound brown trout was taken a number of years ago. Several *Field & Stream* records have come from that river in the past. Flaming Gorge Reservoir produced a 33-pound, 10-ounce brown trout in 1977—a possible world's record, plus many other brown trout of the 20-pound class. This water may develop into a real producer.

Strawberry River in the central-eastern part of the state is also a good bet for rocky mountain trout and cutthroat trout.

For further information on fishing in Utah, write the Department of Fish and Game, 1596 West North Temple, Salt Lake City, Utah 84101.

This is a rugged state, much of it desert, but the timbered mountains in the east offer rugged climbs and scenery, with some trout in the fast and tumbling brooks and canyon streams.

For more information, write the Division Wildlife Resources, Salt Lake, Utah 84116.

MAP 116

MAP 117

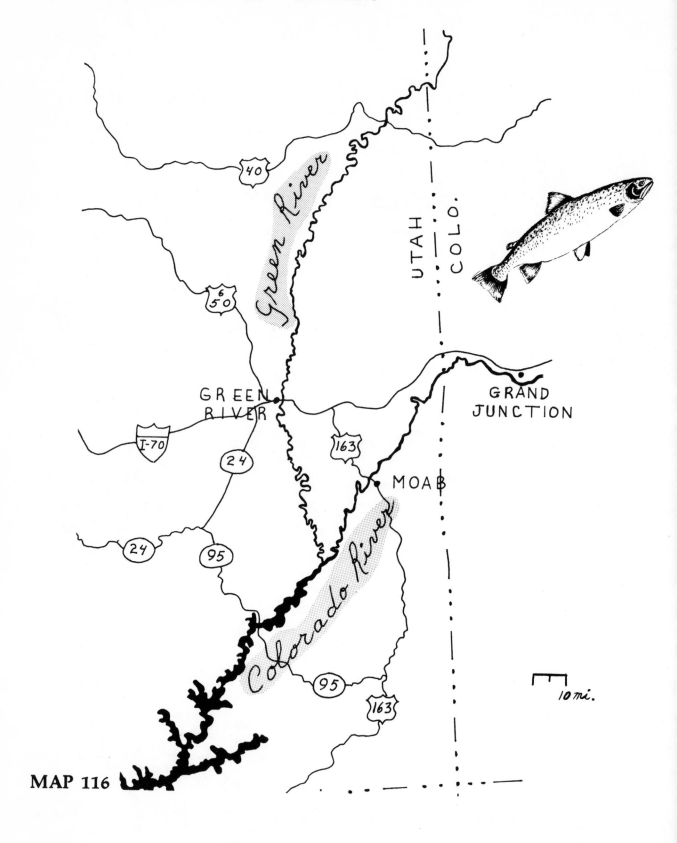

MAP 116

10 mi.

**MAP 117**

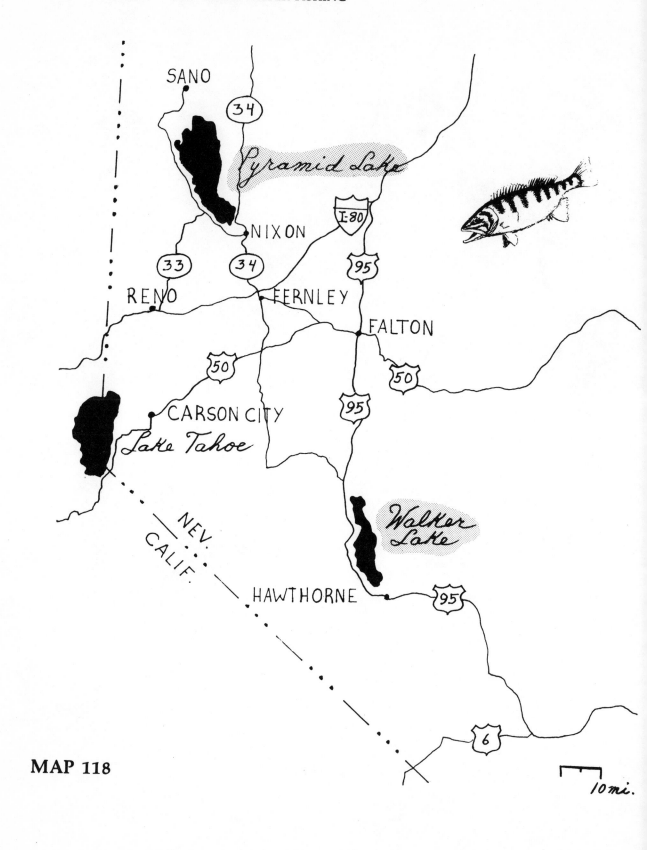

**MAP 118**

10 mi.

# ARIZONA

A desert state, but it boasts the famed Colorado along its border with Arizona containing bass and trout. The Lahontan trout, a cutthroat, native only to western Nevada, has been caught as big as 41 pounds from Pyramid Lake. Topaz, Catnip and Summit Lakes are good bets, as is Walker. U.S. 95 skirts the west shore of Lake Walker.

The best bass fishing to be had is in famed Lake Mead. It is a big lake, 246 miles in area, with 550 miles of shoreline. It has been written up for some years now as a top fishing water of the United States. Write to the Department of Fish and Game, P.O. Box 10678, Reno, Nevada 89501 for up-to-date fishing conditions, since they vary in this state as to quality.

# NEVADA

Lake Mead on the Nevada border is the headliner at the site of the famous Hoover Dam. This is shared with Nevada and has some 550 miles of shoreline and a lot of big bass and panfish. There is some good rainbow trout fishing in the area just below the dam.

In the Colorado chain of lakes, Lake Havasu above Parker Dam is another good spot for bass. The Greenbelt area in the north-central section is mountainous, with small and good rainbow trout streams.

Also look into Kaibab National Forest in the northwest. There are small streams containing rainbow trout of small size. Facts are up-to-date from the Game and Fish Department, 222 W. Greenway, Phoenix, Arizona 85023.

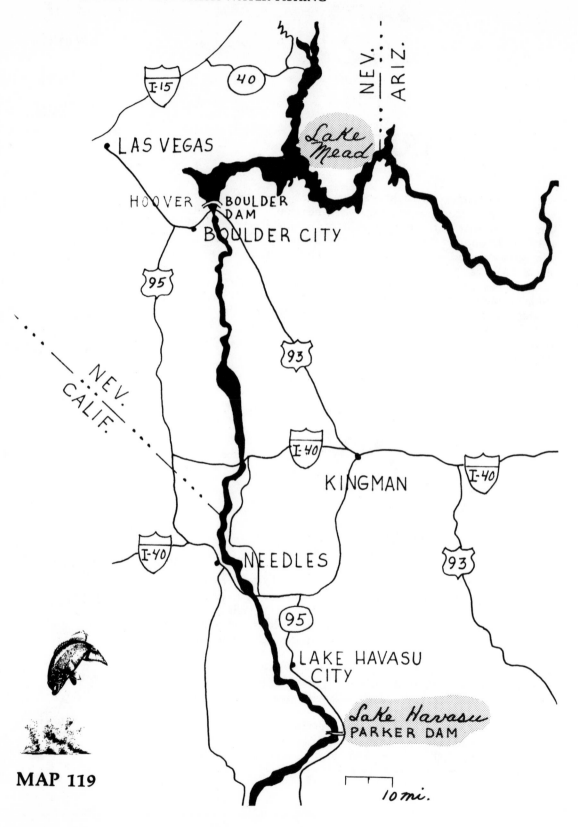

I-15

40

NEV.
ARIZ.

*Lake Mead*

LAS VEGAS

HOOVER    BOULDER
DAM

BOULDER CITY

95

93

NEV.
CALIF.

I-40

I-40

KINGMAN

I-40

93

NEEDLES

95

LAKE HAVASU
CITY

*Lake Havasu*
PARKER DAM

MAP 119

10 mi.

# WASHINGTON

In the early forties I had the experience of fishing many of this state's waters while working for a Seattle radio station, and later as an Army Private at Fort Lewis, near Olympia. I'll never forget it, and as I look back, the entire state is one big steelhead trout fishery. It is difficult to home in on any one stream or any choice—since they are all different, they produce better at different seasons and each offers something special.

The streams that enter the mighty Columbia are the state's best. Those on the extreme West Pacific Coast area, up to and including the northern streams along the Straits of Juan de Fuca, and the streams on the peninsula and around the Puget Sound area on the mainland clear to Canada have still other characteristics. So there is no choice of a Number One stream in this state.

This makes it hard to tell you where to go except to say that in season, take your choice. To understand this problem, one has to know something about the steelhead and how to catch it. Reports indicate that you have a 46% chance of catching a steelhead, which is better odds than I'd give you on New York's Beaverkill when fishing for browns and rainbows there. Statewide, there are about 200,000 steelheaders, plus you, the outsider. But there's also plenty of room, as our map and descriptions will show.

Similar to the fish runs in Oregon, there are two seasons for steelhead fishing and they differ considerably in conditions, tackle and technique. December and January are the best months for

MAP
120

199

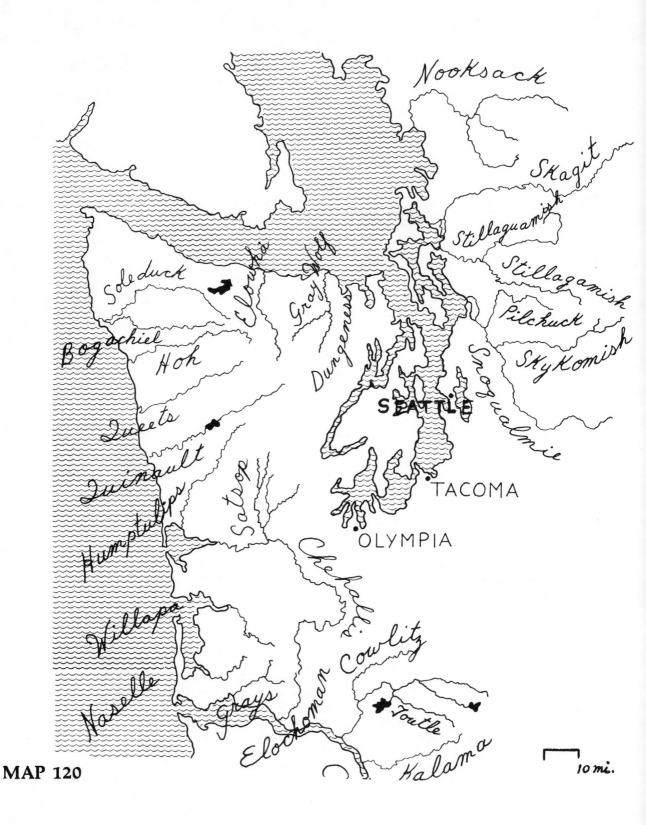

**MAP 120**

10 mi.

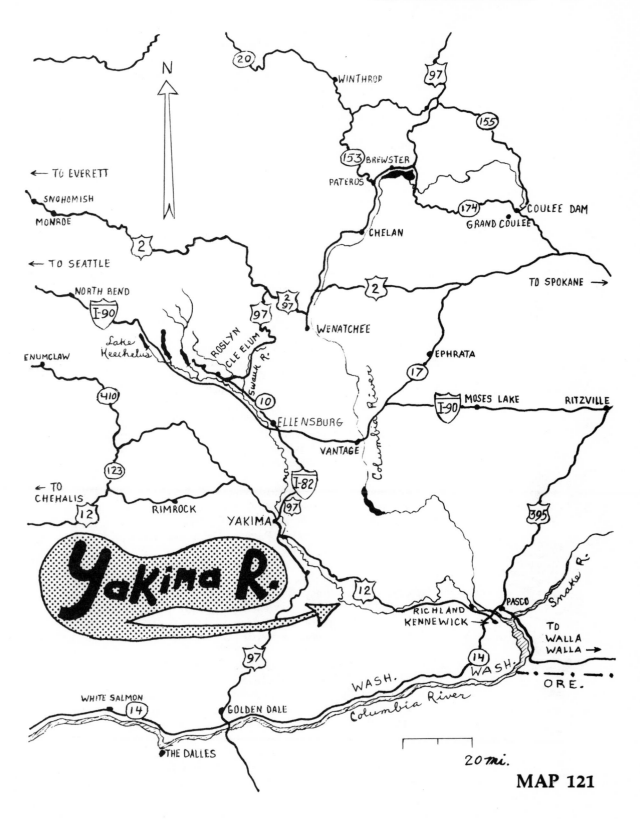

MAP 121

winter fishing, with good takes in November and February and on into March, if conditions are favorable. These fish, of course, are migratory, living most of their lives in the ocean and annually ascending the rivers to spawn. While in the ocean they put on weight and strength for the battle of migration.

Some of the best known steelhead streams that ordinarily provide their largest catches in December include the Cowlitz, Humptulips, Skykomish, East Fork Lewis, Bogachiel, Chehalis, Elochoman, Naselle and Willapa. The take of winter-run steelhead on the lower Columbia is also best in December, but this is still well below the catch of summer runs.

The Nooksack and North Fork Stillaguamish are streams that ordinarily produce best in January. Some waters which alternate between January and December as top months include the Skagit, Toutle, Kalama, Snoqualmie and Washougal. February is usually good on the Satsop, but January and March catches are often higher. The main Stillaguamish and the Dungeness are unpredictable, with the best steelhead fishing coming sometimes in December, possibly in January and likely in February.

The Hoh or Soleduc are waters to try any time from December to March, while the Pilchuck is good in December, January or February. The Skykomish offers good success December through April, with January being the top month. The Wynooche is best in January or February.

Some of the streams that are consistent producers from February on, after many waters have dropped off, include the Elwha, Grays, Queets and Quinault, and the Toutle.

To fish for steelhead in Washington you need a fishing license—unless you are under the age of 16 years—plus a two dollar Steelhead Permit Card, which may be obtained at any of the 1,000 license dealers scattered throughout the state (usually in sporting goods stores).

The general opening of the winter steelhead fishing season in Washington is December 1. Major groups of streams are closed to fishing in February, March and April. Seasons for all streams are listed in the current Fishing Pamphlet available from all hunting and fishing license dealers.

The State Game Department is presently planting over 3,000,000 winter-run and 2,000,000 summer-run steelhead migrants. This hatchery planting program now provides over 50% of the adult steelhead caught each year, and increasing angler interest calls for expansion of the program. To maintain the program and to accomplish planned expansion, additional funds will be needed.

Catching the steelhead is a special treat. Yearly data, taken from Steelhead Fishing Permit cards, shows that about 140,000 individuals actually fish for steelhead each year. But only around 60,000 catch one fish or more. The average annual steelhead catch of successful fishermen is over four fish per season, while the average catch for *all* those who fished is only two fish annually.

Two overlapping "races" of steelhead occur in Washington. Winter-run fish are found in almost all streams west of the Cascade Mountains. Summer-run fish occur in the Columbia

River and its tributaries above Bonneville Dam and in about 20% of the major steelhead streams of western Washington. Winter-runs move upstream from November to June and spawn in the early spring. Summer-fun fish generally travel upstream during June, July, August and September, but may be found as early as February in some streams. Summer-runs lay over in deep pools until the following spring, at which time they spawn. The spawning season for steelhead extends from February through June, usually peaking in March and April. Seaward migrants of both races move downstream with the spring runoff, peaking around the first of May in western Washington and about a month later east of the Cascades.

Much has been done in Washington to increase the numbers of summer-run steelhead, which is now a major fishery. Total annual steelhead catch in Washington now averages around 300,000 fish. Yearly catch of summer-runs is increasing, and now averages about 80,000 steelhead.

The Snake and Columbia Rivers are the largest producers of summer-run steelhead. The Snake normally supplies anglers with around 15,000 fish annually. It produces best in October, but September, November and December are also very good months to try your skill. The lower Columbia River sees best summer-run angling in July with June through September the best overall periods. On the upper Columbia, most summer runs are caught in August and September, with October through May also productive. The Grande Ronde is well known for summer run fishing, with the best fishing in October. The Kalama produces the most summer-runs in July, but is good from May through October. The Klickitat is best in August and September.

## Yakima

The Yakima heads from the eastern slopes of the Washington Cascade Mountains and is fed by three reservoirs and numerous small tributaries. It winds its way through sagebrush and semi-desert country southeast of Ellensburg, through Yakima and down to the Columbia River at Richland. I have fished the Yakima several times for trout and the one point I must accent here is the exact timing required for this waterway. You can get skunked mightily if you are there at the wrong time.

October is the time for fly fishing for some very practical reasons. The summer, which should be the best time, is confused because water is unpredictably dumped into the course from three irrigation reservoirs: Lakes Keechelus, Kachess and Cle Elum. This provides water for the crops in the vast lower valleys, meaning high water. Fish it with spinning gear at that time; I've had little response with flies. But in October when the water is low and clear, break out the fly rod and go to work. The trout are not monsters such as are found in many of the other rivers and streams described in this book, but they are plentiful and full of fight.

Rainbows are the prize here, ranging two to four pounds, on the average. Eastern brook trout and native cutthroat are also

taken, which brings to mind the usual sloughing off of the cutthroat by many anglers and angling writers. Their snubbing of this grand game fish is completely unwarranted, in my option. I wish we had them in many of our Eastern waters. They'll take flies with utter abandon and they grow big!

The upper portion of the Yakima between the mouth of the Cle Elum and Ellensburg is a typical fast mountain stream with boulder-strewn runs, deep pocket water, riffles and deep gorges. Some of it is hard to wade and most anglers therefore resort to boat and float fishing to reach the good pools.

From Ellensburg down, the Yakima flows through a deep and narrow canyon. Despite the natural terrain, the water is smooth and easily wadable once you get down to it but, again, floating is the easier process. Wading can be done to some extent near the mouths of the Teanaway and Swauk Rivers.

The local pattern of floater imitates the grasshopper or stone fly. Big, fluffy bucktails also produce. One trick to remember is that of doping the bucktail to float and swishing it out on the surface.

Interstate 90 borders the Yakima along the south bank from Lake Keechelus to Ellensburg. Along the north bank, Highway 10 from Cle Elum to Ellensburg makes the river available. U.S. 97 takes you along the canyon water below Ellensburg, down to Yakima. Interstate 82 has been opened now and old Route 97 has been designated a scenic route, so take your time on it and have the camera loaded.

Ellensburg is the place to center your activities. If you are there in October, it is bound to be crowded with both fishermen and hunters. Don't overlook the excellent lake fishing to be had in the vicinity. Crab Tree Canyon Lake is one to try while you are there for up to 5-pound rainbows. They'll take trolled flies and occasionally can be lured to floaters.

# OREGON

The two big fish of this state are trout and salmon. While there is some good bass fishing, the angler traveling a thousand miles on a vacation would pass it by—in favor of the salmon, especially.

There are five species of Pacific salmon that migrate from the ocean into Oregon streams: the chinook, silver, sockeye, dog (or chum), and the humpback. The headliners are the chinook, or king, and the silver, or coho. The chinooks will run to 40 and 50 pounds; the silvers are a bit smaller but are just as sporty, nonetheless. They ascend rivers all along the coast. The sockeye, a little less glamorous, inhabits many of the inland lakes and is a good plus to the angler fishing the lakes for trout.

As to location in this big state, you have to think in terms of the major drainage systems of the big rivers. The Columbia River system dominates the northern part of the state. Saltwater trolling for salmon is done at the mouth of the Columbia, but the best angling is done from Rainier, and upstream from there. The spring runs of chinooks start in late February and March, and peak in April. By summer, fish are taken as far upstream as the John Day, Walla Walla, Grande Ronde and the Imnah Rivers.

Western Oregon is dominated by the Willamette River system, the largest tributary of the Columbia. It drains from the Coastal side of the Cascades, emptying into the Columbia at Portland. Some of its tributaries drain from the southern reaches of the state. The salmon come into the Willamette in mid-March and you should connect up to the first of May. Then the fish move into the tributaries; one of the best is the Clackamas, entering the river

MAP
122

205

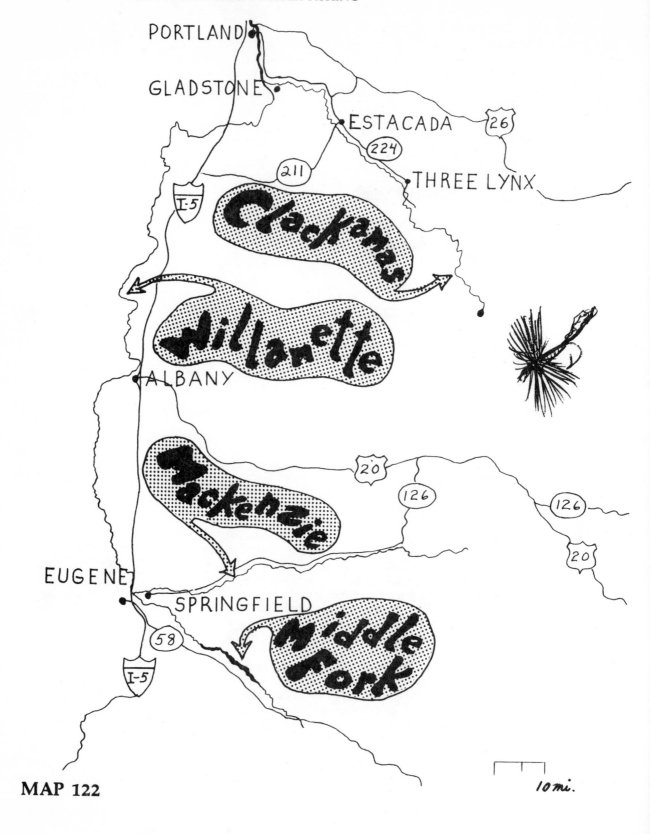

**MAP 122**

10 mi.

at Gladstone and paralleled by State Route 211. Get the facts and your lodgings at Estacada and Three Lynx on State Route 224.

The McKenzie and Middle Fork of the Willamette enter the main river at Springfield on Interstate 5. June is the best salmon month and throughout the early summer these are best streams in the Willamette system.

The Willamette has a winter run of steelhead that you should not miss. From January to June you'll catch the steelies along with native rainbows, cutthroat and salmon.

If you arrive in Oregon in mid-April to May, mid-September to late October, head for Tillamook Bay on the ocean, due west of Portland. The river above the bay is the best salmon fishing in the state, as far as I'm concerned. There are five good rivers feeding into the bay.

The Deschutes River system also has its runs of salmon and steelhead. It enters the big river at The Dalles. This area is vast. There are lakes in this system that contain some of the best trout fishing in the world. Assimilate information from the state and chamber of commerce information centers in order to pinpoint just where and when you want to go fishing. The Oregon Game Commission has also published a booklet entitled, *Oregon Back Country Lakes.* It will blow your mind with possibilities. Order it from

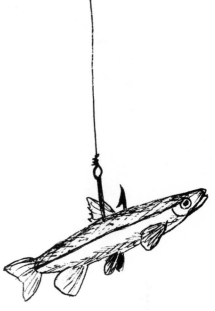

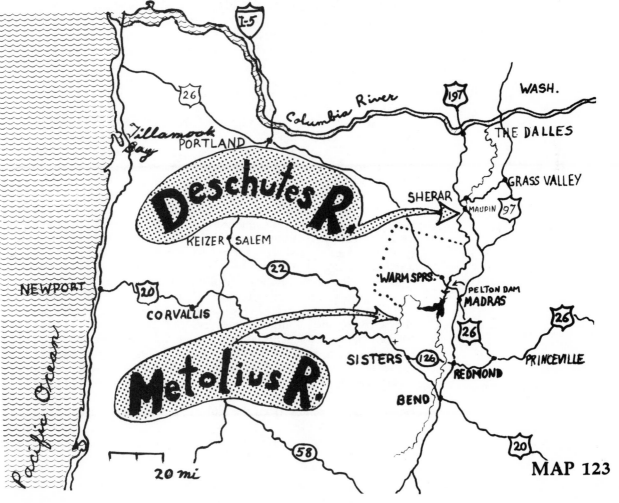

MAP 123

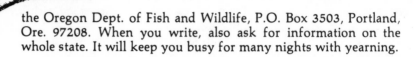

the Oregon Dept. of Fish and Wildlife, P.O. Box 3503, Portland, Ore. 97208. When you write, also ask for information on the whole state. It will keep you busy for many nights with yearning.

## Metolius

Now, to specific trout rivers that have made this state famous. If I were to ask the Creator to design a stream that would please all my wants, I'd give him a blueprint of the Metolius: long, beautiful, blue-green stretches of moving but not overturbulent water; varied bends and coves and alluring deep runs alongside grassy banks; a stream flowing through some of the most beautiful timber country that Oregon can boast. The water is always clear, even in a downpour. The water temperature is a constant 56° almost all season long, which provides an adequate supply of natural insect foods. With a steady parade of hatching insects, the fly fisherman who fishes this water with any regularity can step into the hatching sequence and not fish blindly. Wading is easy.

The width of the river varies from about 30 to 50 feet, just nice for long casts. Fish the shady sides for trout resting along the banks.

There are a few good rapids to break the even flow of the water and to offer a bit of change. These are all wadable and not too strong. The average depth ranges from 3 to 4 feet, with some pools going a bit deeper. There are subtle cross-currents to work beside and around.

This is water specially ordered for the fly fisherman, although many types of angling are performed on it. Dry fly fishing can be superb, since the water is sometimes glassy, sometimes a bit riffled by gentle currents, at times a bit frothy—offering just about every type of surface the fisherman could ask for. Nymphing, especially deep nymphing, should also be done when no flies are hatching. Allow the line to find its way through the cross-currents and eddies of a moderately rocked bottom . . . and sink those flies deep.

The first time I fished this water was some thirty years ago, and a recent visit found little or no change in its curves and courses. Some of the old trees that bordered the river are gone, but new ones hold promise for the future. There are many more fishermen, however. The Metolius is a vacation stream with lots of accommodations and lots of people who come by to visit and casually fish. There are also the devoted experts and fly fishing technicians, especially from the clubs in California who visit this stream regularly.

The Metolius has long been known as a top Oregon fly fishing stream. It reminds one of some of the Pennsylvania streams and even at times of the slow meander of the sandy streams of Long Island.

Born in the mountains of the eastern slopes of the Cascades, it flows in a northerly direction for many miles, only to turn easterly to describe a great arc for about 30 miles, finally emptying into Round Butte Reservoir on the Deschutes River.

In the old days the upper reaches of the river were well fished by both locals and out-of-staters. I fished it first with bait and then spinning tackle. Now, after many of us have realized the value of this water for fly fishing, the upper 8 miles have been reserved for fly fishing only. The lower river below Bridge 99 is open to all legal methods. Last time I was there I counted, during my two weeks' stay, some fifty anglers. Forty of these were fly fishermen. These men were alternating between fishing the water below and fishing the upper part of the river above Second Bridge upstream from Camp Sherman. This is all delightful wading. Below the camp, much fishing can be done from the banks.

The northern portion of the Deschutes National Forest contains most of the Metolius, so there is no access problem throughout its entire length. Some of the river marks the border of the Warm Springs Indian Reservation and a permit is needed to fish if you want to angle from the north bank. Take time off and meet and talk with some of the local Indians; they consider the Metolius a sacred water, just as we should.

Ponderosa pine is the mainstay of foliage along its banks, with just enough brush present to catch flies. By and large, however, the river is free for the casting, since it is wadable throughout. Casting angles can be found which will deliver the fly without hangups. For those who enjoy targeting their casts in under banks and undercuts, this stream is superb. The best fish lie under and along these spots and it takes the pretty cast and long drift to entice them out. Add the spice of a downed ponderosa that protrudes from the bank to collect brush, and you have a tantalizing situation.

Standard patterns of wet flies, nymphs and dries are good here if a selection somewhere near the size and shape of the naturals can be found. I've taken good trout here on strictly Eastern patterns, such as the Lady Beaverkill, Hendrickson, March Brown and Quill Gordon. In fact, that would almost do the selection. I've never had too much success with bucktails and streamers on this water, though there is a good minnow supply. Several big trout that I've kept to open and examine had minnows in their stomachs, so it is a good idea to have some imitations along and fish them deep and slow.

There is no best fishing time on the Metolius. When you are there is the best time. Fish it to closing time in October, a beautiful time of the year.

The rainbows predominate and their sides are redder than most of their tribe in other waters. They are deep, plump fish that not only jump like salmon, but body-roll and pitch to the bottom in the manner of the brook trout and the brown. You'll catch many pan-sizers in the 12-inch class, but with a little subtlety you'll find others that will range upwards of 5 pounds, with browns and Dolly Vardens even larger. If you can reach this water in the spring when the may fly and stone fly hatches are in progress, it will seem as though you are fishing in a hatchery.

Three resorts and many good Forest Service campgrounds are nearby and some along the stream banks. Lodges are also equipped with horses and guides. Visit the Wizard Falls Fish Hatchery and the giant springs at the headwaters of the river. For scenery, Mt. Jefferson and Three Sisters Mountains are about all you'd ever want.

The location is central Oregon off the loop road north of Highway 20 about 12 miles west of Sisters, about 95 miles east of Salem. At this writing a good place to stay is the "House," a lodge on the Metolius; Lake Creek Lodge; Metolius River Lodge; or Camp Sherman. Supplies can be had at the Camp Sherman store and some smaller stores in Sisters.

## Lower Deschutes

Any time from early May on into the last week in October a car license check will find anglers from almost every state of the Union along Oregon's Lower Deschutes River. They'll be hauling campers of all descriptions and will find more than adequate places to camp along this far-from-secret haven for trout fishing. The season in Oregon is longer than in many other states, so the angler can enjoy excellent fishing for a longer period of time and also combine a family vacation.

It is big water, deep and wide, and there are over 165 miles of it to work. This is another stream that would take many lifetimes to really get to know. One of the reasons why this stream is rated high in this book is because it is so readily available to even the most casual vacationer and angler. While the trout are not as big as those found in many streams of other states, the amount of good fishing is surprising even though it is well pounded all season long. This lower river is no better than the upper, but serves as an example of Oregon-style angling if you like the big water for long casts and long stretches to wade or float. The fly fisherman is in his prime when the salmon fly is on the water, beginning about the last week in May. Heavy hatches on may flies and caddis continue along all through the summer and into the fall.

Scenically the Lower Deschutes it is a prime attraction throughout its entire length to where it enters the Columbia River at The Dalles. Many of the experts consider the best water to be from the town of Bend downstream to Maupin. Here are almost 90 miles of superb fishing from bank, wading or boat, although some of the water is restricted against boat fishing. While the water is seldom crystal clear, this can be an advantage, since the fish are not as easily spooked in the greenish water. Below Bend, boat fishing is prohibited. The boat can offer ready access to a larger amount of water, however. The angler merely has to disembark and begin fishing. When a new stretch is desired, he climbs back in and floats downstream to the next hot spot. Many gravel bars and islands and reefs afford landing spots where a lunchtime campfire can be set. In the stretch between Redmond to Bend, fly fishing is excellent and the water affords all kinds of challenges that the experts like to solve with casting presentation techniques, using everything from big dry flies to big minnow imitations of streamers and bucktails. Access roads of both paved and unpaved variety afford entry.

Another popular stretch is from the big bridge about a mile or so east of Warm Springs. I suggest inquiring at Madras or Warm Springs about just where to go. I would also strongly advise hiring a guide to go along with you. He'll save you time and offer suggestions on fly patterns, fishing spots and techniques. Often an angler used to other types of water can be fooled by this river, for it has its own pet idiosyncracies that can cause you to go fishless until you know its secrets.

Those who have the pleasure of fishing the Deschutes develop their pet sections and visit them time after time. I am subject to this habit, and I've found the stream in its Warm Springs Indian Reservation area as my haven. The first few times I did this stretch I hired a guide and enjoyed both his company and his wisdom of fishing this river. I found my eastern Beaverkill techniques sadly lacking if I wanted to connect with really good fish. The Indians supply maps and intelligent instructions as to the ways to reach the hot spots, particularly those which do not get excessive use.

If you choose to fish the Deschutes from Maupin, upstream, there is a public access road to Sherar which continues on up to Mack's Canyon. You'll find two improved campgrounds just below the Sherar Bridge. Beavertail Campground, about 10 miles above the bridge, is where you'll find me, but at the other end of the road is the campground at Mack's Canyon.

For picturesque fishing, try the stretch in the canyon down stream from Sherar. This is fast, tumbling mountain stream-type water, with a few glassy stretches to break the flow. Here, then, is every type of water for the sophisticated angler to deal with. Again, a guide is fun to have and he can save you much time in getting to the big fish.

There are many places to stay in Bend, Madras, Maupin and Redmond. There's a large state park at Round Butte Reservoir some miles southwest of Madras, where you can camp. Try the public park at Pelton Dam slightly northwest of Madras.

Contact for local information and guide service can be had with Oscar Lang, Oscar's Sporting Goods, in Madras.

All along its length from Bend, through central Oregon to its entry into the Columbia, you'll encounter variety water, big water, fast water, slow glassy water, with accompanying scenery and conveniences that can make a trip to the Deschutes a memorable experience for yourself as well as the family.

## North Umpqua

In company with the Metolius and the Klamath, the McKenzie and the Rogue, the Deschutes and the Williamson, the North Umpqua River holds its crown high as a fine stream of the West Coast. It has steelhead, but rainbows too, along with big native cutthroats. The North Umpqua starts its majestic course from ice pockets and crystal springs high in the Cascade Mountains at the famous Diamond Lake, flowing steadily downward and westward for a hundred miles, where it rushes to join the South Umpqua a few miles west of Roseburg. The last 40 miles are open to all types of fishing, and many consider boat fishing superior to wading or bank casting. In the water below Winchester Dam, there is excellent fishing from the shore. Beginning at Rock Creek upstream to a posted section below Soda Springs Dam, the stream is restricted to fly fishing. You'll find big pools, small pools, bedrock bottom, and the fishing is excellent for all species. The summer steelhead is the glamour fish, however, and everybody is after them. It is a hard stream to go fishless in, since the native cutthroats will hit flies even if the steelheads are sulking at the moment you are there. Big, red-sided, heavily spotted rainbows afford a chance at a creel limit and are so brightly colored that they are often mistaken for salmon.

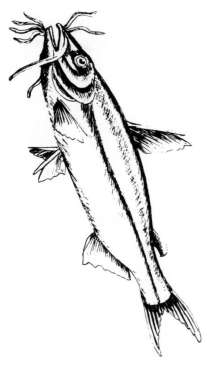

The most popular section for steelhead is between Bogus Creek Campground and Steamboat. Try to fish it some time between the middle of July and the middle of October. A very popular water for cutthroat and rainbows is the section between Horseshoe Bend Campground and Soda Springs. I've had good dry fly days there.

Up toward the source at Diamond Lake (a place you should visit even if you only take pictures) is the 30 miles between the fly-only water and the lake. Access is from State Highway 138 that runs along its course, making every foot of the river easily accessible.

For local information try the Umpqua Gun Store in Roseburg or Glide Sporting Goods and Steamboat Inn. You can stay comfortably at Winchester-Roseburg Hotel and at Diamond Lake Lodge. Of course the entire area is spotted with camping facilities so you should have little trouble with accommodations and provisions.

This stream is well known in the West, but very few Easterners have heard much about the Umpqua. It is not a tourist stream per se, but many of the locals swear by it.

For tackle I'd suggest the big rods and reels with plenty of backing. Be prepared to use the large-size steelhead flies, but carry a box full of big nymphs and conventional wet flies. The big, puffy, dry flies are also good in midsummer when the steelhead will come to them. The water is clear for the most part. Carry and use a wading staff and also bring chains and felts for changeable boot bottoms. The underwater paths on this river can be quite slippery.

There's a good supply of native cutthroat here. They are no monsters, but during a hatch of small may flies they are fun to

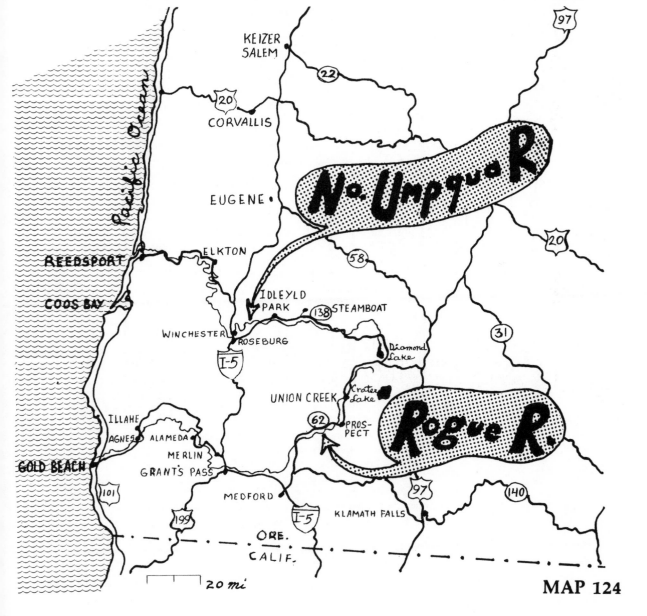

**MAP 124**

work over even if you have to take time off from your steelheading to enjoy them.

Northern California and southern Oregon are about the last real semi-wilderness areas where wild trout can be found on the U.S. West Coast. Streams that can afford good rainbow, brown and cutthroat, and, in addition, the Pacific version of the Atlantic salmon quality fishing, are becoming fewer and fewer. There are numberless streams entering the Pacific that have all the trout with the exception of the brown. Some have never been extensively written about. Explore all this water to the limit of your time off. You are in for some surprises.

## The Rogue River

The Easterner who visits the West and doesn't fish the Rogue is just not one of the boys. It is a must on the agenda of the angler aspiring status in the piscatorial community. And the Rogue is certainly not without its rewards. It is mighty, glamorous and thrill-packed, whether you float it, wade it or fish it from the bank. The fish are big: rainbows, cutthroats, steelheads and salmon.

The lower river from Grant's Pass to the ocean is mainly salmon and steelhead water with a goodly supply of coastal cutthroats. Although good fishing is found along the entire length of some 200 miles, the canyon country adds the spectacular scenery for which the Rogue is noted. A good deal of the best water is not available from the road and must be floated or fished from jet boats.

From the mouth of the river where it crosses U.S. 101, there are several paved roads following both sides of the river for about 10 miles upstream. It is well sprinkled with campsites. For the vacationer there is an interesting boat trip from Gold Beach to Agnes. Get information on this at Gold Beach, Oregon.

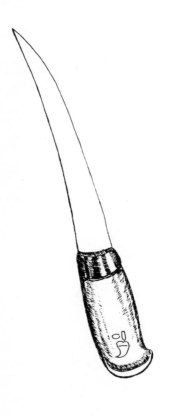

In this lower part of the river the spinning tackle and spinners and spoons, plus other hardware are used for the big migratory fish just entering from the ocean. July, August and September are the best months. From Grant's Pass to Alameda there are good roads, but no good roads are available from Illahe, and float fishing is IT. Fishing can be had from the bank and access from the road from Illahe to Agnes. Float trips can be arranged from Grant's Pass clear to Gold Beach. The five-day trip cost me about $250 a few years ago, and whatever the current price, it is well worth it as an experience in itself as well as for the fishing to be had.

Make this trip at least once.

The best fly fishing, however, is above Grant's Pass in the so-called upper water and is my favorite locality. The farther upstream, the smaller the river. Boating is still popular and recommended, however, at least as far as Prospect. Here there are six very good tributaries branching out and each is perfect wading and fly casting water. Try Red Blanket Creek, Middle Fork, Bear Creek and South Fork. Small water but lots of fish, and it's uncrowded even at the peak of the summer season. There's just too much water! This is where the spawners go, including the magnificent salmon, and the best fishing is enjoyed immediately after the spring runoff.

Since there is so much river coupled with varying conditions, it is best to inquire from the locals and guides as to the best techniques and spots to fish. The regulations vary considerably and a local check is a must.

North of Medford, Oregon, State Highway 62 follows the river in a northeasterly direction for about 60 miles to Union Creek Camp. There are also three state parks plus many private campgrounds, resorts, informal cabin lodges and motels.

I'd suggest starting your inquiries by contacting Lucas Ranch, at Agnes, Oregon, or Morrison's Lodge at Merlin, Oregon. Another good contact is Jerry Boice at Gold Beach. As usual in this country, the local sporting goods store is the source of local and up-to-date information when you arrive on the scene.

Your first experience on the Rogue will not be your last. There are hidden magnets in that river that will attract you back again and again. Those big salmon and the manner of catching them is a new and thrilling experience even for the sophisticated Atlantic salmon angler. Those cutthroats, even the pansizers, are excellent for an early breakfast. The Rogue rainbows that can be lured to the dry fly, or at least to large steelhead flies, will thrash you unmercifully.

There's something about the Rogue that is different from most other streams. The country for one thing . . . it has its special kind of friendly breed. And don't miss taking that float trip. Bring the youngsters. It will be a prized time in their lives.

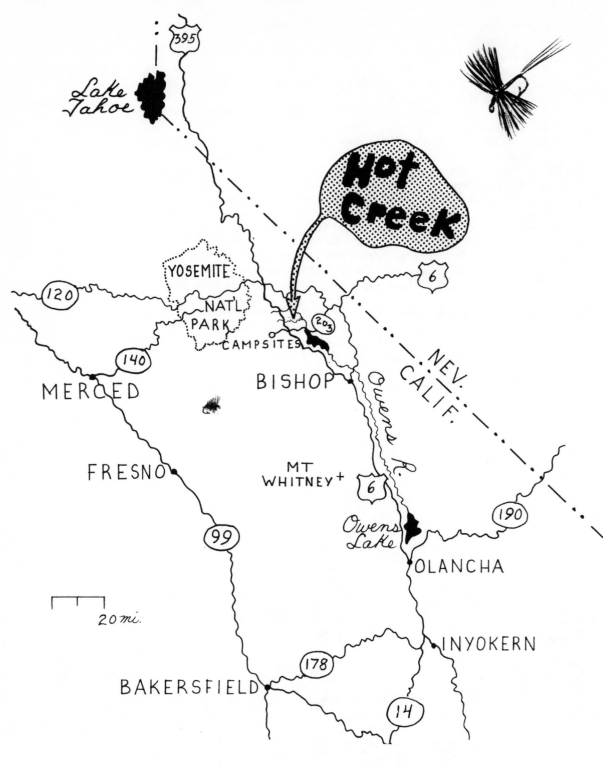

**MAP 125**

# CALIFORNIA

### Hot Creek

MAP
125

I'm thankful to my fishing buddies who are members of the various fly fishing clubs of Southern California for introducing me to Hot Creek, one of the most unusual trout streams in the entire world.

Hot Creek is unique in all ways that the word implies, especially in the stretch controlled by the Hot Creek Ranch. While it is not good policy in this age to refer to private waters, I do here, and with much respect for the controlled water issue as a necessity to provide examples of prime waters if good trout fishing is to survive. The balance of the stream is almost its equal but, again, the Ranch water is unique and every angler who is really interested in experiencing the utmost in trouting should make the Mecca-like trip sometime in his life. Fish the Kings, the Kern, the Klamath and all the others, but pay your respects to Hot Creek before, during, or afterward. The club is located some 35 miles north of Bishop off Highway 395. Much good information can be had at the state fish hatchery or from Lee Willardson at Hot Creek Ranch, or any one of the sporting goods stores in Bishop. The creek flows from the High Sierras in a southeasterly direction into the desert-like Owens Valley about 2 miles past U.S. Highway 395 to the town of Hot Creek Springs. Then it flows straight east for about 10 miles to where it joins the Owens River, itself a prime trout stream, though difficult to reach unless you like climbing down steep and rock-strewn canyons.

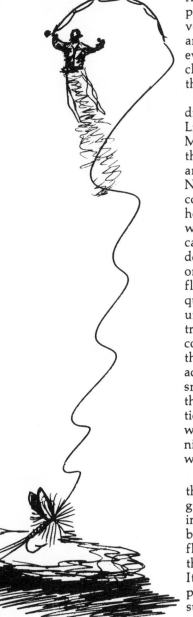

A bright testimony to the wonders of this river is in a well-prepared report sponsored by the Department of Fish and Game in cooperation with CAL TROUT. To quote John Dienstant, who is the head of the Department's Division of Wild Trout: "Hot Creek is amongst the finest chalk streams in the world today." The figures from this report show a massive amount of brown trout production in a slow-moving classic stream with undercut banks, very rich in all kinds of freshwater skuds and shrimp, may flies and immense hatches of very small caddis flies. Many times in the evenings and sometimes in the mornings around 11 o'clock, huge clouds of these No. 18, 20 and 22 caddises will move up and down the river to a point where they literally block out the sun.

Popular flies include the No. 18 Turkey Caddis, among hundreds of California flies designed for the mountain streams. The Light Cahill is another, as are the Blue Dun and the Quill Gordon. Milt Kahl, one of the best of the Hot Creekers from Los Angeles, the head cartoonist for Disney and co-creator of Mickey Mouse and others of that clan, uses just three flies: the Sedge, which is a No. 18 Turkey Caddis, the Little Maryatt (an ancient British concoction), and the Quill Gordon, all in 18, 20's and 22's . . . small hooks for such big trout. Milt's technique is to cast a 21-foot leader with the last 14 feet of flat tippet strength, one or 2 pounds. He casts it across the stream, even into a brisk wind that whistles down from the nearby mountains in sometimes gale force. There, on the opposite bank, the pile of light tippet lands in a bunch. The fly floats in the center of the pile and then drifts casually and quietly down with the current, buffeted perhaps by a slight breeze until all of the leader has been absorbed. By that time a big brown trout has taken the fly. On strike, all of this slack has to be accounted for. A direct straight-leader type of cast would not allow the fly to float convincingly for a respectable distance and so is not acceptable to the trout. Milt is only after the big trout, and the smartest ones. At times he will be seen kneeling, as if in prayer, in the grass beside the water, scanning the bottom between the reflections until he spots a big one; he knows the trout almost by name, where they live . . . probably even their marital status. The scanning takes quite a few minutes, maybe an hour, and then he goes to work.

After leaving the springs and hatchery grounds, it flows through Hot Creek Ranch, which restricts some 2½ miles for their guests. This section of the river passes through a kind of meandering meadowlike basin where angling is done for browns and rainbows from the bank with dry flies only. No wading, no sinking of flies. Most of my friends fish it with barbless hooks and most of them find that the smallest flies—size 18 and smaller—do the trick. It is also catch-and-release. You keep a trout only long enough to photograph it. If you want to eat trout, you get them from the supermarket at Bishop! Many of these trout have been caught many times and they are smart and highly selective. They are leader-shy and very spooky. They grow big because they don't end up in the frying pan. When you hook into a trout here, it's bound to be big and smart. The Ranch record is a 15-pounder taken on a dry fly.

DUNSMUIR •

I-5

*Shasta Lake*

(299)

(299)

MAP 127

REDDING •

(53)

(16)

I-5

(29)

*Lake Berryessa*

SACRAMENTO

(128)

DAVIS

I-5

(128)

I-505

MAP 128

(121)

NAPA •

I-80

5 mi.

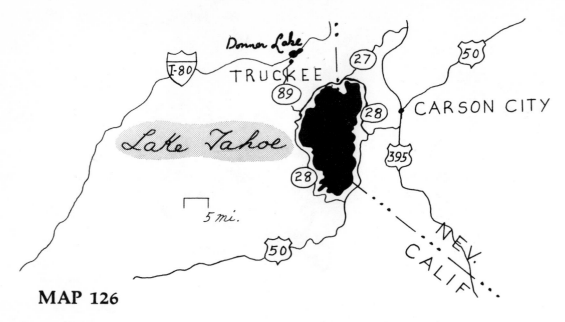

**MAP 126**

## Lakes and Reservoirs

But there's more than stream trouting in this state. There are a number of top lakes with long-time reputations for excellent trout and salmon angling. Lake Tahoe comes to mind first, despite the fact that pollution from nearby resorts has almost wrecked it. It is a deep lake and hard for the uninitiated to connect on, so I suggest a guide. Kokanee salmon, Lahontan trout, Yellowstone cutthroat, Kamloops trout, rainbow and brook trout are available in weights up to 10 pounds. Excellent boat launching facilities, boat liveries and accommodations practically ring the lake.

I-80 borders the lake too, on the north and U.S. 50 on the southeast shore.

Just north of Lake Tahoe rainbows and browns can be taken in famous Donner Lake near the town of Truckee. Big Mackinaw trout are also there. Lake Shasta, the largest man-made lake in the state, has a variety of top quality year-round fishing. It is easily reached by State Route 299 from east or west and Interstate 5 from north or south. There's also some excellent black bass fishing here. Again, I suggest a guide. Since this is so vast an area, shop around at the various sporting camps and stores along the shore before picking either a guide or a camp to fish from.

Smallmouth black bass have been stocked in many reservoirs in the state and have shown phenomenal growth. Northwest of Sacramento the Berryessa Reservoir is a case in point.

Largemouth bass are growing to monster size in some of the lakes in the southern tip of the state, notably Lake Havasu and Lake Mojave on the Colorado River, itself a fine bass producer.

The great Colorado is tops for the bass fisherman all along its length. Try the water from Needles, California, below the Davis Dam just at the point where the three states, Nevada, Arizona and California, join. Lake Miramar and San Vicente, in San Diego County are hot with 15- and 20-pound bass from Florida stock.

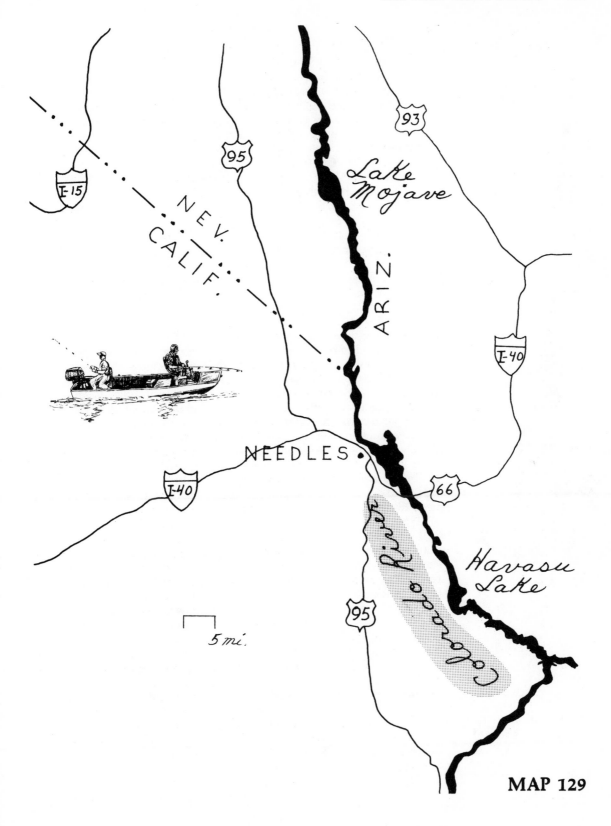

MAP 129

## Kern River

When the name Kern River is mentioned, one particular and exclusively gorgeous trout comes to mind: the magnificent golden trout of the High Sierras. California is first again . . . and there's no doubt about it, although some goldens are stocked in Wyoming.

This is the home grounds of the golden, but by no means the only stream where it is found. Thanks to efforts of fly fishermen, naturalists, conservationists, ecologists and the staunch and stubborn crew of the California Fish Commission, the golden thrives better than it did before the onrush of civilization. There are constant threats to this fish and its waters, mainly from tourism, large scale resort developments, hiking and camping, and too much fishing. This trout can survive only in its native volcanic waters and lives only above the 10,000-foot mark in altitude. There are a few hatcheries turning them out under strict control to maintain the delicate strain. Constant drain on the stream by anglers wishing to sample this trout keep the numbers too low. Some day perhaps it will all be fly-fishing-only water with even more restricted limits. Yet everyone wants to catch a golden, even if a little one. I almost cried when my first one held in the hand glistened back at me, clobbering the eyes with colors never seen before, or since. I wanted to put it back in its natural element, but it had been hooked too deep on a Leadwing Coachman.

The Kern is classified as one of the major streams flowing west out of the Sierra Nevada Mountains into the San Joaquin Valley of central California. The Kern and its region are heavily fished all during the open season. But you can find quiet and serenity and some excellent fishing due to the constant stocking of these waters, plus the natural spawn that seems to be guaranteed at least for the present. California Trout, a branch of Trout Unlimited and also affiliated with the Federation of Fly Fishermen aids in great measure the political pressure which it is hoped will keep these waters forever in condition to represent the epitome of wilderness trouting.

The Upper Kern is a medium-sized stream varying from 50 to 100 feet across in the lower waters to a mere trickle where it is born "up mountains." It is typical mountain stream, rushing and falling fast through rocks and boulders, gravel bars and holes, white water and step pools. It is cold and clear and flows in a southerly direction for about 70 miles, turning finally westerly to flatten out in the valley near Bakersfield. It is easily accessible in the lower region, with roads all along the way and lots of fishermen at the peak periods. The water below Isabella Reservoir is "put and take," but the rainbows are healthy and sometimes quite selective. They do offer good trouting to the many anglers from the burgeoning civilization nearby. Above Isabella there is another stocked stretch that gets heavy pressure. Strangely enough, a great many of the stocked fish live to a ripe old age, and trout of 10 pounds are not uncommon. All these fish are rainbows, not goldens, however. The goldens are found only in the upper river in the high altitudes.

Above the Kernville dam there is some very fine fishing

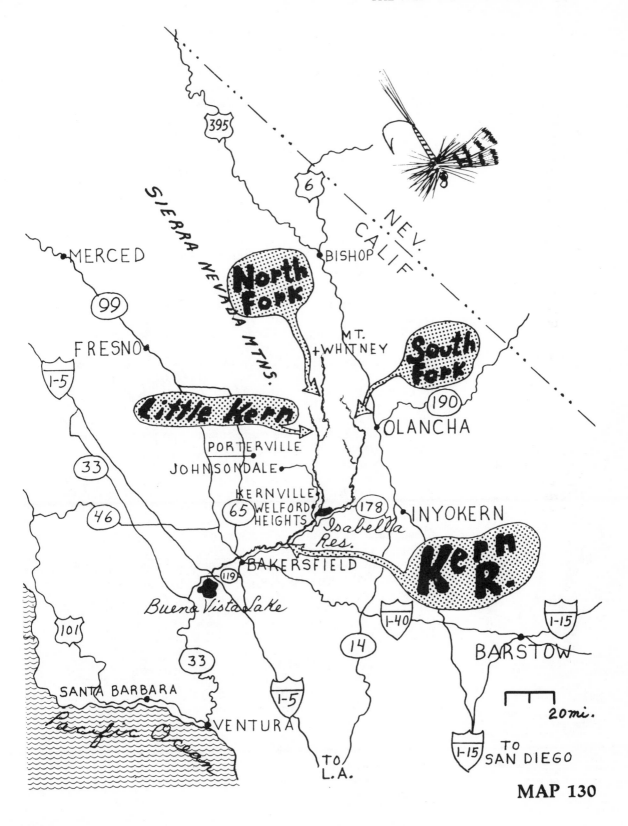

MAP 130

through campgrounds, and it gets better when the road leaves the river and you have to backpack. Big fish, big snakes, big rocks, big holes in the pools, beautiful broken and white water and riffles mark this part of the river. Nymphs and small wet flies work well here, such as the Hare's Ear Nymph, streamers such as the Spruce and Muddler, and any of the shrimp imitations such as the yellow. Green nymphs and the grasshopper also do well. The Sofa Pillow fly, an imitation of the local stone fly, is good evenings and mornings when these flies are hatching out.

The list of prime California streams is long: The Upper McCloud, Klamath, Trinity, East Walker, Lower Hat, Hot Creek, North Yuba, Feather, Truckee, Owens, Kings and Kern. All conjure up memories of gorgeous scenery at breathtaking heights and of trout of more variety than any state in the Union.

## Upper Sacramento

The Upper Sacramento, while not as highly touted as many California rivers, is one of my favorites. It is getting better as increased conservation activity improves it.

The basic stream is not large nor deep as some of the others, ranging from about 20 feet wide near the source to 60 feet across near the lake. It begins high in the mountains near Mount Shasta, and about twenty creeks—all snow runoffs—form the main stream that begins its downward rush in fast, rocky and somewhat roily water. Usually it is clear enough for good fly fishing by July when the waters have lowered and settled sufficiently. In September it is bound to be perfect for the many anglers who visit it. It seldom gets too warm in either air or water temperature.

It is curvy water where the bottoms are rocky. There is a constant change within a matter of few yards, offering every type of water imaginable. As the stream begins to slow in the valley, the long pools become longer, offering flatter water that is the delight of the dry fly fisherman. The stream is constantly on its drive to Shasta Lake. While there is considerable brush along the course, casting angles can be had almost everywhere. Perhaps a little wading is necessary to avoid downed trees and other brush along the banks. Felt-soled boots should be used since the rocks are quite slippery.

Brookies, browns and rainbows are there. Many of the big fish taken come up from the lake. Add to the natural spawn and lake residents the constant stocking by the conservation department, and a mixed creel of 10- to 14-inch fish is not uncommon. Even the hatchery fish will be found firm and fighting and equal to the stream-bred fish in selectivity. The reason for their excellent quality is the amount of natural feed in the stream.

From Lakehead north past Shasta Springs, you'll take Interstate 5, which runs right along the main stream. There are many turnoffs that will put you right into the water, as the river can be seen and photographed from the main road at many places with Mt. Shasta usually in the background. Fortunately there is little posted land since the major portion of the river is in Shasta National Forest.

Base your activity at Dunsmuir on Highway 97 and Route 5 on I-5, north of Redding. Motels and campgrounds abound. Reservations should be made in advance during the height of the summer season. Look up Ted Faye who operates a guide service at Lookout Point Motel. He is a man over 70 years of age and can out-wade and outlast the best of us. Ted uses two flies on a weighted leader. The flies are also weighted. So he goes down for the big ones.

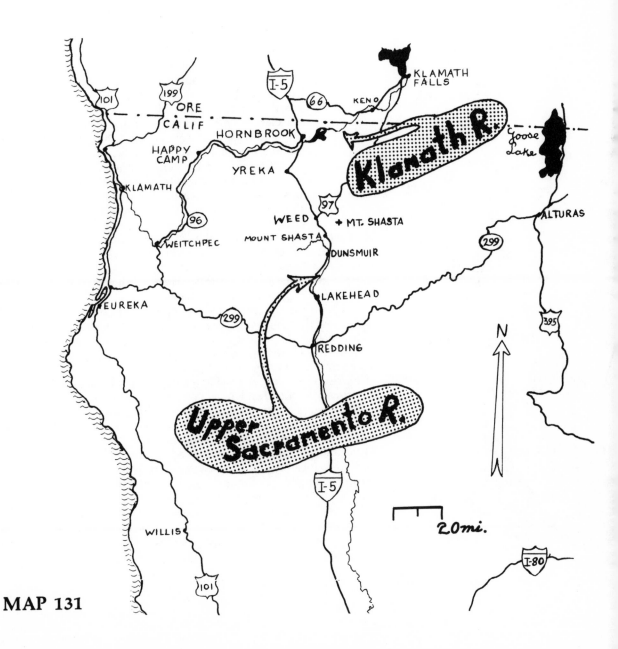

**MAP 131**

The stream itself is a generally free-stone stream and along its banks one of the oldest profitable railroads adds a bit of unusual charm. The banks are strewn with wild rhubarb, ferns, alders, aspens with a few pines and redwoods. Every year some very large fish in the 4- to 6-pound class are taken on flies, and some of the best fly casting is to be had right in the town of Dunsmuir, where the original Mount Shasta resort is still standing.

## The Klamath River

When I think about the Klamath River, fond memories of staunch steelhead and salmon come to mind, not to underestimate the fine rainbow fishing to be had there also. This is, of course, a major river that has been a top name in angling since the earliest days of piscatoria on the West Coast. It needs protection badly, for it seems that every bit of good watershed is subject to the ravages of man in their many deadly forms. The Klamath is not immune.

The river has its source near Klamath Falls, Oregon, heading down to Northern California, flowing through two artifical lakes— Copoc and Iron Gate Reservoir—then flowing some 186 miles to the Pacific Ocean near Klamath, California.

From Iron Gate it works its way through a steep and windy canyon, rushing and pounding down some 2,000 feet to the ocean. This is quoted average of about 12 feet per mile, which makes wading a difficult proposition except in pooled-up sections.

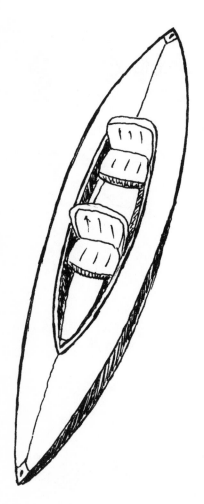

It is a wide stream, ranging from about 150 to almost 300 feet during the normal part of the season. Four main tributaries add to its power, glamor and fishing: the Shasta, Scott, Salmon and Trinity—all good fishing streams in their own right. As usual, in Northern California where the forests are thick and verdant, the scenery always offers more than pleasant backdrops for the catch photos. Particularly attractive are the Salmon-Trinity-Alps and Marble Mountain Wilderness Areas with their jagged peaks towering over green forested slopes.

This is the stream visited by anglers from far away New York and especially singled out by the angling fraternities of southern California.

Trying to home in on a specific spot to fish this river, if you are a stranger in town, is difficult. I suggest contacting Al Kutskey of Hornbrook, California. He's located near Iron Gate Reservoir. Another would be Jim Rhoads at Happy Camp or Bud Clyburn at Ash Creek. The motel and store at Weitchpec is another good reference point. For a complete Klamath River Fishing Guide Book, Jim Freeman in Richmond has a publication that sells for $1.00 and which tells all you need to know. Motels and private parks are located at Yreka, Klamath and Klamath River. There's Happy Camp or Weitchpec, with several Forest Service campgrounds at various points along the river.

Needless to say, the Klamath has every type of water one could wish for, and except for the heavy-water season or high-water conditions due to water release from the dams, it can be waded most of its length. During the steelhead runs, float trips are very popular and the trip down the fast flow is an experience in itself even if you don't fish.

From Klamath Lake in Oregon downstream to Copoc Lake in California the fishing for native rainbows is superb. Search out Keno, Oregon, off Highway 66 and work the stretch for some 10 miles below. This is heavily stocked water and also heavily fished. There is much posted land, but permission to fish can be obtained.

If you become a member of Trout Unlimited and Federation of Fly Fishermen, you'll have ready access to up-to-date information on every detail of the Klamath and I urge here your joining these two groups that are fighting for the lives of streams and watersheds like the Klamath. Good steelhead water is becoming scarce as civilization encroaches. Let us hope that this, one of the greatest monuments of nature, can remain unspoiled. This is one of California's three wild trout streams that have been set aside in Senate Bill 107; thus the Corps of Engineers has been blocked from playing in it for a period of 10 years.

Steelheading is done from the mouth of the river at the beginning of the season well up into the mountains, so there's plenty of room for exercise. Bring a wading staff and big rods and be prepared to make long casts with the big steelhead flies. During the summer, steelies take flies with as much abandon as the native rainbows. Put the Klamath on your list as a "must."

Fishing technique is generally quartering downstream with these wet flies, allowing the current to swing the fly below you. After letting it sink and soak for a minute, you bring it back in a retrieve and then repeat the process as you wade downstream. The rods should be 8 or 9 feet with shooting heads. The newer black monofilament lines are becoming very popular, used behind the shooting head. Fly fishermen do catch Klamath fish into the 7-pound category, but the usual is from 4 to 7. According to my friends, this stream has the nicest weather and nicest fishing of any stream in the country for steelheads, since it has a summer run in the fall and a nice early winter run up until the weather begins to chill in November. October, then, would be the prime time. There are a number of guide services with boats for moving up and down the river, or you can drive along, pick your pool and wade in. Good fishing can be found all the way from the ocean to the Iron Gate Dam. I still like the Happy Camp area, however, to Orleans, a stretch of about 50 miles. In the winter, all manner of tackle is used, from conventional bait and egg fishing with spinning gear all the way up to the lithe fly rod and good patterns of wet flies.

## How to Plan Your Fishing Trip

As I went along in this book detailing first the trout streams and then the waters where the other prime fishing was to be had, I kept wanting to add bits of instruction on fishing styles and forms and to offer travel planning ideas and other pertinent data. But this would have clouded the issue of the book which is, namely, to present the best and most famous fishing spots and how to reach them and discover their potential.

For some 50 years I've been making mistakes and forgetting a lot of things, for planning a trip is not just a matter of jumping in the car and taking off. I can remember one time when I was bound for prime trout water where I was to meet the editor of one of the national fishing and hunting magazines. When I arrived on the scene, I found I'd forgotten my dry fly box with a special selection of flies I'd wanted for the trip.

In order to make your trip as smooth and carefree as possible it is best to know where you are going, what conditions will be encountered, what clothes to wear and what gear to use. In this book I show you how to get to top fishing waters by car. But that is not all there is to planning. Taking off from the information herein, I suggest you write to the conservation departments of the states you intend to visit. Also write to the chamber of commerce of the nearest big town or city for up-to-date resort information. Now you'll be armed with the regulations and some detailed information on the water selected (see section following Appendix on maps and listings).

**Fishing and Boating Regulations:** These have been purposely left out of this book, since these facts can change from year to year and even during a season. Fishing these days is more complicated than it used to be. There are countless situations where specific

228

local regulations are in effect. The same goes for boating regulations: it doesn't hurt to get the correct dope beforehand.

There are also camping restrictions and always new campgrounds being made available as well as fresh boat liveries and launching facilities.

Then there are the roads. It is best to write to the state in which you'll be fishing to find out about road blocks, construction and the general conditions before you leave your front yard. Know about the pitfalls in advance.

With the various resorts recommended by government sources as well as those that advertise in the outdoor magazines, such as *Field & Stream, Outdoor Life* and *Sports Afield,* you'll be able to make a selection of the "base camp" for your fishing excursion. From resort proprietors you can get definite recommendations as to clothing, available launching facilities, boat and motor rentals, camping gear, canoe trip outfittings and guide services.

One word here about guides. If your trip is limited in time and the water is large, it is best to hire a guide to take you out, especially in strange country and under strange fishing conditions. Many guides serve also as outfitters. In many cases you can go to the outfitter with little gear of your own and he'll supply just what you need.

The next step is to make reservations. Don't just drive up and expect everything to fall in place without advance notice. You might literally miss the boat because they are all taken.

If you plan to bed down some distance from the water to be fished, you can and should visit the bait and tackle stores and sporting goods stores. You can pick up needed localized equipment and a lot of advice.

**Fishing Tackle:** If the jaunt is a short one and you are familiar with the water, you can almost gear up unconsciously. You know what to expect there and what you'll be wanting to use while in search of the game fish to be found. Nevertheless, check through the list . . . rods, reels (Are they fully loaded with line?), extra spools for spinning gear changes, terminal tackle such as leaders, swivels and hooks, lures and plugs (plenty of back-ups), the appropriate landing net. A medium- or long-handled net (inspect the bag for tears and worn-out spots) is needed for canoe or boat, a short-handled one for wading. Inspect snaps and bags. Remember to pack the thermometer, the depth string with its weight for lake and river fishing, knife, scissors or clippers, fly dope, compass, camera . . . but don't do what I did recently, shoot thirty-six times with the camera, only to find it wasn't loaded with film! Go through the list of fly boxes and lure boxes, making sure they are loaded and ready. If the trip is a long way from home, or from a base where tackle can be had, bring plenty of back-up equipment, especially terminal tackle and lures. Make sure you have tools and patch-up materials for reels and rods. Oh—don't forget the creel or fish stringer.

Adequate provisions for carrying live bait should be worked out for long treks. Also bring along traps and nets to catch your own if you are a long way from a bait dealer.

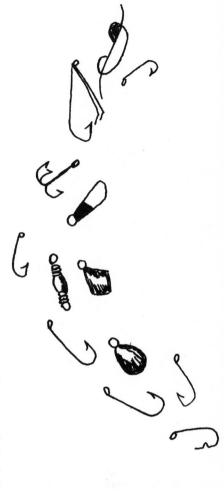

**Clothing, Boats, Waders and Other Necessities:** Selecting the appropriate clothing for an outing, especially in a strange state or one of a different climate, is always a problem. I've fished for shad at Lemon Bluff on the St. Johns River in Florida in February and have suffered from the cold because I thought it was always warm in that state. Similarly, in Newfoundland where one would expect to find cool days and nights, I've sweated it out under flannel shirts. I caught my biggest salmon in the Gander River, fishing in my jockey shorts!

So the best recommendation I can come up with to be safe is to go equipped with everything from heavy-weather clothes to light sport shirts and even short pants, almost wherever you travel. In some places, weather can change in an instant. A nice warm day on the lake can blow up into a storm in a few minutes. Carry everything from moccasins for canoeing and light trail hiking to rubber-bottomed boots for the north country. Check those boots and waders for leaks. Will you need special footgear? Do you have a patching kit? Take extra clothing in case of a dunking. Pack that in the car along with snack foods such as apples, oranges, or other energy foods such as a bag of mixed raisins and nuts. Then load your fishing wallet, which should not be your personal wallet, just in case you get a wetting. Leave the personal one in the car and have your ID duplicate and fishing license in the one you take astream or on the lake.

Rain gear is a must wherever you go. It rains everywhere, sometimes even in the deserts. And rain gear is always a defense against sudden winds.

Also, wherever you go you'll find insects—everything from blackflies and no-see-ums to mosquitoes and horseflies; bring along plenty of non-aerosol repellant.

A first aid kit should be in the car and another one in the boat and a third in your fishing jacket or outdoor coat if you are hiking.

If you wear a hat, have an extra, in case one blows overboard. I like glasses to shelter my eyes from the wind. Polarized lenses are the best since they allow sight penetration into reflective waters. Also, have along a packet of lens cleaners. Bring extra matches even if you have a lighter with its extra flint. Pack extra smokes in plastic bags and either jacket them or put them in the tackle box.

**Accessories:** A compass in your fishing jacket is sometimes handy, as is one in your car or boat. Along with this, a barometer is handy for weather warning. A temperature guage is a must if you are lake fishing. Certainly both a fishing knife and a hunting knife with a good small sharpening stone are good to have, plus a pair of needle-nosed pliers for removing hooks from the fish.

## Car Top Boats and Trailering

Are you thoroughly insured? Are you paid up?

Inspect your boat for any needed repairs and fix-ups. Also thoroughly inspect the car-top carrier for wornout straps and rusted fixtures. Make sure the carrier is mounted on tight and check it often during the trip. When the boat is mounted, make sure *it* is tight and test it too, several times during a long drive, especially if you travel over bumpy roads. When driving in a crosswind, drive at a slower speed than usual. Watch those wind gusts, especially when there is oncoming traffic.

If your boat is motorized, make sure your serial numbers are legible, your sticker up-to-date and that you have the registration in your outing wallet and also in your wallet to be left in the car. Check all needed accessories, such as a standard, attached, red-and-green bow light or a battery-operated one for portable use. (It is a good idea to carry a portable one even aboard a boat that has a full-fledged lighting system.) For a spare for the stern light, bring a flashlight and a means to attach it to the stern light shaft in case of a failure. Bring along at least two flashlights with fresh batteries. I wish I had done this recently when my wife accidentally dropped our only flashlight overboard.

For the trailer, make sure the grease fittings are filled before takeoff and bring a loaded grease gun for grease replacements and to grease the boat motor. For care of the motor, consult the owner's manual for all of those details and make believe you will be a thousand miles from nowhere when you have trouble. Coast Guard approved emergency equipment is a must to check off before your trip.

When driving long distances, do not pack a lot of gear in your boat. It will ride too heavy on car top or trailer, and unless you have a cover it will get grimy and wet from rain or dew. Besides, a lot of loose gear can move about and be available for theft when you stop for that hamburger in the middle of the night. Keep tools and valuables in the car and preferably covered so they cannot be identified as valuable.

Since theft and vandalism are on the increase, I do not venture out of my yard without an adequate and loud buzzer system on the boat and on the car. There are many types of warning systems on the market. Find the one that suits your purpose and install it yourself so you know what to do with it if it doesn't work. Check it out regularly.

Check the trailer lighting system and have flashlight backups, at least for the running lights. Almost needless to say, check the power winch, connection chains and locks and oil them. Most important, check the tires and have a spare trailer tire inflated on a spare wheel and the wheel tight on the trailer. (Many trailer owners don't even own a spare, but trailers get flats and blowouts just as cars do.) Know how to change it. Do you know how to jack up a trailer? Better find out.

Once the boat is on the trailer where it should be in a balanced position for travel, tighten the belt and inspect it regularly while en route. Also have an additional tie-down at the bow so the boat doesn't rock over train tracks and bumps in the road. Install twin driving mirrors even if your boat is small. You'll be backing up and turning a great deal, sometimes in tight places.

When you park the rig for the night, try and get as close to your room or tent as possible, or, in a town, under a street light. When you take off in the morning, give the rig an eye inspection and look for any tampering. (How many people ever look at their tires before taking off on the first trip of the day in their personal car?)

For ease in driving and trying to find your way in the dark, I have found that a listing of each move on the highway taped to the dash in large letters and numbers is a great help. I've also cut out map sections and pasted them up within easy reading distance for quick reference.

And of course don't drive when you are tired. This time it's a vacation, not a marathon. If you want to save time (and also your stomach lining), have some goodies aboard and refreshments in the thermos . . . it's usually better than diner food along the road.

Keep a log of the trip, just for fun. Makes good reading years later, especially when you want to make the same run again, because you can note the things you forgot the last time. It makes good reading also when you are preparing to venture into fresh and unknown territory . . . are you "fully found" as they say in boating? "Fully found" means that everything needed (with a plus) is aboard and all systems are "go."

As to the car itself, routine precautions should prevail as always.

Let's see, now. Have *I* forgotten anything?

## America's Freshwater Game Fish

It is not the province of this book to offer instruction in sport fishing. Several authors' books cover the subject in its many aspects and I humbly suggest you read my *Tactics on Trout* (Knopf, 1969), *Basic Fly Fishing and Fly Tying* (Stackpole, 1973), *Introduction To Bait Fishing* (Stackpole, 1972), *Freshwater Fishing* (Hawthorn, 1976) and *The Trout And The Fly* (Hawthorn, 1977).

**Salmon:** The various species of Pacific salmon are native to Washington, Oregon and northern California. The coho and kokanee have recently been planted in the Midwest Great Lakes with phenomenal success, with fish in the 50-pound class reported. These fish in their native habitat are taken mainly at the mouths of major West Coast rivers and in some cases well upstream in company with the steelhead trout that follow them to eat their eggs, which drift down from the spawning areas.

This is big fish angling, with 80-pounders taken regularly on heavy bait-casting rigs and large-size spinning rods and reels. Heavy trolling and casting of deep-running spoons are the two basic methods of catching them. They are tops in table fare, as is the Atlantic salmon, found only in the northeast Canadian provinces of Nova Scotia, Newfoundland, New Brunswick and Quebec and, to a limited degree, in northeastern Maine.

The Atlantic salmon is limited to fly fishing only. The Atlantic has, because of its equal distribution in northern Europe, become world famous as the sport fish of kings. The Atlantic variety has also been planted in the waters of New Zealand and Australia, where the sport is considered the finest in the world now.

The *Field & Stream* records tell the story very well.

**The Trout:** Trout include Brown, brook, lake, rainbow, Dolly Varden, cutthroat, steelhead and golden.

These are fish that for over two hundred years have dominated the sport of freshwater fishing, especially fly fishing and angling with artificial lures.

The brook trout, originally found only in the Northeast, has found new residence in the mountains of the Rocky Mountain States and the Far West.

The brown trout, originally imported from Germany in the 1800's, has become a native American in all waters where trout can survive.

The rainbow, once found only in the Far West and Mountain States, has done very well in the Northeastern States and even as far south as Georgia and Arkansas.

The Dolly Varden, found in the mountainous West, has not been transplanted but is a fighting game fish as far north as Alaska.

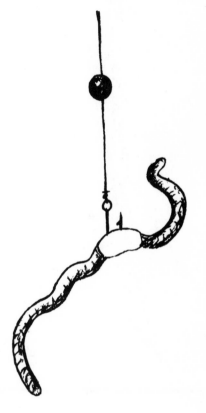

The cutthroat and steelhead, which ascend the coastal rivers from the Pacific Ocean for their spawning, in former times were found only in those areas but now have been transplanted to some extent in Midwest lakes and rivers. All of these species are tough game fighters and avid takers of both bait and artificial lures.

The specific waters singled out for them in this book should be fished in order to experience the delights which famed authors have been reporting for a century. The fly rod, spin-casting rod, light lines and leaders, artificial flies and small shiny metal lures take their toll of fish annually. These trout reside in waters from tiny creeks to magnificent rivers, from ice-cold ponds to extensive lakes and artificial impoundments where they are taken on the surface with flies or deep down by still-fishing with bait.

Study the records of big fish taken, by whom and where in the *Field & Stream* records included in this section.

Limited in range but extravagant in beauty and exotic attraction, the golden trout of the High Sierras is a fish of legend. The trip to its domain is equally attractive to the naturalist-sportsman. The golden trout of New Hampshire is a char.

**Northern Pike, Muskellunge, Walleye, Pickerel:** The muskie is the largest American freshwater game fish, ranging up to 50 pounds. Only the catfish of the Deep South are larger in weight. These hefty game fish abound in Minnesota, Wisconsin, Michigan and the waters of some upper Northeastern States with a few isolated reservoirs in states as far south as Arkansas also containing the fish. Heavy bait-casting and spinning gear is generally recommended, particularly when trolling or casting the heavy live bait used to entice them. Plugs and spinner casting is also effective with medium heavy spinning gear, and a few fly fishermen go after them with heavy fly rods and big flies or live bait.

The pike is found in the same general waters, mostly in large rivers of the North and in the deep lakes. The same gear of heavy stature is recommended, but pike can certainly be caught on light tackle. Both pike and muskies are exceptionally savage fighters and, once aboard, are quite dangerous due to their large teeth. They are excellent as a table delicacy.

The walleye is also found in the same waters and to a larger degree in waters where both largemouth and smallmouth bass are found. They are not generally as sporty as the others but they more than make up the difference in taste. They are also considered easier to catch.

The pickerel is found in most states where the bass are located. They are sporty fare on light tackle, including fly rods, and are classed by many anglers with the panfish such as crappie, bluegills, shad and sunfish.

Study the records in the *Field & Stream* listings. It is good indication of the possibilities and where to go for the record breakers. For techniques and tackle, consult my books listed earlier.

**The Bass:** Largemouth, smallmouth, Kentucky and spotted.

"Pound for pound, the gamiest fish that swims"; so wrote Dr. Henshall in the 1800's in one of the first books on the black bass written in the United States. The bass are the most sought-after freshwater game fish in North America, and the basic two varieties, the largemouth and the smallmouth, are found in all the mainland states. The largest are the Florida largemouth, recently introduced into some Southern California lakes where they grow to a record size of over 15 pounds.

The largest smallmouths are taken in the Northern States from Minnesota to Maine, and good catches can be had as far west as Washington and Oregon.

The Kentucky bass and spotted bass are limited to the Carolinas, Kentucky and Tennessee, with a few found in neighboring states. All methods of fishing are used—fly rod angling with conventional flies, plus the popular art of bass-bug fishing, spinning with bait, artificial lures such as spinners and small plugs, still-fishing and trolling with lures and live bait . . . use 'em all!

With the addition of large artificial impoundments such as the famed TVA lakes in Southeastern U.S., the bass have increased their range and numbers for all to enjoy.

The way to tell the difference between the largemouth and smallmouth bass is to study the relationship of mouth to eye. The jaw of the largemouth extends back beyond the eye. The jaw of the smallmouth extends to a point just below the eye. Both species are powerful fighters even in the warm waters of the Southern States and Florida.

Considered by some to be superior to the trout for dining pleasures, the bass are in the diet of millions of sportsmen. Farm ponds developed for sport as well as food production produce bass harvests of large volume.

Study the *Field & Stream* prize winning bass catches.

**Panfish:** Black and white crappie, yellow and white perch, landlocked striped bass, shad, white bass, bream, bluegills and other sunfish.

These comprise the principal list of panfish, so designated because they fit into a frying pan to be cooked to a delicious brown. They are the main attraction to the beginner fisherman, the vacationer, and the angler who enjoys lazy days on a lake or river, fishing for the small fry with light and ultra-light spinning and fly rod gear.

They take avidly to flies and popping lures, underwater flies, spinners and of course bait: worms or live minnows. They are some of the most colorful fish to be had and delight both old and young because great numbers of them are easily caught. They are found in most small creeks, brooks, small ponds and even open-water swamps as well as the big lakes and impoundments. Catching them when luck with the gamier and bigger fish is hard to come by often saves the day for a bring-home meal of fresh fish.

Study the *Field & Stream* records to get an idea of the potential with these varieties and where they are taken.

# New World-Record Fish

## FRESHWATER RECORDS

| SPECIES | | | | | | CAUGHT BY ROD AND REEL | | |
|---|---|---|---|---|---|---|---|---|
| Common Name | Scientific Name | Lb. | Oz. | Length | Girth | Where | When | Angler |
| BASS, Largemouth | Micropterus salmoides | ★ 22-4 | | 32½" | 28½" | Montgomery Lake, Ga. | June 2, 1932 | George W. Perry |
| BASS, Redeye | Micropterus coosae | ★ 8-3 | | 23" | 16½" | Flint R., Ga. | Oct. 23, 1977 | David A. Hubbard |
| BASS, Rock | Ambloplites rupestis | 3 | | 13½" | 10¾" | York River, Ontario | Aug. 1, 1974 | Peter Gulgin |
| BASS, Smallmouth | Micropterus dolomieui | ★ 11-15 | | 27" | 21⅔" | Dale Hollow Lake, Ky. | July 9, 1955 | David L. Hayes |
| BASS, Spotted | Micropterus punctulatus spp | 8-10½ | | 23½" | 19⅞" | Smith Lake, Alabama | Feb. 25, 1972 | Billy Henderson |
| BASS, White | Morone chrysops | ★ 5-5 | | 19½" | 17" | Ferguson Lake, Calif. | Mar. 8, 1972 | Norman W. Mize |
| BASS, Whiterock | White X Striped | 20 | | 30" | 24½" | Savannah R., Ga. | May 5, 1977 | Don Raley |
| BASS, Yellow | Morone mississippiensis | 2-4 | | 16¼" | 12¾" | Lake Monroe, Ind. | Mar. 27, 1977 | Donald L. Stalker |
| BLUEGILL | Lepomis macrochirus | ★ 4-12 | | 15" | 18¼" | Ketona Lake, Alabama | Apr. 9, 1950 | T. S. Hudson |
| BOWFIN | Amia calva | 19-12 | | 39" | | Lake Marion, S.C. | Nov. 5, 1972 | M. R. Webster |
| BUFFALO, Bigmouth | Ictiobus cyprinellus | 56 | | 44¼" | 33" | Lock Loma L., Mo. | Aug. 19, 1976 | W. J. Long |
| BUFFALO, Smallmouth | Ictiobus bubalus | 32-8 | | 34½" | 29" | Sardis Res., Miss. | Oct. 22, 1977 | Eddie O'Daniel |
| BULLHEAD, Black | Ictalurus melas | 8 | | 24" | 17¾" | Lake Waccabuc, N.Y. | Aug. 1, 1951 | Kani Evans |
| CARP | Cyprinus carpio | 55-5 | | 42" | 31" | Clearwater Lake, Minn. | July 10, 1952 | Frank J. Ledwein |
| CATFISH, Blue | Ictalurus furcatus | 97 | | 57" | 37" | Missouri River, S.D. | Sept. 16, 1959 | Edward B. Elliott |
| CATFISH, Channel | Ictalurus punctatus | ★ 58 | | 47¼" | 29⅛" | Santee-Cooper Res., S.C. | July 7, 1964 | W. B. Whaley |
| CATFISH, Flathead | Pylodictis olivaris | 79-8 | | 44" | 27" | White River, Indiana | Aug. 13, 1966 | Glenn T. Simpson |
| CATFISH, White | Ictalurus catus | 10-5 | | 25" | 17½" | Raritan R., N.J. | June 23, 1976 | Lewis W. Lomerson |
| CHAR, Arctic | Salvelinus alpinus | 29-11 | | 39¾" | 26" | Arctic R., N.W.T. | Aug. 21, 1968 | Jeanne P. Branson |
| CRAPPIE, Black | Pomoxis nigromaculatus | 5 | | 19¼" | 18⅝" | Santee-Cooper Res., S.C. | Mar. 15, 1957 | Paul E. Foust |
| CRAPPIE, White | Pomoxis annularis | ★ 5-3 | | 21" | 19" | Enid Dam, Miss. | July 31, 1957 | Fred L. Bright |
| DOLLY VARDEN | Salvelinus malma | 32 | | 40½" | 29¾" | L. Pend Oreille, Idaho | Oct. 27, 1949 | N. L. Higgins |
| DRUM, Freshwater | Aplodinotus grunniens | 54-8 | | 31½" | 29" | Nickajack Lake, Tenn. | Apr. 20, 1972 | Benny E. Hull |
| GAR, Alligator | Lepisosteus spatula | 279 | | 93" | | Rio Grande River, Texas | Dec. 2, 1951 | Bill Valverde |
| GAR, Longnose | Lepisosteus osseus | 50-5 | | 72¼" | 22¼" | Trinity River, Texas | July 30, 1954 | Townsend Miller |
| GRAYLING, American | Thymallus arcticus | ★ 5-15 | | 29⅞" | 15⅛" | Katseyedie R., N.W.T. | Aug. 16, 1967 | Jeanne P. Branson |
| KOKANEE | Oncorhynchus nerka | ★ 6-9¾ | | 24½" | 14½" | Priest Lake, Idaho | June 9, 1975 | Jerry Verge |
| MUSKELLUNGE | Esox masquinongy | ★ 69-15 | | 64½" | 31¾" | St. Lawrence River, N.Y. | Sept. 22, 1957 | Arthur Lawton |
| PERCH, White | Morone americanus | 4-12 | | 19½" | 13" | Messalonskee Lake, Me. | June 4, 1949 | Mrs. Earl Small |
| PERCH, Yellow | Perca flavescens | 4-3½ | | | | Bordentown, N.J. | May 1865 | Dr. C. C. Abbot |
| PICKEREL, Chain | Esox niger | ★ 9-6 | | 31" | 14" | Homerville, Georgia | Feb. 17, 1961 | Baxley McQuaig, Jr. |
| PIKE, Northern | Esox lucius | ★ 46-2 | | 52½" | 25" | Sacandaga Res., N.Y. | Sept. 15, 1940 | Peter Dubuc |
| REDHORSE, Silver | Moxostoma anisurum | 4-2 | | 20½" | 14" | Gasconade R., Mo. | Oct. 5, 1974 | C. Larry McKinney |
| SALMON, Atlantic | Salmo salar | 79-2 | | | | Tana River, Norway | 1928 | Henrik Henriksen |
| SALMON, Chinook | Oncorhynchus tshawytscha | ★ 93 | | 50" | 39" | Kelp Bay, Alaska | June 24, 1977 | Howard C. Rider |
| SALMON, Chum | Oncorhynchus keta | 27-3 | | 39⅜" | 24½" | Raymond Cove, Alaska | June 11, 1977 | Robert A. Jahnke |
| SALMON, Landlocked | Salmo salar | 22-8 | | 36" | | Sebago Lake, Maine | Aug. 1, 1907 | Edward Blakely |
| SALMON, Coho | Oncorhynchus kisutch | 31 | | | | Cowichan Bay, B.C. | Oct. 11, 1947 | Mrs. Lee Hallberg |
| SAUGER | Stizostedion canadense | 8-12 | | 28" | 15" | Lake Sakakawea, N.D. | Oct. 6, 1971 | Mike Fischer |
| SHAD, American | Alosa sapidissima | ★ 9-2 | | 25" | 17½" | Enfield, Connecticut | Apr. 28, 1973 | Edward P. Nelson |
| STURGEON, White | Acipenser transmontanus | 360 | | 111" | 86" | Snake River, Idaho | Apr. 24, 1956 | Willard Cravens |
| SUNFISH, Green | Lepomis cyanellus | 2-2 | | 14¾" | 14" | Stockton Lake, Missouri | June 18, 1971 | Paul M. Dilley |
| SUNFISH, Redbreast | Lepomis auritus | 1-8½ | | 11" | 12⅝" | Suwannee R., Fla. | Apr. 30, 1977 | Tommy D. Cason, Jr. |
| SUNFISH, Redear | Lepomis microlophus | 4-8 | | 16¼" | 17¾" | Chase City, Virginia | June 19, 1970 | Maurice E. Ball |
| TROUT, Brook | Salvelinus fontinalis | 14-8 | | 31½" | | Nipigon River, Ontario | July 1916 | Dr. W. J. Cook |
| TROUT, Brown | Salmo trutta | Record being reviewed | | | | | | |
| TROUT, Cutthroat | Salmo clarki | 41 | | 39" | | Pyramid Lake, Nevada | Dec. 1925 | John Skimmerhorn |
| TROUT, Golden | Salmo aguabonita | 11 | | 28" | 16" | Cook's Lake, Wyoming | Aug. 5, 1948 | Chas. S. Reed |
| TROUT, Lake | Salvelinus namaycush | ★ 65 | | 52" | 38" | Great Bear L., N.W.T. | Aug. 8, 1970 | Larry Daunis |
| TROUT, Rainbow, Stlhd. or Kamloops | Salmo gairdneri | ★ 42-2 | | 43" | 23½" | Bell Island, Alaska | June 22, 1970 | David Robert White |
| TROUT, Sunapee | Salvelinus aureolus | 11-8 | | 33" | 17¼" | Lake Sunapee, N.H. | Aug. 1, 1954 | Ernest Theoharis |
| TROUT, Tiger | Brown X Brook | 17 | | 31" | 21" | L. Michigan, Wis. | Aug. 2, 1977 | Edward Rudnicki |
| WALLEYE | Stizostedion vitreum | ★ 25 | | 41" | 29" | Old Hickory Lake, Tenn. | Aug. 1, 1960 | Mabry Harper |
| WARMOUTH | Lepomis gulosus | 2 | | 12" | 12½" | Sylvania, Ga. | May 4, 1974 | Carlton Robbins |
| WHITEFISH, Lake | Coregonus clupeaformis | 13 | | 32¼" | 19" | Great Bear L., N.W.T. | July 14, 1974 | Robert L. Stintsman |
| WHITEFISH, Mountain | Prosopium williamsoni | 5 | | 19" | 14" | Athabasca R., Alberta | June 3, 1963 | Orville Welch |

Fresh-water Records compiled by FIELD & STREAM          ★ Winner in Annual Field & Stream Fishing Contest

**Reprinted from FIELD & STREAM, February, 1978**

# Index

Abilene, Texas, 159
Absaroka Primitive Area, Montana, 169
Accessories and fishing tackle, 229
Adirondack State Park, New York, 43, 44
Agnes, Oregon, 214, 215
Alabama, 77; *chapter on*, 105; Fisheries Section, Alabama Dept. of Commerce, 105
Albany, New York, 41
Albemarle, Lake, Mississippi, 107; *map*, 109
Alexander City, Alabama, 105
Alexandria, Louisiana, 153
Alexandria Drafting Co., (maps), Virginia, 69, 73
Alf, Dick, Fly Shop, Idaho, 190, 192
Allaben, New York, 43
Allagash River, Maine, 4-6; *map*, 2, 3
Allegheny Mountains, Pennsylvania, 57
Allegheny National Forest, Pennsylvania, 60; *map*, 59
Allegheny River, Pennsylvania, 57, 60, 64; *map*, 59
Allen County, Kentucky, 100
Altamaha area, Georgia, 77, 80
Alturas Lake, Idaho, 192; *maps*, 186, 191
American Legion State Park, Connecticut, 29
Amnicon River, Wisconsin, 125; *map*, 128
Amsterdam, New York, 39
Andalusia, Louisiana, 141
Anderson, Jack, 172
Animas River, Colorado, 173
Apalachicola River, Florida, 87; *map*, 88
Apopka, Lake, Florida, 85; *map*, 82
Appalachian Mountains, Pennsylvania, 57; the Carolinas, 71, 73; Tennessee, 101

Arizona, *chapter on*, 197; Game and Fish Commission, 197
Arkabutla Reservoir, Mississippi, 107; *map*, 108
Arkansas, 89, 100, 143; *chapter on*, 147-153; Game and Fish Commission, 150, 151
Arlington, Vermont, 19
Armour Lake Canoe Outfitters, Wisconsin, 130
Armstrong Creek, Montana, 171
Arrowhead Country, Minnesota, 135
Arrowhead Lake, Texas, 160; *map*, 161
Asheville, North Carolina, 71
Ashokan Reservoir, New York, 41, 42; *maps*, 37, 40
Ashton, Idaho, 181, 188
Atchafalaya River, Louisiana, 153; *map*, 154
Athens, Alabama, 105
Atlanta, Georgia, 77
Augusta, Maine, 5, 6
Au Sable River, Michigan 124; *map*, 123
Ausable Forks, New York, 44
Ausable River, New York, 44, 46; *map*, 45
Averill, Vermont, 14

Back Lake, New Hampshire, 8; *map*, 10
Bailey, Dan, Tackle Shop, Montana, 171, 172, 181
Bailey, Nelson, Maine, 5
Bakersville, California, 222
Bangor, Maine, 5
Bangor Pool, Maine, 1, 5
Barkhamsted, Connecticut, 29
Barnes, Pat, Tackle Shop, Montana, 181
Barnett, Ross; Reservoir; Mississippi, 107; *map*, 110
Barre, Vermont, 13
Barrett's Diversion Dam, Montana, 166

Bartlett's Ferry, South Carolina, 76
Barton River, Vermont, 13, 14; *map*, 12
Bass, landlocked striped and white, 234
Basswood Lake, Minnesota, 135; *map*, 138
Batesville, Arkansas, 148
Baton Rouge, Louisiana, 153
Battenkill River, Vermont, 13; *section on*, 19; *map*, 20
Baxter State Park, Maine, 5; *maps*, 2, 3
Bay of Fundy, Maine, 4
Bayou Access, Arkansas, 150
Bayou Bartholomew, Louisiana, 153; *map*, 152
Bear Creek, Oregon, 214
Beaverhead River, Montana, 162, 169; *section on*, 165-169; *map*, 164
Beaverkill River, New York, 19, 38, 41, 43, 189, 199; *section on*, 38-39; *map*, 37
Beaver Lodge, Kentucky, 100
Beavertail Campground, Oregon, 211
Belgrade Lakes, Maine, 6; *map*, 3
Bemidji, Minnesota, 135; *map*, 136
Bend, Oregon, 211
Bennington, Vermont, 19
Berghofer, Carl, New Mexico, 185
Bergman, Ray, 51
Berkshires, Massachusetts, 26
Berlin Reservoir, Ohio, 89; *map*, 92
Berryessa Reservoir, ·California, 220; *map*, 219
Big Brush, Kentucky, 100
Big Dan Hole Pond, New Hampshire, 8; *map*, 9
Big Flat Brook, New Jersey, 51; *map*, 52
Big Fork River, Minnesota, 137
Big Hole River, Montana, *section on*, 163-165; *map*, 161
Big Sky Motels, Montana, 165
Big Springs, Idaho, 187; *map*, 186
Big Timber, Montana, 169

Birmingham, Alabama, 105
Bishop, California, 217
Black River, Michigan, 119; *map*, 120
Blackshear Lake, Georgia, 80; *map*, 81
Blackstone, Massachusetts, 26
Blackwood Lake, New Jersey, 56
Blakeley Mountain Dam, Arkansas, 148
Blanco, New Mexico, 183
Blanding, Louisiana, 141
Blazes, Lake Helen, Florida, 83
Bloomfield, Vermont, 14
Bluegills, 234
Blue Mesa Reservoir, Colorado, 173
Blue Ridge Lake, Georgia, 77; *map*, 76
Blue Ridge Mountains, North Carolina, 71
Bluff Lake, Illinois, 141
Boating regulations, 228
Bogachiel River, Washington, 202; *map*, 200
Bogus Creek Campground, Oregon, 212
Boice, Jerry, Oregon, 215
Bois Brule River, Wisconsin, 128; *section on*, 133; *maps*, 128, 131
Bonneville Dam, Washington, 203
Boulder Dam, Nevada; *map*, 198
Boulder Junction, Wisconsin, 125
Boulder River, Montana, 169; *section on*, 169-171; *map*, 170
Boulder River Ranch, Montana, 171
Bowling Green, Kentucky, 100
Box Canyon, Idaho, 187, 188
Boysen Reservoir, Wyoming, 177; *map*, 178
Bozeman, Montana, 181
Brainerd, Minnesota, 135; *map*, 136
Branson, Missouri, 143
Brazos, Texas, 159; *map*, 159
Bream, 234
Bright, Bob, Missouri, 143
Bristol, Connecticut, 29
Brown Paper Co., Maine, 5
Brownsville, Texas, 159
Bruce Creek, Arkansas, 148
Bruin, Lake, Louisiana, 153
Bruin, Lake, Missouri; *map*, 109
Brule River, Wisconsin, 133; *map*, 132
Buck, Pennsylvania, 61
Buckley, Wayne, Florida, 87
Buford, Colorado, 176
Buggs Island Lake, North Carolina, 69; *map*, 68
Bull Shoals Lake, Missouri, 143, 148; *map*, 144
Burkesville, Kentucky, 95
Burlington, Connecticut, 29
Burlington, Vermont, 13
Burlington Lake, Georgia, 77; *map*, 76
Bushkill, Pennsylvania, 57
Byrdstown, Kentucky, 95

Cahaba River, Alabama, 105; *map*, 106
Calais, Maine, 6

Calhoun, Georgia, 80
California, 8, 19, 208; *chapter on*, 217-227; Dept. of Fish and Game, 218
Callico Rock, Arkansas, 148
*Cal Trout* organization, 218, 222
Camden, New Jersey, 56
Cambridge, Vermont, 19
Camp Sherman, Oregon, 209, 210
Canada, 1
Canandaigua, Lake, New York, 46
Candlewood Lake, Connecticut, 32; *map*, 34
Canton, Ohio, 89
Cape Vincent, New Jersey, 46
Cary, Idaho, 189
Cascade Mountains, Washington, 202, 203, 205, 209, 212
Catahoula Lake, Louisiana, 153; *map*, 154
Catnip Lake, Arizona, 197
Catskill Mountains, 4, 29, 38
Catskill Mountain State Park, New York, 41, 51; *map*, 37
Cayuga, New York, 46
Celina, Tennessee, 95
Chain-O-Lakes region, Illinois, 141; *map*, 140
Challis National Forest, Idaho, 190, 192
Chama River, New Mexico, 183
Chamberlain Lake, 4, 6, 13; *maps*, 2, 3
Champlain, Lake, Vermont, 13, 44, 46; *maps*, 20, 45
Channel Lake, Illinois, 141
Charleston, South Carolina, 73
Chassahowitzka River, Florida, 87; *map*, 85
Chattahoochee River, South Carolina, 76, 77
Chattanooga, Tennessee, 80, 101
Chattooga River, South Carolina, 73; *map*, 74
Chatuga, Georgia 77; *map*, 76
Chaubunagungamaug, Lake, Maine, 23; *map*, 24
Chaumont, New York, 446
Chautauqua, Lake, Illinois, 141; *map*, 139
Chautauqua, Lake, New York, 46; *map*, 47
Cheboygan River System, Michigan, 114
Chehalis River, Washington, 202; *map*, 200
Chickopee River, Massachusetts, 26
China Lake, Maine, 5
Chippewa River, Wisconsin, 129; *map*, 126
Chotard, Lake, Mississippi, 107; *map*, 109
Clackamas River, Oregon, 205; *map*, 206
Clark Canyon Dam, Montana, 166
Clark Hill Reservoir, Georgia, 77; *map*, 76
Clark River, Montana, 166, 171

Clayton, Georgia, 73
Clayton, Idaho, 192
Cle Elum, Washington, 204; reservoir, 203; stream, 204
Clinton, Iowa, 141
Clyburn, Bud, California, 226
Coffee Pot Rapids, Idaho, 187
Colorado, *chapter on*, 173-176
Colorado River, 159, 193, 197, 220; *maps*, 194, 221
Columbia, Pennsylvania, 61, 75
Columbia River, Washington, 199, 203, 205, 210, 212, 292; *maps*, 201, 207
Columbia, South Carolina, 73
Conejos River, Colorado, 173
Connecticut, *chapter on*, 27-36; Conn. Board of Fisheries and Game, 36; State Dept. of Environmental Protection, 27, 36
Connecticut River, 13, 14, 17, 21, 29, 36; *section on*, 29-32; *maps*, 10, 11, 18, 25, 28, 31, 32, 33
Connecticut River Lakes, 8; *map*, 10
Conowingo Lake, Pennsylvania, 57, 61; *map*, 60
Continental Divide, Montana, 163, 177; *map*, 164
Cooks Falls, New York, 39
Copoc Lake, California, 226, 227
Copper Range Campground, Wisconsin, 133; *map*, 131
Cornwall, Connecticut, 29
Corpus Christi, Texas, 159
Cowlitz River, Washington, 202; *map*, 200
Crabtree Canyon Lake, Washington, 204
Crappies, black and white, 234
Crescent City, Florida, 85, 87
Crescent Lake, Florida, 85; *map*, 82
Crivitz, Wisconsin, 128; *map*, 132
Cross City, Florida, 87
Crystal Lake, Vermont, 14; *map*, 15
Crystal River, Florida, 87; *map*, 85
Culver, New Jeersey, 56; *map*, 52
Cumberland, Lake, Kentucky, 96; *map*, 98
Cumberland River, Kentucky, 100
Curran River, California, 222
Current River, Missouri; *map*, 145
Curry, New York, 41

Dale Hollow Lake, Kentucky, 95; *map*, 96
Dallas, Pennsylvania, 61
Dallas-Fort Worth, Texas, 159, 160
Dalles, The, Oregon, 207, 211
Danbury, Connecticut, 32
Danville, Kentucky, 95
Day, John, River, Oregon, 205
Decatur, Alabama, 105
Deerfield River, Massachusetts, *section on*, 23, 24; *map*, 25
De Land, Florida, 83

Delaware River, 38, 39, 43, 51, 57, 64; *maps*, 37, 52, 55, 59
Delaware River Water Gap, Pennsylvania, 57; *map*, 58
Dennison, Texas, 160
Dennys River, Maine, 5, 6; *map*, 3
Derby Center, Vermont, 14
Deschutes National Forest, Oregon, 209
Deschutes River, Oregon, 207, 209, 210, 211, 212; *map*, 207; Lower Deschutes, *section on*, 210-212
De Soto National Forest, Mississippi, 107; *map*, 110
Detroit, Michigan, 112
Devoe Lake, Michigan, 122
Deward, Michigan, 119
Dew Spring Hole, Arkansas, 149
Dexter, New York, 46
Diamond Lake, Oregon, 212; *map*, 213
Diamond Lake Lodge, Oregon, 212
Dienstant, John, 218
Dingman's Ferry, Pennsylvania, 57
Dinwoodie Glacier Area, Wyoming, 179
Diversion Lake, Texas, 160; *map*, 161
Divide, Montana, 165
Doe Creek, Tennessee, 101
Dog River, Vermont, 13
Donner Lake, California, 220; *map*, 220
Dooley Pond, Connecticut, 36
Dora, Lake, Florida, 85; *map*, 82
Double Top Mountain, New York, 41
Douglas County, Wisconsin, 133
Drumore, Pennsylvania, 61
Dubois, Wyoming, 179
Dufresne Pond, Vermont, 19
Duluth, Minnesota, 135
Dungeness River, Washington, 202; *map*, 200
Dunnellon, Florida, 87
Dunsmuir, California, 225, 226
Dylan, Montana, 166

Eagle Chain Lakes, Wisconsin, 125
Eagle Lake, Louisiana, 153; Massachusetts, 4; *map*, 2; Mississippi, 107; *map*, 109
Eagle River, North Carolina, 71
East Dorset, Vermont, 19
East Fork Lewis, Washington, 202
East River, Colorado, 173
East Walker River, California, 224
Eau Claire, Wisconsin, 125
Edmonds, North Carolina, 71
*Eighty-Eight Top Trout Streams*, 175
Ellensburg, Washington, 203, 204
Ellenville, New York, 39
Eleven Point River, Missouri, 144; *map*, 145
Ellis, Idaho, 192
Elochoman River, Washington, 202; *map*, 200
Elowha River, Washington, *map*, 200
El Paso, Texas, 159
Elwha River, Washington, 202

Ely, Minnesota, 135
Enfield, Connecticut, 29
Enfield Dam, Connecticut, 29
Enid Lake, Mississippi, 107; *map*, 108
Ennis Lake, Idaho, 181
Erie, Lake, 46, 60, 61, 87; *maps*, 47, 59, 62, 67, 90
Erwin, Tennessee, 101
Escanaba Area, Michigan, 115; Wisconsin, 125
Esopus River, New York, 39, 41, 42; *map*, 40
Estacada, Oregon, 207
Etowah River, Georgia, 80
Eufala Lake, Alabama, 105

Farmington River, Connecticut, 6, 26, 32; *section on*, 27-29; *map*, 28
Faye, Ted, California, 225
Feather River, California, 224
*Federation of Fly Fishermen*, 167, 222, 227
Finger Lakes, New York, 46
Fire Hole River, Wyoming, *section on*, 179; *map*, 180
Fishing Regulations, 228
Fishville, Louisiana, 153
Flag River, Wisconsin, 128; *map*, 128
Flaming Gorge Reservoir, Vermont, 193
Flathead River, Montana, *section on*, 167-169; *map*, 168
Flat Top Wilderness Area, Colorado, 176
Flint River, Georgia, 80; *map*, 81
Florence County, Wisconsin, 134
Florida, *chapter on*, 83-88; State Game and Fish Commission, 87; State Hunting and Fishing Association, 87
Fontana Lake, North Carolina, 71; *maps*, 70, 102
Forest County, Wisconsin, 134
Forney, North Carolina, 71
Fort Kent, Maine, 5
Fort Washakie, Wyoming, 179
Foulton, Louisiana, 141
Four Corners Area, New Mexico, 183
Francis Lake, New Hampshire, 8; *map*, 10
Franconia Village, New Hampshire, 8
Frankfort, Kentucky, 100
Frank's Sport Shop, Montana, 165
Freeman, Jim, California, 226
French Creek, Pennsylvania, 60; *map*, 62
Frying Pan River, Colorado, 173
*Fruitland Peninsula Sportsman's Association*, Florida, 87

Galena Summit, Idaho, 192; *maps*, 186, 191
Gallatin River, Montana, 171
Galveston, Texas, 159
Gannett River, Idaho 189
Gardiner, Montana, 172
Garrison Dam, North Dakota, 157

Gary, Indiana, 94
Gasconade River, Missouri, 144; *map*, 145
Gaston, Lake, North Carolina, *map*, 68
Gaylord, Michigan, 119
Gentry Creek, Tennessee, 101
George, Lake, Florida, 85; *map*, 82
George, Walter F., Reservoir, Alabama, 105
Georgia, *chapter on*, 77-81
Gibbons River, Wyoming, *section on*, 179; *map*, 180
Gilboa Dam, New York, 39, 43; Reservoir, *map*, 37
Glacier National Park, Montana, 166
Gladstone, Oregon, 207
Glenwood Springs, Colorado, 176
Glide Sporting Goods, Oregon, 212
Goat Rock Reservoir, South Carolina, 76
Godfrey, Will, Idaho, 188
Gold Beach, Oregon, 214
Grafton, New Hampshire, 8; Grafton Pond, *map*, 7
Grand Junction, Colorado, 176
Grand Lake Chain, Maine, 5
Grand Lake Stream, Maine, 6; *map*, 3
Grand Marais, Minnesota, 135; *map*, 138
Grand Teton National Park, Wyoming, 177
Grande Ronde River, Oregon, 205
Granny Creek, Tennessee, 101
Grant's Pass, Oregon, 214
Grayling, Michigan, 119, 124
Gray River, Washington, 202; *map*, 200
Gray Wolf River, Washington, *map*, 200
Great Averill Pond, Vermont, 14; *map*, 14
Great Smoky Mountains, North Carolina, 71
Green Bay Peninsula, Wisconsin, 129; *map*, 132
Green County, Kentucky, 100
Green River, Colorado, 175
Green River, Utah, 193; *maps*, 194, 195
Greenbelt Area, Nevada, 197
Greenfield, New York, 19
Greentown, Pennsylvania, 61
Greenville, Maine, 1, 5
Greenville, North Carolina, 72
Greenwich, New York, 19
Greenwood Lake, New Jersey, 56; *map*, 53
Greenwood Lake, Minnesota, 135; *map*, 138
Greers Ferry Trout Hatchery, Arkansas, 148, 150
Grenada, Mississippi, 107; *map*, 108
Groves Creek, Idaho, 189
*Guide To Tennessee Fishing*, 101
Gunflint Trail, Minnesota, 135
Gunnison River, Colorado, *section on*, 173-175; *map*, 174

Guntersville Lake, Alabama, 105; *map*, 104

Haddam Island State Park, 32; *map*, 32
Haddam Meadows Park, Connecticut, 32; *map*, 32
Hancock, New York, 39, 41
Hancock County, Mississippi, 107
Hanover, Louisiana, 141
Happy Camp, California, 227
Harding Lake, Georgia, *map*, 79
Hardy Swimming Beach, Arkansas, 150
Harlan County, Kentucky, 100
Harriman Ranch, Idaho, 188
Harris Lake, Florida, 85; *map*, 82
Harrisburg, Pennsylvania, 61
Hartford, Connecticut, 29, 32
Hartland, Connecticut, 29
Hartwell, Georgia, 77
Hartwell Reservoir, *maps*, 74, 76
Harvey's Lake, Pennsylvania, 61; *map*, 66
Hattiesburg, Mississippi, 107
Havana, Illinois, 141
Havasu, Lake, Nevada, 197, 220; *maps*, 198, 221
Hawley, Pennsylvania, 61
Hayward, Wisconsin, 128
Hazel River, North Carolina, 71
Hazelgreen, Missouri, 144
Heber Springs, Arkansas, 150; *map*, 146
Hebgen Lake, Idaho, 181
Helen Blazes, Lake, Florida, 83
Henry's Fork, Idaho, *section on*, 187-189; *map*, 186
Henson Creek, Colorado, 175
Herrington Lake, Kentucky, 95; *map*, 98
Hibbing, Minnesota, 137
High Lakes, Wisconsin, 125; *map*, 127
High Springs, Florida, 87
Highlands, North Carolina, 71
Hinsdale County, Colorado, 173; Chamber of Commerce, 175
Hoh River, Washington, 202; *map*, 202
Holtwood, Pennsylvania, 61
Holyoke, Massachusetts, 21
Homosassa Springs, Florida, 87
Hoover Dam, Nevada, 197; *map*, 198
Hopatcong, Lake, New Jersey, 51; *map*, 50
Horespasture River, North Carolina, 71; *map*, 70
Horseshoe Bend Campground, Oregon, 212
Hot Creek, California, *section on*, 217-220; 224; *map*, 216
Housatonic River, Connecticut, 29; *maps*, 30, 34
Hudson River, Vermont, 19; *map*, 37
Humptulips River, Washington, 202; *map*, 200
Huntsville, Alabama, 105

Huron, Lake, Michigan, 112; *maps*, 116, 117, 120, 121, 123

Idaho, *chapter on*, 187-192; Fish and Game Dept., 190, 192
Idetown, Pennsylvania, 61
Illahe, Oregon, 214
Illinois, *chapter on*, 141
Illinois River, Illinois, 141; *map*, 139
Imnah River, Oregon, 205
Indiana and Ohio, *chapter on*, 89-94
International Falls Chamber of Commerce, Minnesota, 137
International Paper Co., Maine, 5
Iowa, *chapter on*, 141
Iron Gate Dam, California, 227
Iron·Gate Reservoir, California, 226
Iron River, Wisconsin, 128; *map*, 128
Isabella, Missouri, 144
Isabella Reservoir, California, 222; *map*, 223
Island Park Area, Idaho, 188
Island Park Dam, Idaho, 187
Island Pond, Vermont, 14; *maps*, 12, 16

Jack's Fork, Missouri, 144; *map*, 145
Jackson Hole, Wyoming, 177
Jackson Lake, Georgia, 80
Jackson, Mississippi, 107
Jackson, Montana, 163
Jalbert, Greg, 5
Jamestown, Kentucky, 100
Jefferson County, Mississippi, 107
Jefferson River, Montana, 163, 166, 171

Kachess, Lake, Washington, 203
Kaibab National Forest, Nevada, 197
Kalama River, Washington, 202, 203; *map*, 200
Kalispell, Montana, 167
Katherine, Lake, Illinois, 141
Keechelus, Lake, Washington, 203, 204; *map*, 201
Kemp, Lake, Texas, 160; *map*, 161
Keno, Oregon, 226
Keowee, Lake, South Carolina, 76; *map*, 74
Kentucky, *chapter on*, 95-100; Dept. of Fish and Game, 100
Kentucky Lake, Kentucky, 95; *map*, 97
Kern River, California, 217; *section on*, 222-224; *map*, 223
Kernville Dam, California, 222
Kerr, John H., Reservoir, Virginia, 69; *map*, 68
Ketchum, Idaho, 190, 192
Kettle Creek, Pennsylvania; *map*, 59
Kickapoo Lake, Texas, 160; *map*, 161
Kierl Camp, Arkansas, 50
Kilpatrick Bridge, Idaho, 190
Kings Lodge, Wisconsin, 130
Kings River, California, 217, 224
Kingston, New York, 41

Kittatinny Lake, New Jersey, 56; *map*, 52
Klamath Falls, California, 226; *map*, 225
Klamath River, California, 42, 212, 217, 224, 226, 227; *section on*, 226-227; *map*, 225
*Klamath River Fishing Guide*, 226
Klickitat River, Washington, 203
Kutskey, Al, 226

Lac du Flambeau Area, Wisconsin, 127; *map*, 127
Lackawaxen River, Pennsylvania, *map*, 58
Lake City, Colorado, 175
Lake County Chamber of Commerce, Florida, 89
Lake Creek Lodge, Oregon, 210
Lake Fork River, Colorado, 173
Lake of the Ozarks, Missouri, 143; *map*, 142
Lake-of-the-Woods, Minnesota, 137; *map*, 137
Lake Mead, Arizona, 197
Lake Placid, New York, 44
Lamoille River, Vermont, 13
Lampe, Missouri, 143
Lancaster, New Hampshire, 8
Lancaster, Pennsylvania, 61
Lang, Oscar, 212
Lanier, Lake Sidney, Georgia, 77; *map*, 76
Last Chance, Idaho, 188
Laurel Bloomery Creek, Tennessee, 101
Lebanon, New Hampshire, 8, 13
LeBlanc, Homer, 112
Leesburg, Florida, 85, 87
Leesville Reservoir, Ohio, 89; *map*, 91
Lehman, Pennsylvania, 61
Lemon Bluff, Florida, 83
Lesh, Al, Charter Service, 112
Lewbeach, New York, 41
Lewis and Clark Lake, Nebraska, 157; *map*, 156
Lexington, Kentucky, 95
Lick Creek, Kentucky, 100
Lilli, Bud, Trout Shop, Montana; 172
Lionhead Ranch, Montana, 171
Little Calumet River, Indiana, 94; *map*, 93
Little Red River, Arkansas, 148, 150; *map*, 146
Little River, Louisiana, 153; *map*, 154
Little Rock, Arkansas, 149
Little Wood Creek, Idaho, 189; *map*, 186
Livingston, Montana, 171, 172
Logan River, Utah, 193; *map*, 195
Long Island Sound, Connecticut, 29
Long Lake Camps, Maine, 5
Louisiana, *chapter on*, 153-154; Wildlife and Fisheries Comm., 153
Louisville, Kentucky, 100

Lower Deschutes River, Oregon, section on, 210-212; map, 207
Lower Hat River, California, 224
Lower Mesa Falls, Idaho, 187
Lucas Ranch, Oregon, 215
Lumber City, Georgia, 80
Lutie, Missouri, 144

Machias River, Maine, 5, 6; map, 3
Mackenzie River, Oregon, 207; map, 206
Mack's Canyon, Oregon, 211
Mack's Inn, Idaho, 187
Mad River, Vermont, 13
Madison, Wisconsin, 130
Madison River, Montana, 165, 171, 179; section on, 181; map, 180
Madras, Oregon, 211
Maine, chapter on, 1-6; Maine Tourist Development Commission, 5
Maine Wilderness Canoe Basin, 5
Makin, Illinois, 141
Mammoth Springs, Arkansas, 150; map, 146
Manchester, Vermont, 19
Manasquam River, New Jersey, 56; map 55
Manistee River, Michigan, 119; map, 116
Manistique Area, Michigan, 115
Manitowish River, Wisconsin, 127
Many Islands, Arkansas, 150
Marble Mountain Wilderness Area, California, 226
Marcy Dam Pond, New York, 44
Marion, Lake, South Carolina, 73, 75; map, 75
Marshall, Bob, Wilderness Area, Montana, 167
Martin, Lake, Alabama, 105; map 106
Maryland, 61
Mason, Phillip, 175
Massachusetts, chapter on, 21-26; Bureau of Wildlife Research and Management, 21; Division of Fisheries and Game, 21; Division of Fisheries and Wildlife Field Headquarters, 26
Matagorda, Texas, 159
Mattamuskeet, Lake, North Carolina, 72; map, 72
Maupin, Oregon, 211
Maynard, Ed, Ranch, Idaho, 181
McKenzie River, Oregon, 207, 212; map, 206
Mead, Lake, Nevada, 197; map, 198
Medford, Oregon, 215
Meeker County, Montana, 175-176
Melrose, Montana, 165
Memphis, Tennessee, 107
Memphremagog Lake, Vermont, 13; map, 12
Menominee River, Wisconsin, 128, 134; map, 132
Meridian, Mississippi, 107
Merlin, Oregon, 215

Metolius River, Oregon, section on, 208-210; map, 207
Metolius River Lodge, Oregon, 210
Michigan, chapter on, 112-124; Dept. of Natural Resources, 119
Michigan, Lake, maps, 93, 115, 116, 117, 118, 120, 121, 123, 140, 207
Middlefork of the Willamette, Oregon, 207; map, 206
Middletown, Connecticut, 32, 36
Milford, Pennsylvania, 57
Millers River, Massachusetts, 26
Minnesota, 112, chapter on, 135-138
Mio Pond, Michigan, 124
Miramar, Lake, California, 220
Mississippi, chapter on, 107-111, 129, 143; Game and Fish Comm., 111
Mississippi River, maps, 126, 131, 139, 154
Missouri, chapter on, 143; Dept. of Conservation, 144
Missouri River, Missouri, 143, 144, 157; maps, 145, 156
Mohawk River, New York, 46
Mojave Lake, California, 220; map, 221
Moline, Iowa, 141
Moncks Corner, South Carolina, 75
Monroe, Louisiana, 153
Monroe, Lake, Indiana, 94; map, 93
Montana, chapter on, 163-172; Montana Conservation Dept., 165; Dept. of Natural Resources, 138
Montgomery, Alabama, 105
Monument Falls, New York, 44
Moosehead Hotel, Maine, 5
Moosehead Lake, Maine, 1; maps, 2, 3
Moose River, Vermont, 14; map 18
Morgan Center, Vermont, 14
Morrison's Lodge, 215
Mosquito Creek Reservoir, Ohio, 89; map, 92
Moultrie, Lake, South Carolina, 73, 75; map, 75
Mount Jefferson, Oregon, 210
Mount Shasta, California, 224, 226; map, 225
Mullet Lake, Michigan, 119; map, 118
Murphy Dam, New Hampshire, 8
Musconetcong, Lake, New Jersey, 51; map, 50
Muskellunge, 233
Myatt Creek, Arkansas, 150

Namekagon River, Wisconsin, 128; map, 129
Narrows Dam, Arkansas, 148
Naselle River, Washington, 202; map, 200
Nashville, Tennessee, 101
Natchez, Mississippi, 107
Navesink, New Jersey, 56; map, 55
Navajo Dam, New Mexico, 183; map, 182
Nebraska, chapter on, 157; Parks and Game Commission, 157

Needles, California, 220
Nevada, chapter on, 197; Dept. of Fish and Game, 197
Neversink River, New York, 39, 41; map, 40
New Britain, Connecticut, 29
New Brunswick, Canada, 1, 5
New Hampshire, chapter on, 8-11; Economic Div. of Tourism, 8
New Hartford, Connecticut, 29
New Jersey, 38, chapter on, 51-56; Dept. of Fish, Game and Shellfish, 56
New Mexico, chapter on, 183-185; Dept. of Game and Fish, 184, 185
New Philadelphia, Ohio, 89
Newton, New Jersey, 51
New York City, 19, 27, 38, 57, 69
New York State, chapter on, 38-48; Dept. of Environmental Conservation, 41, 46
Nicolet National Forest, Wisconsin, 134
Noland, California, 71
Nolin River, Kentucky, 100; map, 99
Nooksack River, Washington, 202; map, 200
Norfork Dam, Arkansas, 48, 151; map, 146
North Adams, Massachusetts, 26
North Carolina, chapter on, 71-72; Wildlife Resources Comm., 72
North Dakota, chapter on, 157; State Game and Fish Dept., 157
North Fork River, Arkansas, 148, 151; map, 146
North Fork Stillaguamish, Washington, 202
North Platte River, Nebraska, 157; map, 156
North Umpqua River, Oregon, section on, 202-214; map, 213
North Yuba River, California, 224
Northern Highland State Forest, Wisconsin, 125
Norwich, Connecticut, 32
Notteley, Georgia, 77; map, 76
Nulhegan River, Vermont, 14; map, 16

Ocala National Forest, Florida, map, 82
Ocmulgee, Lake, Georgia, 80; map, 81
Oconee River, Georgia, 77; map, 78
Ogenaw County, Michigan, 122
Ohio, chapter on, 89-94
Okatibbee Lake, Mississippi, 107; map, 110
Okeechobee, Lake, Florida, 85, 87
Okefenokee Swamp, Georgia, 80
Oklahoma, chapter on, 158
Oklawaha River, Florida; map, 82
Old Faithful Inn, Idaho, 181
Oliver, Lake, South Carolina, 76
Oliveria River, New York, 41
Olympia, Washington, 199
Onandaga, Lake, New York, 46
Oneida, Lake, New York, 46

Ontario, Lake, New York, 46; *map*, 48
Oostanaula, Georgia, 80
Opelika, Alabama, 105
Orange, Lake, Florida, 85; *maps*, 82, 86
Oregon, 199, *chapter on*, 205-215; Dept. of Fish and Wildlife, 207; Game Commission, 207
*Oregon Back Country Lakes*, 207
Orleans, California 227
Orleans, Vermont, 13
Osage River, Missouri, 143; *map*, 142
Ossipee, New Hampshire, 8
*Outdoors in the White Mountains*, 8
Owasco Lake, New York, 46
Owens River, California, 224; *map*, 216
Owens Valley, California, 217

Pamlico Sound, North Carolina, 72; *map*, 72
Panfish, 234
Pangburn, Arkansas, 150
Parker Dam, Nevada, 197
Parks, Merton, Fly Shop, Montana, 172
Passumpsic River, Vermont, 14; *maps*, 11, 18
Paterson, New Jersey, 56
Paulinskill Lake, New Jersey, 51; *map*, 49
Peachbottom, Pennsylvania, 61
Pelton Dam, Oregon, 211; *map*, 207
Pendergraft, Dan, 165
Pennsylvania, *chapter on*, 57-67; Dept. of Commerce, 61; Pennsylvania Fish Commission, 61
Penobscot River, Maine, 1
Peoria, Illinois, 141
Perch, yellow and white, 234
Peshtigo River, Wisconsin, 128; *map*, 132
Phillipsburg, Pennsylvania, 57
Phoenicia, New York, 41
Picaboo, Idaho, 190
Pickerel, 233
Pickwick Lake, Alabama, 105; Mississippi, 107; *maps*, 104, 108
Pigeon River, Michigan, 119; *map*, 118
Pike, Northern, 233
Pilchuck River, Washington, 202
Pillar Point, New York, 46
Pine Grove Campground, Michigan, 122; *map*, 118
Pine Meadow, Connecticut, 29
Pine River, Colorado, 173
Pine River, Wisconsin, *section on*, 134; *map*, 132
Pipe Organ Lodge, Montana, 166
Pistakee Lake, Illinois, 141; *map*, 140
Pittsburg, New Hampshire, 8
Pittsburgh, Pennsylvania, 60
Placid, Lake, New York, 46
Pleasant Lake, Maine, 5
Pohsimeroi River, Idaho, 192
Poindexter Slough, Montana, 166
Point Pleasant, New Jersey, 56

Pompton Lakes, New Jersey, 56; *map*, 54
Portage, Wisconsin, 125
Port Clinton, Ohio, 87
Port Jervis, Pennsylvania, 57
Portland, Maine, 1
Portland, Oregon, 205, 207
Poultney River, Vermont, 13; *map*, 20
Presque Isle, Wisconsin, 130
Princeton, Maine, 5
Prospect, Oregon, 214
Providence, Lake, Louisiana, 153
Puget Sound area, 199
Pymatuning Reservoir, Ohio, 61, 89; *maps*, 67, 92
Pyramid Lake, Arizona, 197; *map*, 196

Quabbin Reservoir, Massachusetts, *map*, 22
Quality Fishing Waters, Colorado, 175
Quebec, 1, 13
Queets River, Washington, 202; *map*, 200
Quetico Provincial Park, Ontario, 135
Quimby's Camps, Vermont, 14
Quinault River, Washington, 202; *map*, 200

Rabun Lake, Georgia, 77; *map*, 76
Railroad Ranch, Idaho, 188
Rainbow Reservoir, Connecticut, 32; *map*, 31
Rainy Lake, Minnesota, 137; *map*, 137
Rainier, Oregon, 205
Raleigh, North Carolina, 72
Rangeley Lakes, Maine, 1, 6; *map*, 3
Rayburn, Georgia, 77
Red Bank, New Jersey, 56
Redding, California, 225
Redmond, Oregon, 211
Red River Gorge, Kentucky, 100
Red River, Texas, 159, 160; *maps*, 159, 160, 162
Rhinelander, Wisconsin, 125
Rhoads, Jim, 226
Richland, Washington, 203
Rifle River, Michigan, 122; *map*, 121
Rio de los Pinos, New Mexico, 183
Rio Grande, *section on*, 184; *map*, 182
Riverdale, North Dakota, 157
Riverton, Wyoming, 177
Roaring Fork River, Colorado, 173
Rochester, Vermont, 17
Rock Creek, Montana 171
Rock Creek, Oregon, 212
Rockwood, Maine, 5
Rocky Fork Creek, Tennessee, 101
Rodney Lake, Mississippi, 107
Rogue River, Oregon, 212; *section on*, 214-215; *map*, 213
Rom, Bill, 137
Rome, Georgia, 80
Roscoe, New York, 38, 39, 41
Roseburg, Oregon, 212
Rosman, North Carolina, 71

Ross Barnett Reservoir, Mississippi, 107
Round Butte Reservoir, Oregon, 209, 211
Rowe, Massachusetts, 26
Royalton, Vermont, 17
Ruby River, Montana, 163
Rutland, Vermont, 13, 19

Sabine River, Texas, 159
Sackets Harbor, New York, 46
Safe Harbor, Pennsylvania, 61
Saginaw Bay, Michigan, 112; *maps*, 116, 117, 118, 120, 121, 123
St. Clair Shores, Michigan, 112
St. Croix River, Maine, 5, 6; *map*, 3
St. Croix River, Wisconsin, 125, 133; *maps*, 129, 131
Saint John, New Brunswick, 4
St. John Lake, Mississippi, *map*, 109
St. John River, Maine, 4; *map*, 2
St. John's River, Florida, 83; *map*, 82
St. Johnsbury, Vermont, 14
St. Joseph, Louisiana, 153
St. Lawrence River, New York, 46; *map*, 48
St. Mary's River, Georgia, 77
St. Petersburg, Florida, 87
Sakakawea, Lake, North Dakota, 157; *map*, 158
Salem Lake Camp, Vermont, 14
Salem Lake, Vermont, 14; *map*, 12
Salem, Oregon, 210
Salisbury, Connecticut, 36
Salmon, 232
Salmon River, California, 226
Salmon River, Connecticut, 32; *map*, 28
Salmon River, Idaho, 192; *map*, 191
Salt River, Kentucky, 100; *map*, 99
San Cristobal, Lake, Colorado, 173
San Diego County, California 220
Sandusky Bay, Ohio, 89; *map*, 90
San Joaquin Valley, California, 222
San Juan River, New Mexico, *section on*, 183-184; *map*, 182
Sante Fe River, Florida, 87; *map*, 86
*Santee-Cooper Country*, 73
Santee-Cooper Reservoir, South Carolina, 73; *map*, 75
San Vicente, Lake California, 220
Sardis Lake, Mississippi, 107, *map*, 108
Satilla River, Georgia, 77
Satsop River, Washington, 202; *map*, 200
Savannah area, Georgia, 77
Schoharie River, New York, 39, 43
Scott River, California, 226
Scranton, Pennsylvania, 61
Sebago Lake Chain, Maine, 1
Sebring, Lake, Florida, 87; *map*, 84
Second Bridge, Oregon, 209
Selma, Alabama, 105
Seminole Lake, Florida, 87; *map*, 88; Georgia, *map*, 81

Seminole Lake, South Carolina, 76, 80
Seneca Lake, New York, 46
Seymour Lake, Vermont, 14; *map*, 12
Seymour, Texas, 160
Shad, 234
Shandaken, New York, 39
Sharon, Connecticut, 29
Sharon, Michigan, 119
Shasta Lake, California, 220, 224; *map*, 219
Shasta River, California, 226
Shasta Springs, California, 224
Sheep Falls, Idaho, 188
Shepherdsville, Kentucky, 100
Sherar Bridge, Oregon, 211
Shrine River, Idaho, 189
Sidney Lanier Lake, Georgia, 77
Sierra-Nevada Mountains, California, 217, 222; *map*, 223
Silver Creek, Idaho, 42; *section on*, 189-190; *map*, 186
Simpson County, Kentucky, 100
Sinclair Lake, Georgia, 77; *map*, 78
Skagit River, Washington, 202; *map*, 200
Skaneateles Lake, New York, 46
Skykomish River, Washington, 202; *map*, 200
Slide Mountain, New York, 41; *map*, 37
Smithville, Michigan, 119
Snake River, Idaho, 187, 203; *maps*, 186, 191, 201
Sneads, Florida, 87
Sneed, Hobart, 167
Snoqualmie River, Washington, 202; *map*, 200
Soda Springs Dam, Oregon, 212
Soleduc River, Washington, 202; *map*, 200
South Carolina, *chapter on*, 73-75; Wildlife Resources Dept., 75
South Dakota, *chapter on*, 157; Dept. of Game Fish and Parks, 157
South Fork, River, Oregon, 214
South Umpqua River, Oregon, 212
Spednic Lake, Maine, 6; *map*, 3
Spivy Creek, Tennessee, 101
Sportsman's Lodge, Melrose, Montana, 165
Springfield, Illinois, 141
Springfield, Missouri, 143
Spring River, Arkansas, 150; *map*, 146
Stanley Basin Recreation Area, Idaho, 190, 192
Stahl, Frank, 192
Steamboat, Oregon, 212
Stillagamish, River, Washington; *map*, 200
Stoddard Hill State Park, Connecticut, 32; *map*, 33
Stoker Creek, Idaho, 189
Stones Bridge, Wisconsin, 133
Stoney Creek, Tennessee, 101
Straits of Juan de Fuca, Washington, 199

Stratford, Connecticut, 29
Stratford, New Hampshire, 8
Strawberry River, Vermont, 193; *map*, 195
Sturgeon River, Michigan, 119; *map*, 117, 118
Sullivan County, New York, 38
Sulphur River, Kentucky, 100
Summerton, South Carolina, 73
Summit Lake, Arizona, 197
Sunapee Lake, New Hampshire, 8; *map*, 7
Sunfish, 234
Sun Valley, Idaho, 190, 192
Superior, Lake, Michigan, 112, 135; *maps*, 115, 128, 131, 132, 138
Susquehanna River, Pennsylvania, 57, 61, 64; *maps*, 59, 60, 63
Suwanee River, Florida, 80, 87; *map*, 86
Swartswood Lake, New Jersey, 51; *map*, 49
Swauk River, Washington, 204; *map*, 201
Swift River, Massachusetts, 21; *map*, 22

Table Rock Reservoir, Missouri, 143; *map*, 144
Tackle and Accessories, 229
Tahoe, Lake, California, 220; *maps*, 196, 216
Tallahassee, Florida, 87
Tallapoosa River, Alabama, 105
Tamiami Trail, Florida, 87
Tampa, Florida, 87
Taneycomo, Lake, Missouri, 143
Tavares, Florida, 85; *map*, 82
Taylor River, Colorado, 173
Tchoutacabouffa River, Mississippi, 107
Tellico, Tennessee, 101
Tellico Creek, Tennessee, 101
Tellico Wildlife Management Area, Tennessee, 101; *map*, 102
Tenaway River, Washington, 204
Tennessee, *chapter on*, 101-103; Wildlife Resources Agency, 101
Tennessee River, Alabama, 105
Tennessee River, Georgia, 77
Tennessee River, Kentucky, 95
Terry Brook, Vermont, 19
Tewsbury Pond, Vermont, 8
Texarkana Lake, Texas, 162; *map*, 162
Texas, *chapter on*, 159-162; Park and Wildlife Dept., 162
Texoma Lake, Texas, 160; *maps*, 159, 160
Thames River, Connecticut, 32; *map*, 33
Three Lynx, Oregon, 207
Three Sisters Mountains, Oregon, 210
Tidioute, Pennsylvania, 60
Tillamook Bay, Oregon, 207; *map*, 207
Tionesta Creek Reservoir, Pennsylvania, 60; *map*, 59

Tippecanoe River, Indiana, 94; *map*, 94
Titerington, Dick, 179
Titusville, Florida, 83
Tocks Island Dam Project, Pennsylvania, 57
Togowotee Pass, Wyoming, 177; *map*, 178
Toledo Bend Lake maps, Texas, 162
Topaz Lake, Arizona, 197
Toutle River, Washington, 202; *map*, 200
Tower Falls, Montana, 172
Toxaway River, North Carolina, 71; *map*, 70
Trail Creek, Indiana, 94
Trammel River, Kentucky, 100
Trapper's Lake, Colorado, 176
Trego, Wisconsin, 128
Trenton, New Jersey, 56
Trinity River, California, 224, 226
Trinity River, Texas, 159; *map*, 159
Trout, 232
*Trout, Unlimited*, 167, 222, 227
Truckee, California, 220, 224
Tsala Apopka, Lake, Florida, 87; *map*, 85
Tugolo Lake, Georgia, 77; *map*, 76
Turnwood, New York, 41
TVA Lakes, North Carolina, 71; Tennessee, 101
TVA Navigational Charts, 100
Twin Bridges, Montana, 163, 165
Twin Lakes, Connecticut, 36; *map*, 35

Union Creek Camp, Oregon, 215
Unionville, Connecticut, 29
Upper Arkansas River, Colorado, 173
Upper Beaver Dam Creek, Tennessee, 101
Upper McCloud River, California, 224
Upper Mesa Falls, Idaho, 188; *map*, 186
Upper Rio Grande, Colorado, 173
Upper Sacramento River, California, *section on*, 224-226; *map*, 225
Upper Salmon River, Idaho, *section on*, 190-192; *map*, 191
Upper Yellowstone River, Montana, 171; *map*, 170
U. S. Army Corps of Engineers, 12, 69, 227
Utah, *chapter on*, 193-195; Dept. of Fish and Game, 193; Division of Wildlife Resources, 193

Velard, New Mexico, 185
Vermont, *chapter on*, 13-20; Fish and Game Comm., 19; Fish and Game Department, 17
Vicksburg, Mississippi, 107
Virginia *chapter on*, 69; 89

Wakeley Bridge, Michigan, 124
Walhalla, South Carolina, 73
Walker Lake, Arizona, 197; *map*, 196
Wallenpaupack, Lake, Pennsylvania, 61; *map*, 65

Warren, Michigan, 112
Washington, *chapter on*, 199-204; State Game Dept., 202
Washington County, Maine, 5
Webster Lake, Massachusetts, 23
Welaka, Florida, 87
West Arlington, Vermont, 19
Westburk, Vermont, 13
Westfield River, Massachusetts, 26
Westkill, New York, 41
Westminster, South Carolina, 73
Westmore, Vermont, 13
West Virginia, *chapter on*, 69; 89
Wetherby's, Maine, 5
Wheeler Lake, Alabama, 105; *map*, 104
White Mountain National Forest; *map*, 11
White Mountains Region Associates, New Hampshire, 8
White River, Colorado, *section on*, 175-176; *map*, 174
White River, Missouri, 144, 147, 148, 149, 151; *map*, 146
White River, Vermont, 13, 14; *map*, 17
White River Junction, Vermont, 17
White Sulphur Springs, Louisiana, 153
Whitewater River, North Carolina, 71; *map*, 70
Wichita, Texas, 160

Wichita Falls, Texas, 160
Wilkes-Barre, Pennsylvania, 61
Willamette River, Oregon, 205, 207; *map*, 206
Willapa River, Washington, *map*, 200
Williston, North Dakota, 157
Willoughby Lake, Vermont, 13; *maps*, 12, 15
Willowemoc River, New York, 32, 39, 41
Wilmington Notch, New York, 44
Wilmington Pond, New York, 44
Wilson, Connecticut, 32
Wilson Lake, Alabama, 105; *map*, 104
Wind River, Wyoming, *section on*, 179; *map*, 178
Windsor, Connecticut, 32
Winnebago, Lake, Wisconsin, 129; *map*, 130
Winneboujou Bridge, Wisconsin, 133; *map*, 131
Winnipesaukee, Lake, New Hampshire, 8; *map*, 9
Winterhaven, Florida, 87
Wisconsin, *chapter on*, 125-134; Dept. of Natural Resources, 130; Division of Fish and Game, 156; Recreational Publicity Section, 130; Recreation Association, 130

Wise River, Montana, 165
Withlacoochee River, Florida 87; *map*, 85
Wold, Cliff, 137
Wolfcreek Dam, Kentucky, 100; *map*, 98
World Record Fish, 236, 237
Wolverine, Michigan, 119
Woodruff, Jim, Reservoir, South Carolina, 76; *map*, 79
Woodville, Mississippi, 107
Worcester, Massachusetts, 21, 23
Wyoming, *chapter on*, 177-181

Yakima River, Washington, *section on*, 203-204; *map*, 201
Yampa River, Colorado, 173
Yellowstone National Park, Montana, 172, 179; *section on*, 179; *maps*, 170, 180
Yellowstone River, Montana, 27, 165, 169; *maps*, 170, 178
York, Pennsylvania, 61
Young Woman's Creek, Pennsylvania; *map*, 59
*Your Outdoor Recreation Map*, 59
Yreka, California, 226
Yucatan Lake, Louisiana, 153